Cheers for Tom Adelman's

Black and Blue

SANDY KOUFAX, the ROBINSON BOYS, and the WORLD SERIES That STUNNED AMERICA

"In his richly layered retrospective, Adelman gives life to a generally neglected season. . . . An entertaining and informative portrait of two underappreciated teams in an unforgettable time." — Bob Hohler, *Boston Globe*

"A well-researched, easy-to-read account. . . . Adelman does a nice job putting some zip into his work, sprinkling it with funny stories and good locker room insight."

— Bob D'Angelo, *Tampa Tribune*

"Adelman tells stories [with] verve and insight . . . avoiding most of the clichés and conventional wisdom of traditional sports volumes."

— Patrick Goldstein, *Los Angeles Times Book Review*

"Adelman goes way past the box scores to get information that makes the players more human and the games more dramatic." — John Curtis, *San Diego Union-Tribune*

"A fine intersection of baseball and social history, as astute in its observations about on-field strategy as it is about race relationships. It is at once a chronicle of a baseball season and a portrait of Frank Robinson, a complex man and a proud athlete who chose to answer his detractors in the best possible way, by leading his team to victory."

— Ram Subramanian, CurledUp.com

Also by Tom Adelman

The Long Ball: The Summer of '75 — Spaceman,
Catfish,
Charlie Hustle, and
the Greatest World Series Ever Played

Black and Blue

SANDY KOUFAX,
the ROBINSON BOYS,
and the WORLD SERIES
That STUNNED AMERICA

Tom Adelman

BACK BAY BOOKS
Little, Brown and Company
New York   Boston   London

Back Bay Books / Little, Brown and Company
Hachette Book Group USA
237 Park Avenue, New York, NY 10017
Visit our Web site at www.HachetteBookGroupUSA.com

Originally published in hardcover by
Little, Brown and Company, April 2006

First Back Bay paperback edition, September 2007

Library of Congress Cataloging-in-Publication Data
Adelman, Tom.
   Black and blue: Sandy Koufax, the Robinson boys, and the World
Series that stunned America / Tom Adelman — 1st ed.
      p. cm.
Includes bibliographical references and index.
   ISBN 978-0-316-06901-4 (hc) / 978-0-316-06715-7 (pb)
   1. World Series (Baseball) (1966) 2. Los Angeles Dodgers
(Baseball team) 3. Baltimore Orioles (Baseball team) I. Title.
GV878.4.A316 2006
796.357'646 — dc22   2005027304

10 9 8 7 6 5 4 3 2 1

Q-MART

Printed in the United States of America

Contents

Black and Blue

PART ONE

Robby's Revenge

One cold afternoon in 1965, two weeks after Thanksgiving, the Cincinnati Reds telephoned Frank Robinson, their star outfielder, to inform him that he'd just been traded. He was going south, they explained. To Baltimore.

Frank was stung.[1] Naturally, there had been rumors; there always were. He'd heard that he would be sent to Houston; then it was supposed to be Cleveland, and then New York. He hadn't really believed any of it, hadn't bothered paying much attention. Why trade him? For a decade, he'd been Cincinnati's best player, regularly batting higher than .300, every season averaging more than thirty homers and one hundred runs batted in. In 1956 he'd been a unanimous pick for Rookie of the Year, in 1961 the overwhelming choice for Most Valuable Player. He was the greatest run producer in the history of the Reds. The previous year, he'd knocked in 113 runs, hit .296 with 33 home runs. Why deal your strongest hitter? It made no sense.

"Well," asked Robby, "who'd you get for me?"

"Pappas, Jack Baldschun, and Dick Simpson."

"Okay."[2]

They'd gotten three guys in exchange, not bad. Baldschun was a workhorse in the bull pen, Simpson a young, speedy outfielder — solid talents certainly, but essentially throw-ins, addenda. The main guy was Milt Pappas. He was a right-hander with a swift fastball, a nasty slider, and, by late 1965, the best record of any starter in Oriole history. He was also nobody's favorite, ostracized by his own teammates for behaving like a snot, viewed by the Baltimore organization as a hypochondriac, disdained by umpires and official scorers alike for his on-the-field tantrums.

Knowing little of this, Bill DeWitt, the owner of the Cincinnati ball club, welcomed the trade. His Reds, though powerful, were just shy of championship caliber. In 1965 they'd hit and fielded better than any other team in the league, remaining in contention until the season's last week. DeWitt's pitching staff, however, had given up too many walks and too many runs. Falling fast, Cincinnati had finished in fourth place. DeWitt was intent on fixing things, and his big idea was to unload Robby before it was too late. He saw Frank as overvalued, a fading talent increasingly hobbled by leg injuries. When reminded that the perennial all-star was only thirty years old, DeWitt shrugged. "Thirty," he agreed, "but an old thirty."[3]

If there was one thing everyone in baseball knew about Frank Robinson, it was this: never make him mad. His temper focused his competitive spirit. Phillie manager Gene Mauch fined his pitchers if they brushed Frank back, and Dodger manager Walter Alston warned his staff against "waking the beast," growing frustrated whenever his head-hunting hurler Don Drysdale worked Robby inside.[4] Frank savored every challenge. He performed best when he had something to prove — during pennant drives, in televised matches, with a game on the line. Beanballs and boobirds only fueled Robby's concentration. Anger improved the quality of his play. And DeWitt's comment infuriated him.

It was in this context that Frank Robinson, a muscular,

ambitious African American every bit as seething and rancorous as the country itself, was dispatched down to Baltimore.

Had he hopped on a plane to fly there, Robinson would have soared above a nation on the brink of ignition. Crime and poverty were on the rise, along with claims of discrimination and police brutality. The civil rights movement had lost its patience. Peaceful sit-ins and freedom marches were giving way to increasingly militant demonstrations for racial equality. The Southeast Asian conflict was shifting into the Vietnam War. Seventy-five million baby boomers were coming of age, many of whom were being randomly drafted to fight meaningless battles in a jungle half a world away.

The northern inner cities were growing progressively more restless, and the declining neighborhoods around Cincinnati's Crosley Field, Cleveland's Municipal Stadium, Detroit's Tiger Stadium, Chicago's Comiskey Park, Pittsburgh's Forbes Field, and Washington's D.C. Stadium were particular flash points. Baseball season was being supplanted by riot season, the long, hot summers of the mid-1960s less an invitation to ballpark repose than a call to urban warfare.

Raised mostly by his mother in a rough patch of West Oakland, Robby had grown up poor, across the Bay from San Francisco, the youngest of eleven children. His manner, from infancy, was swift and intense. He needed to be forceful just to survive, he later said, sharing a dinner table with that many siblings, with only their mom to keep the peace.[5] He was a tall, skinny kid, somewhat shy, with a tendency to slouch, but he adored the game of baseball, and he gravitated every afternoon to the diamond near his mom's house, playing into the evening and up to the very edge of darkness.[6] From his absentee dad, Frank got one thing: an obstinate determination to show him up. "Frank will never make a big-league baseball player," his father told Frank's brothers. "There's no way he can make it."[7] So began a lifelong mission to prove his detractors wrong.

In high school, Robinson came under the tutelage of an exceptionally decent man named George Powles, a white coach who shaped many impoverished black children into professional ballplayers. Powles expected his players to devote themselves fully to the game. He taught Frank to think positively and play aggressively.[8] Thanks to him, one week after graduating from McClymonds High School, at age seventeen, Robby signed a contract with the Cincinnati Reds. His bonus was $3,500. The year was 1953.

He was in the minor leagues for two years, and it was there, out and about in America for the first time, that the talented teenager suddenly encountered racism. Movie theaters and restaurants turned him away for being the wrong color.[9] Fans encouraged him to go back to Africa. His name seemed no longer to be Frank Robinson but "Hey Nigger" or "Coon Boy."[10] He accompanied his club through Utah and Idaho, around Oklahoma, from South Carolina into Georgia, unable to leave the back of the team bus to get food or even to use the bathroom. When at last they'd arrive at their destination, Robby would have to stay somewhere else, across town in a room without air-conditioning, at a YMCA or in a private home. It was always crowded, and in the morning he'd have to locate a "Negro Cab" to get to the ballpark. Once he took the field, the fans howled with indignant taunts and jeers. His every movement was mocked, his sexual preferences maligned, his family's name impugned. What could possibly have prepared him for this? He had had an attentive and caring mother, loving siblings, enthusiastic encouragement from classmates and coaches of every color. Poor, yes, but a different America. Segregation floored him. "You get angry," he acknowledged later, "but one person isn't going to throw the thing down." His response, as always, was to turn their invective into incentive, to drive himself all the harder in order to climb.

Robinson entered Cincinnati's lineup on Opening Day 1956, twenty years old, vengeful and magnificent. What he'd endured in the minors had sharpened his cutthroat style to perfection. He positioned himself even with the plate, crowding the strike zone with his upper torso to guard the outside corner. National League pitchers saw him hanging over the plate like a question mark, asking to be hit. They were only too willing to oblige — most often Don Drysdale, who once, when told to give Robby a base on balls, followed the order by hurling four straight fastballs at his head.[11] Through the late 1950s and early 1960s, besides always being among the best in slugging percentage, Frank also led in beanings. This was fine. When they dropped him, he would take his base, then take it out on their infielders. No black major leaguer had ever dared slide so hard, so nakedly combative. "I feel it's good to bump a guy," downplayed Frank, "even if I know I'm out."[12] It was never just a bump. Unapologetically, he barreled through second basemen, knocked shortstops into left field, tore their stockings with his cleats, ripped tendons and ligaments, broke limbs. It mattered not whether they were white, black, or Latino. "My creed is to play all-out," Frank explained, "always to go all-out." The base paths belonged to him. Whoever got in his way had to accept the consequences. "The possibility of the infielder being wounded by spikes," he said, "is part of baseball." To break up a double play, he cut Don Zimmer of the Dodgers, flattened Johnny Logan of the Braves.[13] He sliced open the arm of Dodger catcher John Roseboro so badly that Rosey bore a long scar for the rest of his life.[14] "He's trying to maim people," LA's Don Newcombe accused. A loner who rarely smiled, Robinson was always admired but seldom liked. "Deliberately vicious," one opponent described him.[15] One famous, spikes-high slide into Milwaukee third baseman Eddie Mathews during the 1960 pennant race initiated baseball's first fistfight between black and white stars.[16]

Frank Robinson is decked by a Dodger pitcher. A familiar scene when Robby played for Cincinnati. (AP / Wide World Photos)

The same year he fought Mathews, Robby purchased an Italian Beretta .25. He often carried a lot of cash on him and figured he needed the protection. He practiced shooting targets at the police firing range in Cincinnati, where the cops would snicker at the small size of his gun.[17] Frank never needed even to brandish it until late on February 9, 1961, in a coffee shop, when a short-order cook gestured threateningly from the kitchen. In those days, he had a quick fuse; he would let things bug him until he exploded. From his right jacket pocket, Frank withdrew the loaded Beretta. "You think you're a big man," he hollered at the cook. "Come on!"

The cook froze. Two policemen happened to be sitting across the restaurant. "Hey," the cook called out to them, "that guy's got a gun!"[18]

Almost reluctantly, they took Robby in and booked him for carrying a concealed weapon. The holding cell was very hot. He lay down, with his jacket as a pillow, and asked himself what in the hell he was doing. "For the first time I began to realize that I wasn't a kid anymore and that I better stop acting like one."[19] He made bail, pleaded guilty, and paid a $250 fine.

Then the teasing began. "Hey, Colt .45!" the fans would jeer. "Who do you think you are — Wyatt Earp?" When he'd get called out on a play, people would taunt him, asking why he didn't pull his gun on the umpire.[20] "All those remarks, all that jockeying served a purpose," Frank recalled. "It was like waving a red flag in front of me constantly. It was a reminder, a goad."[21] Before the year was out, Robby had homered in a World Series, won the Most Valuable Player Award, and married Barbara Ann Cole. He finished the 1961 season with a .323 batting average, having hit 37 home runs and batted in 124 runs. His totals in 1962 were even higher — a batting average of .342, 39 home runs, and 136 RBIs.

He'd grown comfortable in the National League. He knew what to expect from the pitchers, and they knew enough to respect him. Cincinnati had made its peace with him, and he with it. As of December 9, 1965, however, that whole chapter of his life was over. He was going to the American League, to Baltimore. And he had no idea what to expect.

Robby's next stop, it turned out, was not so different from his last. Like Cincinnati, Baltimore was a hilly waterfront town with an industrial past, filled with low-slung brick buildings and the descendants of German immigrants. A century and a quarter earlier, it had been, after New York, the nation's second largest city. Now, in 1966, it was the sixth, and falling

fast. "A little town," Oriole pitcher Wally Bunker remembered.
"A little cow town."[22] The actor known as Divine, recalling
his own childhood there, noted, "When you live in Baltimore,
you don't think anything could ever happen."[23] Yet it possessed charms — its neighborhoods of old-fashioned row
houses; its numerous churches, bridges, and monuments; its
downtown tower one million bricks high; its reputation for
amiability, for religious tolerance, for discerning social clubs.
The largest neon sign on the East Coast was an advertisement
for Domino sugar in Baltimore Harbor, its bright red light
glistening on the aged docks where stevedores continued as
always to carouse with merchant sailors and roustabouts.
Men in the blue-collar sections still raised racing pigeons in
lofts, and sidewalk vendors — "Street A-rabs" — sold straw-
berries out of horse-drawn carts, as they had since Baltimore's heyday. "People there never talked about it as a city,"
film director and Baltimore native Barry Levinson recalled.
"They always called it 'The Town.'"[24] The odor of cinnamon
and cloves wafted through, generated by the resident spice-
makers. "I loved the feel of it," said John Fialka, a reporter
back then for the *Baltimore Sun.* "Someone once compared
liking Baltimore to 'falling in love with a woman who has a
broken nose.' That covers me."[25]

But more than her nose was broken. For more than a
decade, the city had been losing both jobs and whites to the
suburbs, and the tens of thousands of southern blacks arriving in Baltimore of late could find no work. The flour mills
and coffee warehouses from which Baltimore had garnered
much of its wealth were closed, and many of its factories and
shipyards were in sad shape. An urban renewal project was
displacing many of the poor, their apartment buildings being
bulldozed and no immediate housing alternatives being provided. "In the 1960s, in the name of this concept of rebuilding," Levinson remembered, "they began to destroy some of
the city's stronger, more colorful aspects."[26] The white middle

class, though living still in the county of Baltimore, had largely abandoned the city, while its most privileged citizens had removed themselves still further, to exclusive neighborhoods as far north as the Pennsylvania line. They attended private schools and elite functions, registered their daughters as debutantes, had themselves listed in the blue book, and spent weekends perusing society columns to find out who wore what at the cotillion. By the early sixties, Maryland had earned a reputation among black activists as the most segregated state in the North, while Baltimore was being called the largest segregated city in the country.

This characterization was not entirely unfair, nor unexpected. This was not, of course, the Deep South, yet technically Baltimore was below the Mason-Dixon Line. The first blood of the Civil War had been spilled there when gangs of Confederate sympathizers had fired on Union troops traveling to Washington, D.C. Maryland, as a border state, had fallen on both sides of the conflict, divided against itself. John Wilkes Booth, fleeing the capital after shooting the president, had felt safe once he'd crossed into the state. Ninety-nine years later, the presidential candidacy of George Wallace, segregationist governor of Alabama, had tapped into a groundswell of support in Maryland.[27]

By the time of Wallace's campaign, however, racial integration was well under way and could not be undone. In the face of the bravery exhibited by black GIs, in the wake of the aid and hard work provided the war effort by the country's African American communities, official justifications for segregation sounded hollow. Still, the clock ticked slowly in Baltimore. The city's institutions were mostly integrated by 1966, but encouraging the creation of diverse, multiracial neighborhoods had proved difficult. Real estate speculators — "blockbusters" — spread rumors that plummeting property values were caused by blacks, fueling white flight and profiting handsomely as a result. Middle-class African Americans who sought property were shown a limited number of offerings, tear-down homes for the most part, blatantly overpriced. If they moved in, white neighbors threw rocks and smeared their windows with mud. And so racial separation persisted.

Perhaps no single individual came to symbolize postwar integration more than Jack Robinson, a black ballplayer whose appearance in a Brooklyn Dodger uniform in 1947 was said to have pried open minds everywhere. But before the Dodgers could break the major-league color barrier, they first had to integrate the minors, and it was then, suited up as a member of the Montreal Royals, that Robinson had first passed through Baltimore.

Already, the port city had seen organized baseball dock, then set sail countless times. At one time or another, Baltimore had hosted a team in the National Association, the American Association, the Union Association, the Eastern League, the National League, the American League, the Federal League, and the Negro Eastern League. All of them had left. By 1946 only two teams remained. The Baltimore Orioles (distinct from the major-league team that would arrive in 1954) was the southernmost AAA team in the all-white International League, while the Baltimore Elite Giants played in the Negro National League.

During all those many decades, through all those leagues, every ballplayer who visited Baltimore came with his team only to oppose players of the same skin color. This ceased after the Royals — and Jack Robinson — arrived on April 27, 1946. While the white fans who sat behind his wife, Rachel, complained vociferously about "that nigger son of a bitch," Jack got a hit, stole a base, scored a run, and led his team to victory.[28] This continued all season long, and by year's end Jack possessed the league's highest batting average and fielding percentage. His team went on to win both the pennant and the Little World Series, and he was named the International League's Most Valuable Player. Setting an example

Frank Robinson would later follow, Jack Robinson had competed less against the opposing team than against the white fans who turned out to greet him with bellicose threats and obscene taunts. He had fought the bigots of Baltimore through baseball and had emerged a hero.

In the wake of Frank's trade, as he busily readied himself to play in the new league, Barbara had traveled to Baltimore to locate a suitable home for them and their two young children. Her husband was one of the highest-paid baseball players of the era. (He would earn $68,000 in 1966.) Finding a decent four-bedroom in a metropolitan area inhabited by almost two million people should not have been difficult.

And indeed, over the phone to Mrs. Robinson, the real estate agents dwelled on the many available options. They talked up the elementary schools and the cozy, safe homes of Baltimore, streets silent but for the gentle breezes blowing through the porch rockers, the pedaling of cherubic paperboys bicycling along tree-lined avenues, or the occasional housewife scolding her poodle. Then the realtors met Barbara and immediately clammed up, backed away, suggested other firms that might be more suitable. All along they'd been thinking that her husband, "Mr. Robinson with the Baltimore Orioles," played third base, that she was Mrs. Brooks Robinson, that she was entitled to suburban comfort, that she was white.

The other two African Americans who played for the Orioles, Paul Blair and Sam Bowens, had accepted homes in black neighborhoods. (Blair, for example, lived in the Beacon Hill apartments.)[29] Eventually, Barbara did the same. She telephoned her husband in discouragement. She had found a place on Cedardale Road in Northwest Baltimore. It was grimy and infested with bugs, its floor covered with dog feces.

Welcome to Baltimore, Frank thought sourly.[30]

In March 1966, Robby drove himself to Florida. He reported to the Orioles' spring training site on the seventh. His daughter had fallen ill, his car had broken down, his new baseball contract was taking time to resolve, and by the time he got to camp, the whole team was out on the field, shagging flies, playing catch, practicing hitting, perspiring in the Miami sun. Alone in the clubhouse, Frank pulled on his new uniform and the stirrup socks of black and orange, a combination of colors that dated back four hundred years to the family crest of Lord Baltimore. The team had a new logo that year, their formal, stitched bird insignia replaced by a smiling, googly-eyed Woody Woodpecker knockoff. Nobody liked the change.[31]

As Frank emerged from the dugout carrying a bat, his new teammates got their first good look at him. His legs were long and slender, his waist narrow, his shoulders broad. He was tall, with a strong upper body and an astonishingly small face — squint-eyed, button-nosed, unsmiling, and intense.

As he strode up to the batting cage, Oriole infielder Luis Aparicio and pitcher Dave McNally turned rather lazily to watch. Leaning side by side against the cage, these two might at first have seemed to have little in common. McNally was from Montana, Aparicio from Venezuela. McNally was at the dawn of his career, Aparicio in the apparent twilight. Whereas "Mac" had yet to achieve much of anything, "Little Looie" was famous, during a lead-footed "slow ball" era in the league of the plodding slugger, for almost single-handedly reviving the moribund running game, stealing bases like no American Leaguer had since the days before Babe Ruth.

What these two distinctly different men shared, however, was a wry sense of humor. They were ballplayers, yes, but just as important, both were wiseasses.

As Robby neared the batting cage, Little Looie knitted his brows in consternation. "Is this all we got for Pappas?" he snorted, feigning disappointment.[32]

Mac grimly shook his head. "Yeah," he said dubiously. He

eyed the thin, stiltlike legs that had earned Frank the childhood nickname "Pencils" and asked, "Robinson, if you take
your shoes off, do those things stick in the ground?"[33]

Whereas many in Baltimore were still scratching their heads
over this trade, not knowing what to think and fearing the
worst, worrying that the club had exchanged Baltimore's
finest pitcher for Bill DeWitt's damaged goods, McNally and
Aparicio could not have been happier. McNally, winner of just
eleven of twenty-nine starts in 1965 despite posting a personal best 2.85 ERA, anticipated plenty of run support with
Robby in the lineup. Aparicio, still one of the best leadoff hitters in the history of the game, though coming off his most
disappointing season, savored the prospect of being aboard
when Frank came to bat, grabbing an extra base as the pitcher
concentrated on the threat at the plate, advancing further if
Frank flied to right, scampering home whenever Frank drove
anything deep. Both foresaw a vast improvement in their own
statistics as a result of the trade.

They were not alone. "Frank," said Brooks Robinson, beam-
ing as he cut over to the batting cage to shake the new guy's
hand, "you're exactly what we need."[34]

There were many reasons for Brooks to feel otherwise. A
former MVP himself, he had every right to feel crowded, to
begrudge the new guy any attention — an American Leaguer
skeptical about a National Leaguer's dedication to teamwork.
Brooks had been the big bat in the lineup. He was about the
same height, weight, and age as Robby, arguably even more
talented, if not as well known nationally. He was clean-cut
and outgoing, not moody, not a loner. He'd never in his life
started a brawl or been picked up carrying a gun. He'd spent
the entirety of his brilliant professional career in Baltimore's
small, struggling market, where he'd become as synonymous
with baseball as Johnny Unitas was with football. He was a
proud and perennial Gold Glover, an infielder of uncommon

grace, and thus possibly wary of Frank's reputation for occasional lapses in the outfield.

And of course he was a white man from the Deep South, namely the capital of Arkansas, that contentious battleground of desegregation, and had attended none other than Little Rock Central High School before blacks were allowed (under protection of the army's 101st Airborne Division) to attend. Brooks Robinson never played a single integrated sports game or shared a changing room with an African American until he got to the major leagues. In fact, Frank would be the first black star he had ever played alongside.

Most would have forgiven this pushed-aside, taken-for-granted white southerner if he had sought in spring training to create a little conflict, if he had wished, at least initially, for Frank to fall flat on his face. Remarkably, in real life, the magnificent Gold Glover from Little Rock, the American League's Most Valuable Player in 1964, the resident star of the Orioles seems never once to have felt that way.

As a boy, Brooks had dreamed only of getting signed to a baseball contract, of making the majors.[35] Now he dreamed of winning a pennant, of getting a chance to play in the ultimate contest, the World Series. Three times his team had come quite close. It was very much to his credit that they'd played so well. They'd settled in Baltimore as the Orioles only a decade earlier. Before then, they'd been the tragicomic St. Louis Browns, indisputably the single worst team in the history of major-league baseball. The club that Baltimore had inherited was a junker, but late in the 1960 season, inspired by its hardworking twenty-three-year-old third baseman, the youthful team, after only seven years of playing in Memorial Stadium, had surged dramatically toward the league championship. They'd ultimately fallen to — of course — the far mightier Yankees and finished second. Pursuing the Yankees in a much tighter race four years later, Brooks and company had ended up closer, just two games out of first place. And then in 1965, they'd had another promising start but a humiliating finish.

Having been an Oriole much longer than either Dave McNally or Luis Aparicio, Brooks firmly held that they had only to fine-tune the team, to add just one more ingredient to the mix, before Baltimore would achieve true excellence. With prescient clarity, Brooks understood that Robby was it, the final piece.

A twenty-year-old pitcher named Jim Palmer, his cartoonish eyebrows weighing heavily on his fresh, freckled face, observed from the sidelines as Robby stepped into the batting cage. The first pitch was a slider. Frank got out on his front foot, keeping his weight back, and smashed a clean double down the third-base line. It was the first time young Palmer had ever seen Frank swing the bat. Marveling, he turned to a teammate. "I think we just won the pennant."[36]

With the addition of Robby, the Orioles now had sluggers spread about the diamond, or, in the words of their elated general manager, "cannons at the corners" — Curt Blefary in left field, Frank Robinson in right, Boog Powell at first base, Brooks at third. With the exception of Aparicio at short, however, unproven players manned the remaining positions — rookies Andy Etchebarren behind the plate, Davey Johnson at second, and Paul Blair in center. It was a fragile, even scary, combination. The pitching staff mirrored that mix: inexperienced starters backed by a bull pen of wizened relievers.

As the Orioles traveled around Florida playing preseason exhibitions, the starters threw badly, and the absence of a proven stopper was keenly felt. More than once, reporters found raspy-voiced manager Hank Bauer cursing out his pitchers while pounding the desk in his clubhouse office.[37]

"Hank would get pissed off at you," Brooks Robinson recalled. "Not at the big guys, but the other guys. He had a little doghouse. And if you got in Hank's doghouse, you didn't play for a while."[38]

Increasingly, there were second thoughts about trading Milt Pappas. In the dark of winter, the trade had appeared so alluring. "Whoa," Barry Levinson remembers thinking the morning he picked up the *Baltimore Sun* and read of the trade. "Whoa. That seems very good, very good." Now, in the warm, lambent spring, with a carpet of crocuses blossoming back home in the archbishop's garden on Charles Street, hard questions were being asked. Had they made a mistake?

Charlie Lau didn't think so. And Lau, the team's second-string catcher, possessed many keen insights. He'd been around, bouncing from the Tigers to the Braves to the Athletics to the Orioles. He was not a great player, but he noticed things; he had a baseball mind. (Years later, he would be credited with turning George Brett into one of the game's best pure hitters.)

In the days preceding the Pappas trade, Hank Bauer had sought Lau's counsel. Lau hadn't been bothered by the prospect of losing Pappas. Load up the bull pen with a replacement arm, the second-string catcher said, and he'd scarcely be missed. Lau had a particular arm in mind, attached to the right side of a guy named Moe Drabowsky. Lau had worked with Drabo in Kansas City, and his catching instincts told him that despite all statistics to the contrary, Moe still had good stuff. "Get Moe," Lau advised softly, "and we'll win the pennant."[39] Others predicted a championship based on Baltimore's acquisition of all-star Frank Robinson; only Lau foretold it with the addition of a roaming itinerant Pole.

Myron Walter Drabowsky was a stocky, curly-haired, blond right-hander. Since 1956 he'd played with five clubs in the majors and four in the minors. He was thirty-one years old.

It was amazing how far he'd come, a journey that had begun in Poland, where he'd been born in the village of

Olanna in 1935. He had memories of Poland, but he didn't
know if the memories were really his or just visions created by
his mother's and father's stories.[40] He could recall an un-
painted barn, splintery stables, pens full of angry geese, enig-
matic goats. There was a stream behind the barn, he was
pretty sure. He could certainly picture it — the blue trickle of
water, the mottled shadows in the woods. He would try to
catch tadpoles with his bare hands. He must have been about
three years old. Soon after, he and his mom fled Hitler for
America. His dad joined them later. They settled in Connecticut, and Moe grew improbably athletic. In high school, he became a pitching phenomenon, and at age eighteen he signed
with the Chicago Cubs for $75,000, very big money in those
days.

At first Moe didn't stand out as a starting pitcher in the
majors. Then, on June 2, 1957, beginning the first game of a
doubleheader against Cincinnati, he beaned three Reds in a
row, including Frank Robinson. Two innings later, he beaned
Robby again. With this, Drabo tied the National League record
for most hit batsmen in a single game. In 1958, pitching to
Pittsburgh's Bob Skinner, he tried to put something extra on a
fastball, and his elbow popped. Arm troubles ensued, and the
problem turned psychological. His confidence was drained
further by misfortune. First, he lost a game to Early Wynn,
who was forty-three years old and in the final season of his
Hall of Fame career. It went in the record books because it
was Wynn's 300th (and final) win. Then he gave up a hit to
Stan Musial, also forty-three and in the waning days of his career. This too landed in the record books because it was Stan
the Man's 3,000th hit. Moe also surrendered a home run to
Chicago White Sox outfielder Dave Nicholson. The ball traveled 573 feet — one of the longest home runs in major-league
history.

Moe's only winning season was 1960. He won three games
and lost one. His ERA was 6.44. His elbow hurt. So he pursued

a fallback plan. He earned a degree in economics from Trinity College in Hartford, Connecticut. He wrote his thesis on a monthly investment plan in the New York Stock Exchange. During the off-season, he sold stocks and bonds on Chicago's LaSalle Street for the firm Freehlin & Company.

Sell short — that was how to invest in Drabowsky. Moe finished the 1965 season by winning one and losing six for tenth-place Kansas City. He'd been demoted to Vancouver, sold to St. Louis, demoted to Jacksonville, and then put up for sale. He was just one more bonus baby gone bust. He was 48–81 and had decided to retire unless some club picked him up to use in the majors. Lounging in the minors, he was strictly nowhere.[41] But the majors seemed very far away.

And then Lau issued his prophecy, sending Oriole executives to Fort Lauderdale, where they paid the Cardinals $25,000 for Drabowsky's contract. Baltimore then offered Moe $10,000 for one year's service as a heavy-duty, middle-inning, long reliever. He refused. He was a starting pitcher, not a bullpenner. He'd rather work as a stockbroker, he assured the Orioles. He could earn a good living without the humiliation and rejection.

Baltimore then upped its offer to $12,500.

Drabo did the math, shrugged, and said okay.

And so he came to camp. Attention was focused elsewhere. There was Frank Robinson to photograph and the youthful pitching rotation, the so-called Kiddie Corps or Baby Birds, to worry about. Aparicio and Powell still needed to return to form. Catcher Dick Brown had become terribly ill. Jerry Adair and Russ Snyder were seeing significantly less playing time.

All the while, in the background, Drabo played catch with Charlie Lau. The knowledge that Moe was now a reliever turned out to have a surprisingly calming effect on his control. His fastball came back. He also worked with Lau on a hard slider, in those days often a euphemism for a spitball, an illegal pitch.

When the regular season began, Drabowsky was the first Oriole reliever to appear, pitching an inning and two-thirds in relief of Steve Barber at Fenway Park. Baltimore beat the Red Sox that day 5–4 in thirteen innings. Within a week, having finished a home game started by Jim Palmer against the Washington Senators, Moe earned his first save as a member of the Orioles.

As for Robby, his American League career began in typical fashion. In the first inning of the season opener against Boston, Frank was beaned. He homered in the fifth, and then, as if to make sure that Bill DeWitt heard, he homered in the next two games as well. Three home runs in the first three games; only 159 more games to go. A reporter asked, "Do you think you can hit 162 homers?" Frank blinked a few times. "I don't know how to answer that," he averred. "Even if I could think of something, I wouldn't say it in a room full of men."[42]

He was batting third, with Brooks Robinson behind him, and for the first few months, the Robinson boys tore up the league's pitching. ("I don't see why you reporters keep confusing Brooks and me," Frank teased the press corps. "Can't you see that we wear different numbers?")[43]

Their team started the season at a fabulous clip, losing only three of their first fifteen games. Somehow, despite this, they fell in behind their old rivals the Cleveland Indians, who didn't suffer a loss until the nineteenth day of the season. By May 5, when the Indians arrived in Baltimore for a four-game series, Cleveland's record was 14–1. Already, the Indians' fast, lanky southpaw "Sudden Sam" McDowell had hurled back-to-back one-hitters, while their youngest right-hander, Luis Tiant, had successively shut out the Red Sox, Athletics, and Yankees and had yet to surrender a single run in 1966.

The first meeting between the two teams lasted fifteen suspenseful innings before Baltimore pulled out the victory. They lost the next game, on a Saturday afternoon, in the ninth inning, when the Indians exploded for six runs.

At the time, Robby was not in perfect health. There was nothing extraordinary in that. He was taped up and limping throughout most of his career, always playing with injuries. A few days before the arrival of the Indians, in a game against the Senators, he'd stolen third and banged up his left shoulder. Afterward, it had bothered him to raise his left arm. He'd told nobody; he didn't like complainers. Instead, unconsciously, he started dropping his arm down when he batted so it wouldn't hurt. This adjustment made his bat weigh a ton — which meant he couldn't push it out in front — and also forced Frank to pull his head out. It wasn't until batting practice on Sunday, May 7, in the hours before the series-closing doubleheader against Cleveland, that Frank even realized he was doing it. "I think I've found what I'm doing wrong," he suddenly exclaimed to his teammates, by way of explaining why his batting average had fallen off in recent days from .438 to a mere .371.[44] Immediately, he experimented with various stances. Despite the discomfort, he forced his arms and hands back up where they belonged. The bat no longer seemed heavy, and he could see the ball much better. Consequently, in the first game of the twin bill, Frank homered and doubled. Baltimore won 8–2, lowering Cleveland's record to 15–3 and moving the Orioles to within one game of a first-place tie.

In the second game, they faced Tiant, who was still sporting an ERA of 0.00 on the season. With one on and one out in the bottom of the first, Frank walked to the plate. Indian catcher Duke Sims signaled for a first-pitch fastball, down and in. Tiant nodded and threw. Reminding himself to keep his arms high, get his bat out in front, and keep his head in, Frank ripped the pitch deep down the left-field line. "See you later," he remembered thinking.[45] The ball possessed tremendous height as well as distance. It caught a favorable breeze and flew over the football press box. It cleared fifty rows of left-field seats near the foul pole, as well as a twelve-foot television camera stand atop the bleachers. Drabo, sitting that evening with the other relievers, watched from the bull pen. "We saw that it was crushed," he recalled. "It came right over our heads. We were wondering where it was going to hit. It just kept carrying and carrying."[46]

Two dark-haired teenagers, Mike Sparaco and Bill Wheatley, happened to be passing through the stadium's parking lot at the time.[47] The boys, ninth-grade buddies from a local high school, heard the crowd scream as the ball came soaring over the top of the stands. It bounced over a wire enclosure and rolled to a rest beneath an automobile, 540 feet from home plate. Sparaco dropped down, crawling on his belly, and retrieved the ball from under the car. One fan immediately offered him five dollars for the ball. Another offered ten dollars, then twenty. "I almost took the man's twenty," Sparaco remembered, "but the man's wife gave him a dirty look. I didn't know what to do."[48]

Robby circled the bases. All the while, Tiant, furious at having lost his shutout after twenty-seven consecutive innings, glowered at him.

Boog Powell was moving to the on-deck circle as Robby crossed the plate and headed to the dugout. Powell, tall and wide, only twenty-four years old but already renowned for his own tape-measure blasts, extended a hand. "Did you get it all?" he inquired with a straight face.

Reaching out to accept the congratulations, Frank's hand momentarily vanished within Boog's enormous paw, a twig swallowed by a loaf of bread. "Oh," he shrugged, "just a tiny piece."[49]

Boog snorted.

"It went all the way out," another teammate assured Frank once he got back to the bench.

"Yeah," chuckled Frank. "Right."[50]

Brooks Robinson, in the meantime, grew worried.[51] He was the next man up, the number-four hitter. Stepping warily into the batter's box, Brooks fully anticipated a knockdown pitch as Tiant's response to Robby's wallop. Brooks made no mention of the home run and discreetly avoided the pitcher's stare. The pitch came; it looked low. "Strike one!" called the umpire. Brooks turned his head to disagree, and Duke Sims piped up.

"Hey Brooksie," the awestruck catcher asked, now that he had his attention, "did you see where Frank hit that ball?"[52]

When the Orioles returned to the field in the top of the second, the public-address announcer made a historic pronouncement. "Ladies and gentlemen," rumbled Bill LeFevre's deep, authoritative voice, usually reserved for broadcasting ballplayers' names and uniform numbers, "we are pleased to announce that Frank Robinson's home run in the previous inning was the first ball ever hit completely out of Memorial Stadium."

All 49,516 spectators — working-class and white, most of them — leapt to their feet in the warm Maryland night and began to cheer. As the applause rolled on, wave after wave, Frank numbly realized that his teammates had been telling the truth. Humbled, he repeatedly raised his hand to touch the peak of his cap. "Up to then I felt the Baltimore fans were holding off their approval of me, saying, 'We'll just wait and see if he's really good, if he's really got it.'" The ovation overwhelmed him. *Yes*, he thought, *this is where I belong.* "I felt I was at home."[53]

Two hours later, the Orioles won the game, tying Cleveland for first place in the American League.

"Sometimes," Drabowsky said later, "you can point to an incident as the big one in a season. To me, when Frank hit that ball, it galvanized the whole team. It was like, 'We're going to be tough to beat this year.'"[54]

Eventually, but not yet. They stumbled through the next two weeks, losing close games because of balks, errors, uneven pitching, and sloppy fielding. It did not help that Boog Powell, their powerful first baseman, was hitting just .180, worse than any other Baltimore starter. The deepening slump mirrored his falloff of the previous season, when his batting average had plummeted forty-two points. Either too loyal or too lazy to change his lineup, manager Bauer kept with him, continuing to bat the left-handed Powell fifth after the right-handed Robinsons.

Boog tried everything he could think of to turn himself around. Frustrated, he took extra batting practice; messed with his mechanics; used lighter, longer, and thinner bats, then heavier, thicker, and shorter bats; sought superstitious charms. He did everything but diet. ("Only two things will keep Boog Powell from the Hall of Fame," a broadcaster once joked. "A knife and a fork.") At last he moved back in the box and off the plate, retreating like a supplicant, and abruptly the heavens smiled. His recovery came in a mounting deluge, at the tail end of a losing home game on May 21. Facing Denny McLain in the ninth, in the last at bat before the contest was called on account of rain, Boog thundered a home run, his sixth of the season. Suddenly, everything shone brighter.

In the dugout, Robby slapped Powell on the back. "You got it now," Frank said. "We're rolling. It's over."

They concluded May by winning six of nine with timely hitting and devastating power. "If I didn't get 'em," Boog recalled, "Frank would, or Brooks would."[55]

They went 25–8 in June, then began July by sweeping a five-game series against the previous year's American League champions, the Minnesota Twins. At the all-star break on July 10, the Orioles' lead was eight games, and their winning percentage was .667.

Four Orioles made the all-star team that year: the two Robinsons, pitcher Steve Barber, and catcher Andy Etchebarren.

Indisputably, Barber belonged. He led the league in victories and ERA. To some, however, the selection of Etchebarren seemed questionable. His statistics were not gaudy. He represented, it was thought, all the youngsters who were doing so much to kindle Baltimore's pennant hopes: Davey Johnson, Paul Blair, Jim Palmer.

At twenty-three, Etch got no respect. He was kidded for being ugly (big ears, craggy nose, a thick unibrow), for having an unspellable last name (it was Basque), for striking out too much (once every four at bats), for hitting well only with men on board (he couldn't concentrate with the bases empty because he was too busy pondering what pitches to call the following inning). It was true that he had received the gift of a starting position only because Baltimore's first-string catcher (Dick Brown) had a brain tumor and their second-string catcher (Charlie Lau) required elbow surgery. But almost immediately, Hank Bauer had granted him full responsibility for calling the games (only Steve Barber was allowed to shake off Etchebarren's signs), and Etch had responded brilliantly, bringing coherence to an erratic crew of knuckleballers, flamethrowers, sinker ballers, southpaws, spitballers, and spastics, guiding them — some over-the-hill, some immature, some both — to an astoundingly low team ERA of 3.12.[56]

Additionally, there was his bat. In crucial games, with the score tied and both sides stymied, when something needed to happen, Etch (slotted low in the lineup) always managed to make contact or earn a base on balls, keeping the inning alive long enough to bring up the top of the order and get a rally going. "It might be Frank or Brooks Robinson," recalled pitcher Tommy John, in naming the Orioles he least wanted to face during a close game, "or it could be Andy Etchebarren, their number-eight hitter, if he was hot."[57] And if it wasn't Etch, it was one of the other clutch youngsters, Johnson or Blair, stepping to the plate to deliver some seemingly insignificant contribution — not a home run or an extra-base hit, just getting on, advancing ninety feet, just far enough to shake up the opposing pitcher and force him to face the dreaded Robinsons or the revived Boog one more time.

Neither Etchebarren nor Barber saw any playing time in the 1966 all-star game. Only two days earlier, Barber had pitched seven innings, and the week before, Etchebarren had been hit in the head by a pitch and carried off the field. They flew to St. Louis nonetheless, where the thirty-seventh mid-summer classic was to be held in the new, modern stadium the Cardinals had built to replace old Sportsman's Park. The stands of the new palace, named Busch Stadium after the team's owner, could be reshaped to accommodate either football or baseball. This was the newest in a cookie-cutter style of multipurpose stadia, a trend begun by D.C. Stadium, the Astrodome, and Atlanta–Fulton County Stadium, then concluded by Oakland–Alameda County Coliseum, Riverfront Stadium, and Three Rivers Stadium. All these parks were circular, symmetrical, and immeasurably drab; most were formed from heavy concrete panels and equipped with artificial turf.

Both Etch and Barber were particularly pleased to watch this particular game from the bull pen, as the day was the hottest in memory.[58] Busch Stadium's synthetic grass made the field even hotter. Simply jogging out to the first-base line for the introductions, then returning to the dugout had been enough to make most of the players feel faint.

The Busch Stadium ushers were elaborately dressed in "riverboat fashion," while the entire city was bedecked in celebratory bunting, anticipating a big hug that never came. Instead, St. Louis found itself mired in the gruesome heat wave that was blanketing the entire Midwest. In Chicago, two hundred miles to the north, black youths desperate for relief opened up fire hydrants, which brought the police, which led to four nights of rioting, two deaths, and hundreds of arrests.

St. Louis, having for months readied itself for this close-up, thankfully managed on this occasion to avoid riots, although it did suffer severe power outages.

Dodger left-hander Sandy Koufax, who'd won the previous year's all-star game, was the National League's starting pitcher. With one away and no score in the top of the second, Brooks came to bat. Koufax had retired four consecutive batters, including Frank, without apparent difficulty. Catching a fastball on the inside of his bat, Brooks smashed it toward Atlanta superstar Hank Aaron in left field.

Busch Stadium's customers were dressed in the somewhat formal attire that was customary for a ball game at the time. The men wore dark slacks, white dress shirts, and stubby black ties. They'd shed their jackets in the scorching heat, however, and Aaron lost Brooks's line drive in the sea of white shirts. He started in late, then slipped. The ball skipped past him, and Brooks took third. It would be the only hit the American League managed to get off Koufax, who followed with a wild pitch. Brooks scurried in, and the American League had a run — their only run, as it turned out.

The National League scored a run in the fourth, and there it stayed for ten miserably feverish innings, 1–1, until Dodger shortstop Maury Wills finally brought home Cardinal catcher Tim McCarver with a single to right-center that won the game.

It was, on the whole, a day dominated by the temperature, by the pitchers, and by Brooks. Neither his offense nor his defense suffered in the debilitating heat. He seemed scarcely to notice it. One coach observed that Robinson's fielding was so superb that "he even makes the ball feel bad." After the game, Ron Santo, the National League's starting third baseman, called Brooks "a human vacuum cleaner."

"When the ball was hit down the third-base side of the field, I found myself in the outfield just standing there, watching him," Frank Robinson said. "He's the best I've ever seen at that position."

Typically smooth and inexhaustible, Brooks had played all ten innings (just as he had played all but 4 of the 902 regular season games from July 1959 until he broke his thumb in early 1965). He'd scored his team's only run, collected three of their six hits, and set an all-star game fielding record. He'd been the American League's top vote getter for many weeks, and now, even though his team had lost, he was unanimously named the game's Most Valuable Player.

Perhaps more valuable than his steady play was his role with the Orioles. A quiet, compassionate man, Brooks had always paid close attention to fostering a sense of team purpose. His genial personality had led teammates to call him "Brooks McKeldin," after the city's number-one politician, the amiable Mayor Theodore McKeldin.[59] The challenges the stellar third baseman faced in 1966 proved to be the greatest of his career. "Frank was coming over with a reputation," Brooks explained. "He had a strong personality, and it took a little while for everyone to get used to one another."[60]

Davey Johnson echoed this sentiment. "Frank kind of carried a chip on his shoulder," he recalled, "and dared everybody to knock it off."[61]

With racial sensitivities high, Brooks also worked to guarantee that the twenty-two white Orioles got along with their three African American teammates. Although it was uncommon for black and white players to fraternize off the field, the diplomatic gentleman from Little Rock made it happen. Brooks regularly invited Frank, Paul Blair, and Sam Bowens to join him and Boog for postgame food, drinks, and baseball chat. Frank hadn't experienced that sort of inclusiveness before joining the Orioles and never experienced it again with any other team. The credit, he said, belonged to Brooks.[62]

In the newspapers of the time, African Americans remained "Negroes." In the sports section, Kareem Abdul-Jabbar was a shy seven-foot-one UCLA sophomore named Lew Alcindor (who'd chosen UCLA because his hero, Jack Robinson, had gone there), while the announced desire of the young boxer Muhammad Ali to be called by something other than his "slave name," Cassius Clay, was actively ignored. Everywhere but on the Orioles, it seemed, race relations were deteriorating.

On July 18, as the third-place Indians battled the fourth-place Angels inside windswept Municipal Stadium, rumors swirled through the slums of Cleveland that a white bartender had refused to give a drink of water to a thirsty black man. An outraged mob formed, yelling angrily at police, hurling bottles and bricks. Then — as had already happened that summer in Omaha, Brooklyn, Los Angeles, and Chicago, and over the next few weeks would occur in dozens of other urban centers across Michigan, New Jersey, Ohio, Georgia, and California — a gun went off, the confusion of screams escalated, and the mob grew, met more gunfire, broke windows, set fires, looted, and lost all control. The Cleveland rampage proved to be the summer's worst, killing four, injuring fifty, and causing widespread property damage. Lasting five long nights, it was blamed by U.S. attorney general Nicholas Katzenbach on "generations of indifference by all the American people to the rot and rust and mold which we have allowed to eat into the core of our cities." Until the end of the 1960s, this same pattern — rumors, rhetoricians, roadblocks, riflemen, riot police, regrets, recriminations — repeated itself again and again all over the country.

At the same time, down south in Mississippi, civil rights marchers who were weary of constant police harassment began to chant for "Black Power." They meant it as an affirmation in beleaguered times, a defiant cry of solidarity, but to white America the slogan sounded like code for the slave uprising they'd always known was their karmic due. A nationwide "white backlash" arose in response. Law-and-order politicians suddenly enjoyed a resurgent popularity. That year, for the first time in Lyndon Johnson's presidency, Congress did not pass a civil rights act.

Most of these events passed without much notice by Frank Robinson. He rarely read the front half of a newspaper. He refused all appearances and endorsements on behalf of any civil rights organization. He played baseball, that was all. Five or six games a week, plus two on Sunday, from April to October. He'd pulled a muscle in the back of his leg, his right knee was bad, his left shoulder kept stiffening, but he continued, between the baselines, to display an altogether different kind of black power.

At home on July 27, the Orioles played the Indians. The former league leaders were now fifteen games behind first-place Baltimore. In the seventh inning, with two on and the Orioles leading 4–1, Robby drove a Dick Radatz pitch into the stands of Memorial Stadium for his thirtieth home run of the year. It was his eighth in his last nine games, and from that night on, and for the rest of the season, Frank led the AL in home runs.

The next night in Baltimore, several thousand white teenagers suddenly ran wild.[63] They burst out of Patterson Park after attending a segregationist rally and flooded the streets of black neighborhoods. "We're damn sure gonna kill all the niggers," the rally leader had assured them, preying on their fears about miscegenation, "if it takes that to keep us white."[64] Large with hate, white teenagers sprinted down North Montford Avenue and North Collington Avenue. "Kill the niggers!" they chanted. "Kill the niggers!"[65] They cornered a sixteen-year-old African American named Jimmy Lee in an alley and set about beating him. A black youngster who happened to be out walking his dog was thrown to the ground and choked with belts.[66] A long street battle broke out, with whites throwing rocks and metal pipes at blacks.

The Baltimore police acted swiftly to defuse each of these

situations. But wounds had been opened that would not heal for decades. Racial animosities would harden through the 1970s and 1980s. The city's chronically underemployed blacks would find themselves isolated in dangerous housing projects, feeling hated and forgotten. The streets of East Baltimore would ultimately bisect some of the toughest drug-dealing terrain in the nation, and the town as a whole would develop a reputation as one of the deadliest American cities, boasting a homicide rate that was three times greater than Los Angeles's and five times greater than New York's.

"Barbara," Frank Robinson answered testily, defensively, when his wife tried to thrash out what was happening in the world around them, "I cannot be coming home and discussing racial issues in baseball and in society every night."[67] He scarcely viewed himself as a concerned citizen, much less a civic leader. He was Frank — not Jack — Robinson. He was not Willie Mays, whose hastily taped radio commercials encouraging Bay Area baseball fans to stay home and listen to the Giant game would help to halt San Francisco's civil disturbances later that summer.[68] Frank's position was simple: "Those issues are going to be there every day no matter what I say or do." Later, he would recognize the maverick role his story could play in raising the spirits of his race, but for now he was just too focused on getting back at Bill DeWitt.

Focusing on DeWitt was easy, since the Cincinnati owner continued to defend his trade for Pappas by deriding Robby. "As the season went on," Frank remembered, "Mr. DeWitt kept up the barrage. . . . 'He never had a year like that for us. . . .' 'Wait until July, August. . . .' 'Wait and see how he comes out at the end of the year. . . .' 'In the ten years he played for us we won only one pennant.' "[69]

Cincinnati fans, to whom DeWitt directed these remarks in the main, might have been understanding, or at least more forgiving, were Milt Pappas pitching better. But he was surrendering nearly five runs per game and had lost four and won just one since the all-star break. Having attracted a million spectators the year before, the Reds in 1966 would draw 300,000 fewer fans. DeWitt found himself hanged in effigy in downtown Cincinnati, wearing a label across his chest that read DIMWIT.[70]

Pappas owned a record of 9–10 by mid-September, while Robby had assumed the league lead in runs scored and runs batted in. He still led the American League in home runs but was second in batting average to Minnesota's sensational Tony Oliva. Asked to name his team's most valuable player, Hank Bauer looked at Blair and Snyder, platooning in center, each hitting well; at Etchebarren, that great strength behind the plate; at the well-balanced bull pen that eventually would appear in 137 games, winning 39 and saving 53; at McNally and Aparicio, enjoying their best years thus far; at Blefary and Boog, who'd gradually gotten hot but were hurt now. Brooks Robinson's batting average was on the decline. Bauer sighed. "If Brooks had kept up the pace," the manager said, "this would be tough. There is only one choice, though."[71] He pointed down the dugout at Frank Robinson.

No one disputed the call.

"It was the closest-knit group I've ever been around," Steve Barber recalled. "There were no cliques. Everyone could run with everyone. It was just terrific."[72] They liked to laugh as much as they liked to win. "We were a young club and had the type of fellows who liked to joke a lot," Frank remembered. Perhaps it was their sense of humor that kept them comrades as they traveled a country coming rapidly undone. Bored, standing interminably around in airport terminals and hotel lobbies, teammates mercilessly roasted one another about anything that came to mind. Robby mocked Boog for having the legs of an elephant and then, as if it weren't insulting enough to have been nicknamed after a piece of congealed snot, honored Powell's southern fried upbringing, his white trash diet, and his enormous size by christening him "Crisco."[73] He teased Curt Blefary about his errors in the field, calling him "Clank," implying that he fielded not with a leather glove but a chunk of inflexible metal.[74] Luis Aparicio complained that he was tired of making Brooks Robinson look like a solid third baseman.[75] "The humor has no boundaries," observed a reporter who was traveling with them. "It can be profane. It can be irreverent. It can be about the color of a guy's skin."[76] Paul Blair gave Brooks a hard time about growing up as an acclaimed athlete in a southern town where he never had to play against blacks.[77] Brooks shot right back with a harsh joke about Blair's batting slump. Soon Frank felt comfortable enough to refer to certain white players as "Pale-Face."[78] "We were pretty open about things," recollected Brooks. "We got on one another and everybody had a good time."

That was true even during the tensest moments. Following the all-star game, the team had met up in Chicago to play the White Sox. Mobs of rioters were roving the city's West Side at the time, looting white-owned businesses, torching buildings, stoning firefighters, and trading sniper fire with the police. Leaving O'Hare Airport, Robby's white teammates maintained they were going to keep behind him: he was black; the mobs wouldn't open fire on him. "Oh no, you're not," Frank insisted. "I'm going to stay away from you. You're not going to get me shot up." As the Orioles were driven to the Sheraton Chicago, they urged him, "Come on, get up to the window so they can see you!" Four thousand National Guardsmen were just then entering the riot area in troop trucks and jeeps. Armed with rifles, bayonets, pistols, machine guns, and tear gas grenades, the Guardsmen had received orders to "shoot to kill" if they were shot at.[79] Frank ducked down. "No, thank you," he said. Crouching, he left his seat on the team bus, plopped down in the aisle, and stretched out on the floor, completely out of sight. "Baby," he informed the team's twenty-three white players, "you're all on your own."

They teased him right back. He always carried an attaché case, which was rare in those days, so they speculated about his other job, secretly working for the government as the guy who carries the nuclear football. Or they kidded him that, while they were receiving twelve dollars a day for meal money, his billfold couldn't hold all the dough he was earning, hence the briefcase. At last Frank opened the case. Out jumped a fake snake. It was found that certain players — Paul Blair, Luis Aparicio, Charlie Lau — were petrified of snakes. Soon rubber snakes were showing up everywhere — in the dugout, in the showers, sailing through the air in the clubhouse. Once everyone grew acclimated and was no longer scared, Moe Drabowsky borrowed live snakes from pet stores, bringing them to the ballpark and hiding them in Blair's uniform, Aparicio's glove, and Lau's shoes, creating mayhem.

If Robby hit the majority of the team's home runs, Moe most often struck their funny bone. Most of his pranks began innocently. Being a stockbroker in the off-season, for example, Drabo had to learn the prices of stocks every weekday afternoon after the New York markets closed. He thus had (or at least could claim to have) a legitimate professional interest in discovering that the phones in most stadia were on a direct-dial system. Upon realizing he had only to dial 9 to get a free outside line, he made all his social calls from the bull pen. So did the other relievers. Sometimes they even ordered take-out food to be delivered to the bull pen.[80]

Moe soon stumbled onto the fact that he could call the opposing bull pen as well. At the end of May, the Orioles visited Kansas City. As the game got under way, Drabo casually picked up the phone in the visitors' bull pen and dialed his former teammate Lew Krausse, a relief pitcher in the A's bull pen. "I called over to their pen," Moe remembered, "to find out what players were in the doghouse, whose wives were expecting babies, just to get caught up on all the local news. When their coach Bobby Hofman picked up the phone, I don't know why but I hollered, 'Get Krausse hot in a hurry!' and hung up the phone."[81]

Krausse jumped to his feet and began to exchange warm-up tosses with a bull pen catcher. From across the diamond, Drabo watched in dumbfounded glee. It was only the second inning, and the A's were batting. Rollie Sheldon, Kansas City's starting pitcher, was still throwing decently. The score was 1–1. The guys in the A's dugout couldn't figure out why someone would be warming up. Their manager, Alvin Dark, glanced down at the sudden activity in his pen. What was Krausse doing? Why was he getting in his throws now?

After a few minutes, Moe called the Kansas City bull pen again. "That's enough," he barked. "Sit him down."

Kansas City ended up losing the game 4–2, but before it was over, Moe had again called the A's bull pen. He asked for Krausse this time. "Lew," he asked, choking back a laugh, "you warm?"

Recognizing Moe's voice, Krausse cursed. "Ah Drabo, you son-of-a-bitch!"[82]

The next night, with two out in the fifth, the phone rang in the Oriole bull pen. It was Hank Bauer. He ordered Drabowsky to get ready. Across the way, Krausse was also warming up. They pitched the next two innings against each other. Lew struck out three, but Moe struck out five and went on to register his first major-league victory since May 16, 1965, when he'd been pitching — naturally — for Kansas City.

A reporter caught wind of the first night's prank and wrote it up in the next day's papers. That night, during the third and last game of Baltimore's series with the A's, the phone in the home team's bull pen rang. As always, Bobby Hofman answered.

"Mr. Hofman?" inquired the voice on the other end. Hofman recognized it as the drawling voice of their team's owner. "This is Finley. I just got back in town and I saw that story this morning about the calls you got Friday night. I'd like to hear your version of the episode."

"Well sir," Hofman said, "although we didn't know it at the time, it was Moe Drabowsky who called and told us to have Krausse warm up. Sounded a lot like our skipper, though." Prompted by Finley, the coach proceeded to give a full account of the incident — until he started to hear smothered laughter on the other end of the line. Hofman blushed. "Okay," he said, with a dawning realization. "Moe, I know it's you."[83] And of course it was.

Drabo pitched in forty-five games that first year in Baltimore. He thrived. "I think people tend to say how crazy he was instead of how good he was," pitcher Wally Bunker would later observe. "Moe was a really good pitcher. Plus he was a wonderful guy."[84] In 1966 Moe compiled his best season ever. He won six and lost none. He struck out 97 in 96 innings, walking only 29. But his clutch pitching performances of 1966 were equaled by his feverishly creative practical jokes, many of which raised the standard for major-league pranks. Before Moe it was deemed sufficient to put hot Capsolin ointment on a jockstrap. Drabo, from the bull pen in the middle of a game, was known to organize surreptitious quasi-military assaults against the opposition, a line of teammates with camouflaged faces crawling furtively behind the outfield fence, popping up at the last minute to throw dirt clods and firecrackers into their opponents' pen, and then scurrying back to their own. "The practical jokes were rarely premeditated," he recalled. "I'd just look around and say, 'Gee, I could probably do something here.' And I always tried to have M-80s around."[85] A lit M-80 was handy, for example, to toss into a bathroom stall when a guy was on the toilet.

Moe was the expert on giving hotfoots, the time-honored

tradition wherein a match was secretly wedged into the sole of someone's shoe and then lit. He gave hotfoots to sportswriters in the clubhouse while they were busy interviewing his teammates. He hid beneath benches and tarps for extraordinary lengths of time to surprise unsuspecting players. Later, in the wake of Baltimore's 1970 World Series celebration, he threaded an elaborate line of lighter fluid around several corners in the locker room to give a hotfoot to the commissioner of baseball. (He succeeded, of course.)

"I used to like to put goldfish in the big clear drinking jugs of the opposing teams' pens," he confessed. "And on occasion I'd whistle some sneezing powder into the other team's clubhouse through the air conditioning system."[86]

Thanks to Frank and Moe, the team also came to expect stirring victories. After the all-star break, only one team remained a threat: Detroit. Like the Orioles, the Tigers possessed powerful veteran hitters and occasionally great young pitchers. They had surged in June, winning nineteen of twenty-four games to come within a game and a half of first place. But they came no closer. The Tigers played well against the front-runners but kept losing to the bottom dwellers, such as the seventh-place A's. By the time Detroit failed to sweep the Orioles at home on August 19–21, they were thirteen and a half games back of first-place Baltimore, which, despite having pulled out just one victory from the series, now owned a record of 80–42.

When the Orioles got home, they celebrated. A local funeral director named Fran Ruck had invited them out to his home in Towson for his traditional team get-together. On the evening of August 22, Baltimore's ballplayers and their wives drove out to Ruck's residence, about ten miles north of Baltimore. He showed the team into his large, ranch-style home; motioned generously toward the backyard, the terraced garden, and the in-ground swimming pool; and encouraged them to have a good time.[87]

As always, the alcohol flowed. The team's owner, Jerry Hoffberger, also owned the National Brewing Company, and plenty of cases of National beer were on hand.[88] Predictably, the pool party soon devolved into roughhousing and high jinks. Curt Blefary ran around the flagstone deck warning everybody to get into the pool or risk being thrown in. Before Drabo even had a chance to change into his swimsuit, Boog and some others chased him through the kitchen, tackling him in the living room. A terrific wrestling match and some bloodletting ensued as they worked to get Moe into the pool fully clothed.[89]

Others grabbed Frank, who was lounging on the portico with his wife, Barbara, beside some of the other players who weren't swimming. "You're going in, Robby."

"I don't swim," Frank said.[90]

They smirked at this. He didn't swim? Growing up, Robby had been one of the Bay Area's greatest athletes. He'd played defensive back for the football team at McClymonds High. His American Legion baseball team had won consecutive national championships. As a guard in basketball, he'd made all-city, and his team had earned a couple of state titles. Maybe he didn't *like* to swim, but surely such an accomplished jock knew how. "You're going in anyway," they told him.

"Okay," Frank said resignedly. Anything for team unity. "Let go of me." He figured he would hop into the shallow end, and they'd leave him alone.[91]

In he jumped, slipping awkwardly on the tile, and under he went. His feet could find no purchase on the pool bottom. He clawed at the water. Helplessly, he slid toward the deep end. He was in the center of the pool, with nothing to hold on to. Air bubbles followed his mad motions. He came up, flailing. "Help!" he sputtered. "Help!" Then he went under.

He had not been kidding. He did not know how to swim. "Lots of blacks never learned to swim," Dodger catcher John Roseboro would later explain, "because they couldn't get in pools and weren't welcome on beaches."[92]

Greatly amused, his wife and many others watched Robby splash around. "Look at him," someone chortled. "What an actor!"

Frank again managed to make his way to the surface. He had never been so scared in his life. He had just enough air left in his lungs to issue a final "Help!" before the silvery water closed over him again. He sank in silence to the bottom, and there he stayed. This time he did not resurface. He saw distorted figures leaning over the rim of the pool, lit like angels. He tried to keep calm. He'd read somewhere that it was best not to struggle. As he drifted in and out of consciousness, Robby could see the next day's headline: BILL DEWITT GETS LAST LAUGH; FRANK ROBINSON DROWNS IN UNDERTAKER'S POOL.[93]

Paul Blair looked on, then got caught up in dunking Charlie Lau.[94]

Steve Barber noticed Frank lying on the bottom of the pool, figured he was horsing around.

Boog gripped a can of beer in his paw. "Frank sure has been down there a long time," he observed mildly.[95]

Fortunately for all, Andy Etchebarren also was watching. The rookie catcher stood poolside, dressed in swim trunks. He wasn't sure if Robby was joking, but he decided it was time to find out. He jumped in and gave Frank a poke. There was no response. Etch swam back up to draw a deeper breath, then again dove down to Frank and dragged him to the surface. Two guys on the side of the pool lifted him out. Robby was coughing water and needed, as Etchebarren recalled, "a little bit of work."[96] They let him lie on the concrete by the side of the pool for about five minutes, then Frank got up.

"It hit us," Paul Blair said, "what could have happened."[97]

No reporters were present. Months would pass before the story made the papers.

The incident at Fran Ruck's was the last crisis of the season. The fielding of the entire team remained a thing of near perfection as, throughout the season, Baltimore led the AL in fielding percentage. No Baltimore player ever amassed more total bases, scored more runs, or hit more home runs than Frank Robinson did that year. The Orioles won despite using hurt players. Andy Etchebarren played for months with a broken hand. Curt Blefary broke out in hives. Davey Johnson fractured his toe and was later spiked so badly that his leg required fourteen stitches. Robby's right knee continually filled up with fluid.

As for Boog, who hadn't started swinging the bat well until his devastating ninth-inning clout off Detroit's Denny McLain on May 21, his contributions largely ceased after August 20, when a belated retaliatory pitch from McLain fractured the ring finger on his left hand. After that, Boog could scarcely even hold the bat. Although 1966 would turn out to be the first year in which Powell hit more than thirty homers and drove in more than one hundred runs (he would do it twice more in his career, including his 1970 MVP year), his season essentially began and ended against the Tigers, lasting only a little more than three months.

All these injuries failed to keep the team from winning. From June 13 on, the Orioles never relinquished first place. That year, as Brooks Robinson puts it, "we just kinda ran off and hid from everyone else."

Baltimore's starting four — McNally, Palmer, Barber, and Bunker — were responsible for only forty-eight of the team's ninety-seven victories. Seven relievers accounted for the rest. No one was more surprised by the bull pen's durability and the steadiness of Etchebarren than their manager. "If I had known," Hank Bauer told a reporter at the end of the season, "that half our pitching staff would come up lame one time or another, and that our number one catcher would be out for the season, I don't think I could have figured us to win."[98]

Bauer's Orioles barely won half the games they played in August and September. During this time, a letter from a fan was received by vice president Jack Dunn. The first sentence read, "What the hell is the matter with the Baltimore Orioles?"[99] Right-handed relief pitcher Dick Hall remembered, "We knew by July that we were going to win the pennant. We were just coasting. But Frank kept driving us. He had an unbelievable killer instinct."[100]

By the time the Orioles finally clinched the pennant on September 22 by beating Lew Krausse and the Kansas City A's, Robby led the league in almost every major offensive category. The Orioles ended that road trip, their last of the season, with a victory over the Angels, then flew home.

The next afternoon, apolitical Frank was dragged into politics.

The mayor of Baltimore, Theodore R. McKeldin, had endured the most trying summer of his long political career. McKeldin was a man of considerable height, garrulous, much loved, fond of poetry and the Bible.[101] His face was long and grave, his gaze both penetrating and farsighted. He had a ruddy complexion and a dark comb-over that emphasized his prominent widow's peak. He identified with working-class outcasts and was admired by ethnic minorities as a civil servant of exceptional character.[102] Unlike most men, he neither drank nor smoked. Unlike most politicians, he was resolved never to lie.

The Congress of Racial Equality (CORE), a long-established but increasingly militant civil rights organization, had made Baltimore its "Target City." In July CORE had convened at Baltimore's Knox Presbyterian Church, advocating black nationalism and self-sufficiency and angrily condemning white liberals and integration. At the same time, in the state capital, not far away, a few of these self-same liberals were trying without success to frame a racially blind open-housing law.[103] Sincerely desiring CORE's help in stamping out discrimination, McKeldin addressed the organization's suspicious delegates. No sooner had he emerged from Knox Church than enraged segregationists descended upon the city.[104] They denounced the high-minded McKeldin as "half Jew and half Negro," called him a "bootlicking nigger lover" and a "nigger stooge," characterized his administration as "Jewish-controlled," and chanted "Mayor McKeldin Go To Hell!"[105]

Without a chief of police (the chief had been fired earlier amid accusations of racism), McKeldin had to coordinate conflicting strategies that would permit the various groups to gather in protest while still containing their most explosive elements. Astoundingly, his balancing act succeeded. (The mayor disarmed one angry street mob by earnestly inquiring, "My brothers, my sisters, what is the problem?")[106] The fact that no one was killed as a result of racial violence in Baltimore during the temperamental summer of 1966 was a significant, though unheralded, triumph for City Hall. Until Dr. King's assassination in 1968, Baltimore was one of the very few large American cities that had not endured a recent riot by its black citizens. This remained a source of pride for McKeldin.

Throughout this time, the mayor grasped the unifying potential of local sports teams and ballplayers. Back in 1944, he'd stood in the crowd at Greenmount Avenue and Twenty-ninth Street, watching both dumbfounded and aghast as the old wooden park of Baltimore's International League team had burned to the ground.[107] It was McKeldin, in his first term as mayor, who'd persuaded the Orioles to move into Municipal Stadium on Thirty-third Street. After renovations, the stadium had been renamed Memorial Stadium, to honor the war dead. This was the current club's home.

Now, again, McKeldin used his mayoral authority to underscore the symbolic value of baseball to the community, reaching across racial lines to make the city's African Americans feel included in the Orioles' success. On Monday, September 26, he went to Frank Robinson's neighborhood in Northwest Baltimore to rename Cedardale Road in honor of the superstar who had, begrudgingly, taken a house there. At a ceremony attended by Frank, Barbara, and their two small children, as well as by several hundred youths and parents of African descent, McKeldin announced the change of Cedardale to Robinson Road. To make it official, he snipped a length of orange and black ribbon (the Orioles' team colors).

Frank accepted the honor by thanking not the city but the road. "It isn't every day that you get a street changing its name for you," he pointed out matter-of-factly.[108] The universe was suddenly crazy with compliments for him. Only a year earlier, he was being booed in his home park. Now a recent letter to the editor in the *Baltimore Sun* had chided the city's citizens for not allowing Robby, "the man who made the difference this year," to purchase a home wherever he wanted. "Until Baltimore is ready to greet the Frank Robinsons and the Paul Blairs as neighbors, rather than only as glorified gladiators," the letter concluded, "such honors as these athletes help bring to our city will continue to have a hollow ring."[109]

After the ceremony, the many youngsters came nearer, encircling the mayor and the ballplayer, seeking autographs. After signing the card of one black girl, McKeldin jotted a brief postscript. "I favor open housing," he wrote.

The little girl read his words and looked up, wide-eyed. "You do?" she asked in astonishment.

McKeldin solemnly nodded. "One million per cent."[110]

Fortunately, no one at the ceremony had pointed out that if open housing were the policy, if more homes in more neighborhoods were available for African Americans, Frank Robinson wouldn't be living in Northwest Baltimore at all.

Having (however reluctantly) satisfied any civic obligation he owed to the city's politicos, Frank went back to work. He was closing in on that rarest of baseball gems, the Triple Crown. Only twelve major leaguers had earned it since 1878. All of them were white. They were judged the greatest hitters of all time, men like Napoleon Lajoie, Ty Cobb, Rogers Hornsby, and Ted Williams. None had accomplished the feat in his first year in a different league, however, as Robby was attempting to do, while confronting new pitchers in unfamiliar ballparks.

He possessed thirteen more home runs than his nearest competitor, Minnesota's Harmon Killebrew, and had batted in thirteen more runs than Boog Powell, who was second in RBIs. These leads seemed safe. During the remaining weeks, attention was focused on whether Robby could hold off Killebrew's teammate, the graceful left-hand-hitting Tony Oliva. "Tony O" was a Cuban outfielder in only his third full major-league season. In his rookie year, he had led the league in batting, hits, doubles, and runs. His performance in Game Two of the previous year's World Series, in which he'd helped the Twins defeat Sandy Koufax, had only enhanced his sterling reputation. In his brief career, Oliva had not lost a major-league batting title, although this year, after August 22, he'd started to struggle at the plate. In September's final weeks, Robinson collected five more hits than Oliva. Still, it wasn't enough to guarantee the crown.

Now, in the last series of the regular season, the Twins came to Baltimore to settle it face-to-face. In a Memorial Stadium doubleheader on September 30, Oliva singled four times in ten at bats. He was now batting .309, while Robinson, who had gone two for four in the first game and then sat out the second, was batting .317. Two games remained. Robby could still lose the Triple Crown.

Apropos of the drama of the showdown, the skies went dark with storm clouds, and the next day it poured rain. The season would conclude with another doubleheader. Everything came down to that. With the lead, Robinson could sit the games out and avoid the risk of lowering his average. If so, Oliva would have to bat eight times and get eight hits to win the batting title.

Frank — bad knee, injured leg, strained shoulder, and all — played.

"As good as Frank was," Dave McNally observed, "it was how hard he played that really made an impact. Even when we got way ahead, he only knew one way to play. You think you're trying hard until you see someone trying as hard as he did. The intensity the man had was just incredible."[111]

Hank Bauer had already announced his starters for the World Series. His pitcher for Games One and Four would be Dave McNally. Jim Palmer would pitch Game Two. Bauer couldn't decide whether Steve Barber or Wally Bunker should start Game Three. Barber's record had sagged to 10–5. Struggling with an inflamed elbow tendon, he'd managed to pitch only fourteen innings since the all-star break. Bunker, at 10–6, had fared little better. After a month on the disabled list, he'd returned to serve out the season as a spot starter.

On the frigid, overcast final day of the 1966 season, the two sore-armed pitchers vied for a chance to start the third game of the World Series. It was obvious which one the fans favored. Barber was a homegrown phenom with a movie star mole on his left cheek. He was a photogenic blue-eyed boy from Takoma Park, Maryland, while lantern-jawed Wally hailed from that other coast. Entering to a great ovation, Barber pitched first. Despite pain that surged through his forearm every time he moved his elbow, he hurled a scoreless first. He began the second inning, however, by walking the bases full, and Bauer pulled him, concluding the opportunity of a lifetime. Barber would be unavailable until the following season; his arm needed rest.

In the second game, Bunker shut out the defending AL champs over five innings before he too was pulled. BARBER OUT OF SERIES cried the next day's headlines, while in minuscule print, far down the page, a side column reluctantly noted, "Bunker Looks Better."

As for Oliva, he managed but one hit all day. The title belonged to Robby, as did the Triple Crown. He was the first ballplayer to conclude a season as the leader in batting average, home runs, and RBIs since Mickey Mantle had done it in 1956, and to this day he remains the only black player to win the Triple Crown. He told reporters that he appreciated what the team and the city had done for him, but he was careful to acknowledge the individual who had done more than anyone to drive him to this new height. "I'd especially like to thank," Frank smiled, "Mr. DeWitt."

For all that had been resolved that day, an issue of paramount importance remained in doubt. Just who were the National League champions? Every season, it seemed, the NL pennant was up for grabs until the very end, and 1966 was no different. For weeks the Baltimore Orioles had known they were going to the World Series. Now they even knew that McNally, Palmer, and Bunker would constitute their three starters. But who and where would they be playing? As yet, no one was sure.

For most of the season, the Pittsburgh Pirates and San Francisco Giants had wrestled each other for dominance of the National League. Now the Los Angeles Dodgers had characteristically come on strong at the finish.

Robby wanted Los Angeles to take the pennant. It wasn't just the prestige of going up against the defending world champions. Pittsburgh and San Francisco were both built around their big bats, like Baltimore. Frank wasn't positive the Oriole staff could quiet the likes of Roberto Clemente and Willie Mays, but he felt confident they could negate that negligible thing the Dodgers called an offense.

And so he and his teammates looked to Philadelphia, where the Dodgers battled future Hall of Fame pitcher Jim Bunning for the league championship. Desperately, Robby hoped for Los Angeles to pull it out.

PART TWO

Sandy's Swan Song

The Los Angeles ball club of 1966 was never expected to compete for the National League flag. They looked weak. Their sluggers — Duke Snider, Wally Moon, Frank Howard — were gone. The remaining stars were injured. Two-time batting champion Tommy Davis had badly broken his ankle. Pitching ace Sandy Koufax suffered from arthritis in his throwing arm. The Dodgers couldn't score, and they lacked consistent hitting. Everybody knew this, but nothing had been done in the off-season to rectify it. Instead, the team had acquired pitcher Phil Regan from Detroit, a seemingly insignificant transaction. They still had no third baseman. In a preseason poll, the nation's press picked Los Angeles to finish in the middle of the pack, in fifth place out of ten.

Few reigning world champions have been so underestimated. Although the box scores could never fully account for their victories, through some sort of mysterious, collective will, they won, drawing walks, advancing on errors, scoring on fly balls. They played a style of small ball that was at least fifty years out-of-date, accentuated by a set of unusual skills. They possessed the major leagues' only all-switch-hitting infield, which left them impervious to the late-inning strategies of opposing bull pens. Their team spirit was unparalleled. They ran a lot and sacrificed often. They had in Don Drysdale a pitcher who doubled as a pinch hitter, and in Jim Gilliam a first-base coach who doubled as a third baseman. They had some superlatives too. Their center fielder, Willie Davis, was one of the fastest men in the country. Their first baseman, Wes Parker, was one of the most flawless fielders in baseball history. Their left fielder, Tommy Davis, had been the youngest man ever to win consecutive National League batting titles. He'd been injured in a slide in the middle of the 1965 season, however, and his status remained uncertain. Likewise, their team captain, Maury Wills, had in 1965 come close to breaking his own stolen base record, until his legs had begun to give way, hemorrhaging from too many bruising slides and too much galloping overexertion.

LA's centerpiece, and biggest question mark, was Koufax. Time and again, almost reluctantly, "the Golden Arm" was called on to deliver in high-visibility games, often on short rest, to clinch a pennant or a championship. Most recently, in the seventh game of the 1965 World Series, he'd struck out ten while shutting out the Minnesota Twins with only one pitch, a fastball. Afterward, Sandy could scarcely lift his bowed left arm, which, rather than growing more golden, was becoming increasingly crippled by every pitch he hurled. While his fellow world champions had sung and drunk and flung shaving cream about the dressing room, Koufax had tiredly assured the viewing public that he felt fine. Why? "I don't have to do this again for four whole months." But even if that much rest had proved adequate for his damaged elbow, it was unclear, as the new season dawned, whether the southpaw would still be a Dodger.

During the off-season, he had met with Don Drysdale at a Russian restaurant in Los Angeles. There the two men most responsible for LA's 1963 and 1965 world championships innocently fomented a revolution. Tired of being used against each other in annual salary negotiations with general manager Buzzie Bavasi, the legendary lefty and righty decided to negotiate their contracts together. "It was a small union, a union of two," Koufax remembered. "But it was a union." Having won forty-nine games between them the previous season, while consistently attracting big crowds to every ballpark in which they pitched, they felt justified asking Bavasi for a million dollars to split between them for three years of their service. Soon they lowered the price to $900,000. And they were going to hold out, to go on strike rather than to Vero Beach for spring training, until their agent received a satisfactory figure.

In issuing these demands, in defying tradition so blatantly, the two athletes were asking for more than a pay raise. They were seeking an elevated mind-set. They were asking baseball's owners (and fans) to reconsider the value of the contemporary ballplayer — of every ballplayer, not just those (like themselves) lucky enough to be famous. They wanted, for example, an acknowledgment of basic cost-of-living increases and inflation adjustments. How much would the $80,000 that Babe Ruth had received in 1930 actually be worth in 1966? And what would a modern-day player have to accomplish to deserve that? What about the debilitating injuries sustained on behalf of one's team and the hospital bills after leaving the game? How were they to eat once their arms wore out? "You've got to be honest with yourself and realize it can't go on forever," Koufax explained. He cited the case of Wally Moon, the Dodger hero of 1959, forgotten by 1966, presumably destitute. "I don't think anyone knows where he is. This will happen to Don and me some day. It's the history of the game. I'm not bitter about it. Everybody in it knows what to expect."[1]

They were asking that a player who contributes substantially to the earnings of his employer — whether by drawing more fans, who of course will pay for tickets and parking and then probably buy concessions and souvenirs, or by being largely responsible for championships that will earn the club a World Series bonus — be compensated accordingly. They were asking for the labor standards that workers in other professions enjoyed — the right to counsel from informed representation, the right to strike for fair reimbursement, the right to bargain collectively, the right to engage in transparent, back-and-forth negotiations with one's boss. None of these were the norm, and the two Dodgers were determined to change that.

Koufax was particularly piqued by Bavasi. When the two pitchers turned down management's pitiful counteroffer, the dome-headed and oily GM barked, "Well, we'll miss you boys," and then fell silent for the rest of February and most of March. "We never intended to make an ultimatum, it was a starting point," Sandy heatedly told a reporter. "But what are you to do when you don't hear from the employer for over a month? What? Baseball has always treated us as if we had no choice but to sign, as if the holdout were just a dumb charade. They just made us an offer and waited for us to crawl up to it like a desert water hole."[2]

At the time, no owner would deal with an agent, nor pay a pitcher more than $100,000 a year. Dodger owner Walter O'Malley, an imposing, flint-featured millionaire who hoarded his immense profits with a rare and ardent devotion, was unwilling to be a pioneer on either count. O'Malley was the most powerful owner in baseball. Both he and Bavasi recognized collective bargaining as a dangerous precedent. Koufax had earned $85,000 in 1965. Drysdale had earned $80,000. Thankfully, the reserve clause from prior contracts still bound the two ballplayers to Los Angeles. They couldn't play for any other professional American team. What could they do? Where could they go? They needed the Dodgers for a paycheck. Eventually, Bavasi knew, they'd be forced to accept O'Malley's terms.[3]

In any other city, in any earlier age, their options would have been seriously restricted. Year after year, Joe DiMaggio had

refused to sign his contract until his salary had been sweet-
ened. The response of the dismissive Yankee brass was essentially, "Fine, go back to San Francisco and fish." DiMaggio
buckled. But things were different for Koufax and Drysdale.
They inhabited the new entertainment capital of the world, at
the freshly paved intersection of the television, film, and
music industries. Concepts of celebrity were becoming increasingly porous. Possibilities of all sorts were opening up.

"It must have been a time," a dewy-eyed groupie, eager to
hear about the swinging 1960s, says to an aging record producer in Steven Soderbergh's 1999 film *The Limey*. "A golden
moment." Standing over a smog-shrouded LA skyline, the
producer takes a moment to admire himself in a mirror before
he responds. "Have you ever dreamed about a place you never
really recall being to before?" he asks softly. "A place that
maybe only exists in your imagination? Someplace far away,
half-remembered when you wake up? When you were there,
though, you knew the language. You knew your way around."
He pauses. "That was the sixties." He turns to her, stops, and
continues, "No, it wasn't that either. It was just '66."[4]

Terms like "synergy" and "cross-marketing" had yet to be
coined, but Hollywood got the idea. Famous in one field meant
potentially famous anywhere. Vocalists hosted variety shows,
dancers performed interviews, models delivered the news. The
Beatles were a successful singing group who made feature
films as well as a Saturday morning cartoon. *The Monkees*
was a hit TV show that spawned a band that made a movie.
"Batman" was a song on the radio, a movie in the theater, and
a program on the tube. Dodger catcher John Roseboro accepted the role of Sergeant Dave Bradford on *Dragnet*. The
team's first baseman Wes Parker played the fiancé of Greg's
math teacher on *The Brady Bunch*. Their second baseman
Jim Lefebvre was a cannibal on *Gilligan's Island*. The cur-
rency of superstardom was redeemable at a growing number
of outlets.

One man who couldn't fully appreciate what this meant was Edmund G. "Pat" Brown, the well-liked Democratic governor of California, who in 1966 was running for reelection against a conservative Republican named Ronald Reagan. Brown found it very hard to take the Reagan campaign seriously. A former B movie actor, Reagan was now more familiar to the electorate as the host, every Wednesday evening at seven, of NBC's *Death Valley Days*. Brown compared the political novice Reagan to a pilot who tells his passengers, "I've never flown a plane before, but don't worry: I've always had a deep interest in aviation."[5] It was pithy; it was apt. But come November, Brown would be out of a job.

Throughout their strike, the two pitchers received the utmost sympathy from Hollywood, particularly those movie stars who watched the home games from Dodger Stadium's dugout-level boxes. "I wish them luck in their pitch for more dough but they'll need a blow torch to get into O'Malley's money belt," Bob Hope quipped. "I hope they get it."[6]

"All they ever did," insisted Chuck Connors, star of the popular ABC western *The Rifleman*, "was to say in the best American tradition that they thought they were worth so much money and ask the Dodgers to give it to them. Look, if Elizabeth Taylor can demand a million to go over and make a turkey called *Cleopatra* and can't even get to the set on time, and the picture loses millions, Koufax and Drysdale are certainly worth what they're asking for a season's work."[7]

Connors's support was especially valuable, for he had been a Dodger infielder before changing careers to become an actor. His own success convinced him that Koufax and Drysdale "would have a very good chance of making it in show business, because they are hot properties. They're big box office before they even prove their talent. You put them in the right format, give them the right director, protect them for a while with other good actors and a good cutter, and they'll make it. Then they'd be making five times what they could with the

Sandy Koufax chats with television star and former Dodger Chuck Connors. (Courtesy of the *Sporting News*)

Dodgers. And the funny thing is nobody would be mad at them then." Connors shrugged off their lack of experience. "This is an easy business. All you need is a little energy."[8]

But Walter O'Malley could discern no connection. "I do not believe we are in competition for the entertainment dollar," the burly man declared, his sour expression cramping around a tight little smile.[9] "If they think they can make as much money playing two-bit extras as they can playing baseball," one Dodger official told the *Los Angeles Times*, "they are welcome to it."[10]

Both pitchers had already done incidental acting on television and stage. They'd appeared in comedy skits, occasionally performed walk-ons. Koufax had been in an episode of *Dennis the Menace*. Drysdale had appeared on *Leave It to Beaver* and *The Donna Reed Show*. Paramount Pictures now offered Koufax the role of a television commentator and Drysdale the part of a detective sergeant in *Warning Shot*, a movie in which a police officer (David Janssen) is accused of murder. Screen Gems desired to put Drysdale under a long-term contract to star in a forthcoming ABC series, *The Iron Horse*, about a man who inherits a train.[11] Bob Hope asked Koufax to guest on his next TV special.[12] The television show *The Hollywood Palace* announced that Koufax and Drysdale would appear on April 9. The program's hosts would be actor Gene Barry and the Mamas and the Papas. "Don is expected to sing with his own guitar accompaniment," a spokesman for the show announced. "Koufax will concentrate on humor."[13]

"It's a wonderful thing what baseball can do for some people," said Buzzie Bavasi, having been informed of the duo's many employment opportunities. The general manager sought to make sure that people understood his part in their success. "Without baseball, I don't think they would be making movies."[14]

Meanwhile, at Vero Beach, the other Dodgers went about their work, stretching, jogging, throwing, swinging, and trying hard not to think about the absence of their two best players. Hearing of the vacancies, seventeen pitchers descended on the LA camp, seeking a job as a Dodger starter. Among them was a determined twenty-year-old named Don Sutton, who not only would succeed at breaking into the majors that year but also would spend the next twenty-two years there.

There were plenty of hopeful signs among the gloom. Maury Wills arrived in camp, saying his legs felt fine and promising that this year he would indeed break his stolen base record. Tommy Davis proved the very picture of dedication as he tried to strengthen his leg and make himself once more invaluable to the Dodgers.[15] But while Tommy used to be fast — he would take third in the footraces, behind Willie Davis and Maury Wills — those days were over. It would be many seasons before he'd again put weight on his back foot in the batter's box. He trained himself, in the meantime, to swing off his front foot.

Handsome, funny, and friendly, Tommy Davis had been a star athlete for Boys' High School in Brooklyn. When he turned seventeen, major-league scouts began to buzz about. The Yankees offered a $4,000 signing bonus, as did the Dodgers. Brooklyn scout Al Campanis got to his mother, and she spoke to her son. "As long as the money is the same," she argued, "you might as well sign with the Dodgers. After all, you're a Brooklyn boy." He wasn't convinced. Wasn't it the Yankees who won each October? Playing for the world champions sounded pretty nice.

Then the telephone rang. Some stranger with a high-pitched voice asked to speak with Tommy. It was Jack Robinson. As young Davis, rapt and trembling, placed the cold receiver against his ear, Jack outlined all the advantages of playing for the Dodgers. What a great organization they are! They sure could use him. Jack had heard about Tommy. Jack was hoping he'd become a Dodger too.

Tommy signed with Brooklyn that afternoon.

Two days later, the Dodgers announced that they were leaving town.[16] Walter O'Malley was a businessman, not a baseball fan. He had not been shy about his desire for a scrap of land on which to build a sports arena more consistently profitable than little Ebbets Field. When New York City officials wouldn't oblige, O'Malley called their bluff, quitting the old monochrome world of subways and brownstones, abandoning Brooklyn's claustrophobic crumble for the booming sprawl of Los Angeles, that Technicolor tomorrowland of freeways and tract houses.

Tommy didn't especially care whether his home games were played in New York or California, but his family, his friends in Bedford-Stuyvesant, and his fellow Brooklynites were not so blasé. The quixotic Dodgers had achieved a perfect resonance with their quixotic borough. The players lived near the ballpark, hung out at local pool halls, ate at neighboring coffee shops, and interacted constantly and easily with the hometown folks — bartenders, barbers, streetcar conductors, laundry women, stickball players, everyone. They played their ball games within the intimate, flavorful carnival of Ebbets Field and knew many of its eccentric ushers, vendors, and patrons by name. Brooklyn had several daily newspapers, which had helped fuel Dodger loyalty. "Brooklyn," Don Drysdale wistfully remembered, "was one big but very close family, and the Dodgers were the main topic of everybody's conversations."[17] It wasn't just that Brooklynites passionately felt the game's importance. For generations, new immigrants had reinforced the team's fan base, devotedly following it through surges and pratfalls, gloriously upraised by its postwar greatness. In their avid attachment to the national pastime, newcomers to the country had declared themselves to be Americans. By sharing a team, Brooklyn's various inhabitants had found a collective identity. Cheering for the Dodgers had helped knit the diverse community together.

No more. "Betrayed" was the word on everyone's lips. O'Malley had betrayed them. No longer would Dodgers stroll the borough's narrow, cracked sidewalks or banter good-naturedly with its "regular guys." Now, years later, the players could be seen in newsreels, hiding behind sunglasses while hobnobbing with show business personalities.

Often it is said that, by hauling his team across the United States, Walter O'Malley broke Brooklyn's heart. Too rarely is it pointed out how O'Malley also broke a little piece of LA's heart.

Helicoptering over the city, the Dodger owner had spied a plateau overlooking the downtown commercial district and chosen it as the site for Ebbets Field's successor. Inhabited by dry brush, eucalyptus, cactus, livestock, condemned structures, and peasant families of Mexican descent, its name was Chavez Ravine. Although a metropolis had exploded around it, with a population that had soared from 100,000 to nearly 4 million in less than half a century, Chavez Ravine had managed to retain the flavor of the traditional pueblo. Photos snapped in 1949 show its goatherds and sheep farmers still living in the simple manner of the original settlers. But this way of life was doomed. This scrap of property had grown too valuable to remain undeveloped. In the early 1950s, the residents had been forced out with a promise that they would be provided more modern housing on the same land. They hadn't been. Instead, the fate of Chavez Ravine had hung in limbo until O'Malley had happened out west on his shopping trip. He had liked the site and asked to buy it. A few remembered that this land had been promised to its former occupants. A referendum had been put on the ballot, Proposition B ("B for Baseball!"). Despite angry cries from the Hispanic community, Proposition B ("B for Betrayal!") had passed, opening the way for O'Malley to purchase Chavez Ravine and develop it into the auditorium of his dreams.

John Roseboro's autobiography recounts the acquisition this way: "Walter O'Malley and Los Angeles both got what they wanted, but a lot of land was taken over and given to us over the protests of a lot of people, including some little old ladies."

While the stadium was being built, the Dodgers played their home games in the Los Angeles Memorial Coliseum, an oblong stadium designed to accommodate track and football. To shoehorn a somewhat respectable major-league baseball diamond into the Coliseum, a 42-foot wall had to be put up in left field. Even so, with that wall only 250 feet from home plate, any left-handed batter with an inside-out swing — like, for example, regular Dodger left fielder Wally Moon — was able to take advantage of the park's peculiar proportions by lofting a pop fly to left for an easy home run.

For this reason, Moon had been ideal for them while the

Dodgers had played in the Coliseum. But once Dodger Stadium was ready, his skills no longer gave the home team an
edge. In Chavez Ravine, the Dodgers needed a line drive hitter with a lot of speed. Up came Tommy Davis; out went
Moon. The year was 1962. Maury Wills, batting leadoff, collected 208 hits. Jim Gilliam, batting next, sacrificed his at
bats so that Maury could steal bases. Patiently, Gilliam took
strikes; he backed up in the box so that the catcher had a
longer throw; he fouled off pitches whenever he sensed that
Maury had failed to get a good jump. Wills earned fame for
stealing a record 104 bases that season, while Gilliam faded
into obscurity. This was the spirit of the team Tommy had
joined.

Because he was followed in the lineup by the immensely
threatening Frank Howard, Tommy saw a lot of good pitches
that year. He took full advantage of each and every one, hitting .346. With Wills and Gilliam frequently on base ahead of
him, he led the league with 153 RBIs. Tommy was twenty-
three years old. No National Leaguer in his lifetime had
driven in that many runs, and thirty-six years would pass before another (Sammy Sosa) would equal the feat. Tommy hit
.326 the next season, 1963, again a league high. His team
went on to play the Yankees in the World Series. Facing the
pitchers who, but for Jack Robinson's phone call, would have
been his teammates, Tommy had hit .400 and helped lead his
team to a stunning upset, a four-game sweep.

He had been an instant phenomenon. He wasn't a sterling
fielder — "he threw almost like a girl," John Roseboro would
later declare — but within two seasons, he had become one of
the greatest right-handed batters in baseball history. He'd
outhit Frank Robinson, Hank Aaron, Willie Mays, and Roberto
Clemente, future Hall of Famers, each of whom possessed
a decade's more experience. His future potential looked
limitless — until May 1, 1965. That night at Dodger Stadium,
in the fourth inning of a game against the Giants, Tommy slid

into second base, thinking to break up a double play. His spikes got caught. He heard something snap, went numb, and looked down to see his ankle weirdly bent, the joint sticking out. He turned over and angrily pounded the dirt. He had both dislocated and severely fractured his ankle. Dr. Robert Kerlan, the Dodgers' team physician, said it would take two years to heal. Tommy couldn't wait that long. He sat for the rest of 1965 but arrived at spring training in 1966 determined to make the opening day roster.

It wouldn't be easy. He still had his batting eye, his sharp reflexes, his snappy wrists, but he would never run well again. Further complicating his comeback was "Sweet Lou" Johnson, a man who had been promoted from Spokane the previous year to take Tommy's place. Johnson's hustle had endeared him to the Dodger brass.

Sweet Lou's instantaneous success in LA had been nothing less than remarkable. In 1965 he'd turned thirty-one years old. He had already played for nineteen minor-league clubs in thirteen years. He'd been praying for a chance to reach the big leagues when Tommy had snapped his ankle. A middle-aged rookie — as Maury Wills had been, a few years before — Sweet Lou was also an uninhibited shout of a player whose high spirits down the pennant stretch lit up the Dodgers. Koufax tapped him as the man most responsible for the '65 pennant, while Drysdale approvingly observed, "He goes everywhere like a guy being shot at."[18] Johnson's enthusiasm was contagious — even if it was, as he would later confess, fueled in the main by cocaine, marijuana, and alcohol.[19] Any teammates who noticed this didn't seem to mind. "I'd be lying if I told you I never saw a baseball player take an upper,"[20] Jim Lefebvre would admit soon after. But Lou's clutch-hitting ability made him immensely popular. "Johnson is my left fielder," Walter Alston proclaimed during the winter of 1965–66, "and it will be up to Davis to win his old job back."[21]

The Dodgers simply had too many outfielders. Yet they would probably need them all. If they could write about fifteen names on the lineup card and ingest the contents of Lou Johnson's medicine cabinet, they might be able to survive the loss of Koufax and Drysdale.

As it was, the defending world champions looked pathetic. They dropped their first six spring training games. Then they flew to Houston, where the Astrodome (new the previous year) had just been fitted with artificial grass. It was called AstroTurf, and was created by Monsanto. (In addition to creating plastic vegetation, Monsanto was simultaneously providing the government with a defoliant known as Agent Orange.) On March 21, the Dodgers and Astros became the first two major-league clubs ever to play on AstroTurf. The Dodgers won by a score of 8–3, after Tommy Davis doubled in two runs in the first inning. But it was still clear to everyone that on real grass or fake, the Dodgers without Koufax and Drysdale posed no threat.

During the 1940s and 1950s, it was the dream of just about every American boy to become a big-league ballplayer. Jim Lefebvre pictured himself playing alongside Mickey Mantle. Wes Parker fantasized about being Gil Hodges. Such reveries were still the stuff of youth in the early 1960s, when a youngster named Nolan Ryan watched Sandy Koufax dominate Ryan's hometown Houston club and therein learned how a hard fastball could turn a man into a hero.[22]

By 1966, though, a new dream had taken hold. Instead of Astros, American boys wanted to grow up to be astronauts. In that regard, what happened inside Houston's domed stadium on March 21 stirred far less romance than what was announced the next day at Houston's space center. The National Aeronautics and Space Administration (NASA) had decided that veteran astronauts Virgil I. "Gus" Grissom and Edward H. White II, along with rookie Roger B. Chaffee, would fly the first Apollo spaceship into orbit around the earth, possibly late that year.[23] The three-man Apollo missions had always been intended to supersede the two-man Gemini flights, but the surprise announcement capped NASA's attempt to counter its worst month since the United States had begun its manned space program in 1959.

The bad news had begun on the last day of February, when the two astronauts scheduled for the May blastoff of *Gemini IX* — Elliot M. See Jr. and Charles A. Bassett II — were killed in a plane accident. See was piloting their craft, a T-38 single-engine supersonic trainer, when it crashed. Ironically, the T-38 had crashed into the roof of the very building that housed their space capsule. (It also contained a production line of Phantom jet fighters to be sent to Vietnam, another example of the "military-industrial complex" about which President Eisenhower had warned the country in his farewell address in 1961.)[24]

Two weeks later, the crew of the aloft *Gemini VIII* — Neil A. Armstrong and David R. Scott — linked up with an Agena target rocket 180 miles above the surface of the earth. Even the Soviet news agency, Tass, acknowledged that Armstrong and Scott had just made history, mooring in space for the first time. But no sooner had they docked than disaster struck. An electrical failure in a small maneuvering thruster triggered a wild tumbling. Even free of the Agena, the capsule continued to spin crazily. The astronauts nearly blacked out. They were supposed to spend three days in orbit. Instead, their mission was aborted only ten hours and forty-two minutes after it had begun. They splashed down in the stormy Pacific. To add ignominy to failure, they got seasick while waiting to be picked up by a U.S. Navy destroyer.[25]

By the time his club had scraped out five victories against twelve blowouts in spring training, Dodger manager Walter Alston had given up hope that Koufax and Drysdale would ever come back. "I'm disappointed, of course," Alston disclosed. But he was still proud of his team. "We'll go at it day by day and do the best we can, and we may surprise a few people."[26]

Others, like pitcher Claude Osteen, were less optimistic. Osteen had been ecstatic to join the Dodgers the previous year. He'd come from the Washington Senators, a weak American League team that hit about as little as the Dodgers, though without any speed or defense to offset it. He'd known that in Los Angeles, he'd still have to scrap fiercely for a win, and indeed, in 1965, the Dodgers had become the only modern team to win a pennant with a batting average as low as .245. But Osteen also had known that a lot of pride and magnificent history came along with the Dodger uniform, that he'd be joining the best rotation in baseball, that the Dodgers were always in the pennant race until the end, and that being a Dodger would bring him nearer to his ultimate dream of pitching in the World Series. To join the '65 Dodgers, he would later put it, was to enter "a whole different realm of baseball."[27] This 1966 spring training team, however, was more like one of his old, dispirited Senator clubs. "Playing without Koufax and Drysdale," Osteen admitted, "will be like trying to drive a car without a steering wheel."[28]

The two pitchers in question remained in Los Angeles, rehearsing lines and blocking out scenes on the set of *Warning Shot*. Drysdale told the newsmen who accompanied them to Paramount Studios that he and Koufax "have got to get out of the game sometime and who knows — maybe now is the time."

Reporters prodded Koufax for a comment, but all he'd say, very quietly, was, "I agree with Don."

One newsman doggedly kept after him. "How about your public image?"

"My image?" Koufax scoffed. "What am I doing that's wrong?"[29]

In fact, all month long, across the country, daily headlines dutifully reported every scrap of gossip about their holdout, and very little of it was sympathetic to the ballplayers. Public sentiment was amply captured by *Los Angeles Times* columnist Jim Murray when he wrote, "The elephants want a share of the circus."[30]

Bavasi loved the publicity; Drysdale didn't mind it; Koufax hated it. "It has got so many other people emotionally involved," Sandy complained. "It's gotten out of hand."[31] He felt particularly aggrieved at how the *Los Angeles Times* stoked the controversy, going to great lengths to print letters from vocal pro-O'Malley fans who were fed up with "greedy players," "megalomaniacs," and "two-bit chiselers."[32] "When you start printing letters from fans," Sandy declared, "it's a little unfair. It's emotional. It's not right or wrong — it's a question of them wanting to see their favorite team win."[33]

Pitching legends Sandy Koufax and Don Drysdale stroll into Dodger Stadium. (AP / Wide World Photos)

At the last minute, Hollywood rode to the rescue. As the Dodgers quit the palmettos and scrub pines of Vero Beach and headed west, Chuck Connors phoned Bavasi and encouraged him to sit down with Drysdale. A summit was arranged. They met on the morning of March 30, in the back of a Sunset Boulevard restaurant near Dodger Stadium. They drank coffee and traded figures. At last Drysdale telephoned Koufax, who agreed with Don's assessment. "It was just a matter of both sides giving a little and taking a little," Bavasi summed up.

After thirty-two days, Drysdale, Koufax, and the Dodgers came to terms. The two pitchers inked one-year contracts. They would earn a collective raise of $70,000.

The team was euphoric. "Yeah, baby!" hollered the perpetually penniless Lou Johnson, who'd struggled to imagine a year with no postseason bonus. "My money was in danger!"

O'Malley emphasized that Koufax and Drysdale were signed by Bavasi "as individuals, with a disparity in salary, without an agent, without three-year contracts and without a no-cut clause."[34] Nonetheless, it seemed to be a substantial labor victory.

Overlooked in the publicity surrounding the holdout was an event of far greater significance. On the seventh day of their holdout, March 5, 1966, representatives of the Major League Baseball Players Association had elected Marvin Miller — a Brooklyn boy who'd grown up a Dodger fan, a former assistant to the president of the United Steelworkers — to be their executive director. Like the office of baseball commissioner, the players association at the time was a weak, essentially symbolic body, its reins of power tightly wrapped about the hands of the baseball owners. But Miller was shrewd and imaginative, and he would change all that by riding the prevailing social conscience and pleading the case against ballplayers' inequitable pay. The average salary of a major leaguer in 1966 was $19,000. When Miller left the job fifteen years later, the average salary would be $185,000.

Given the holdout, the distractions, the stiff competition, and the low overall expectations for the team, few were surprised by LA's slow start. But three National League teams that had been expected to compete — the Reds, Braves, and Phillies — stumbled too, failing to distinguish themselves early in the season and soon falling away.

The laggards were less noteworthy than the teams that got off to a quick start. Because of a suspect pitching staff and a weak bench, the Pittsburgh Pirates had been picked to finish even lower than the Dodgers. But they started the season winning eight of their first nine games. Then the San Francisco Giants won twelve straight, sweeping both Los Angeles and Pittsburgh. A month into the season, the Giants were handily in first place, with a 22–7 record, followed by the Pirates. The Dodgers were fourth, behind Houston, only a game over .500.

Sports Illustrated wrote admiringly of the invincible Giants. *Life* ran a lengthy feature on San Francisco's ace, Juan Marichal, who had won his first ten decisions. *Time* went one better and put him on its cover, calling Marichal "the number one . . . and most complete pitcher in the game," even though he had never won the Cy Young Award, losing four years in a row to Southern California pitchers — Drysdale in 1962, Koufax in 1963 and 1965, and Dean Chance of the Angels in 1964.[35] This year, it was assumed, would be different. Northern California's chance had arrived. Los Angeles was seven games out of first place and looked to be settling in comfortably there. Few recognized the parallels to the previous year, when the under-regarded Dodgers had successfully waged an uphill battle — first against San Francisco, then against Minnesota — that had lasted right up to the ninth inning of the seventh game of the World Series.

Of course, as long as there had been Dodgers, there had
been Giants looming over them. Their rivalry dated from 1890,
when the Giants represented Manhattan. The Bridegrooms
(eventually the Trolley Dodgers, then just the Dodgers) took
to representing Brooklyn, which at the time was autonomous,
its own independent city.

From the start, theirs was a fierce feud. Beating no one else
mattered quite so much. Each time the two teams met, fans
and players alike arrived to act out personal grudges, settle
scores, and establish one community's dominance over the
other. Brawls spilled from the field into the stands and back
again. They were not so much professional clubs playing a
game as rival gangs convening to do battle.

When Claude Osteen joined the Dodgers, he discovered
that the animosity was as intense as ever. "It was war," Osteen remembered of meetings between the two teams. "Really
exciting baseball."

During much of the early twentieth century, the club from
Manhattan was far superior. Throughout this period, while
hot-tempered John McGraw drove his Giants to legendary
heights, Brooklyn steadfastly stood by its losing boys. Whether
because the very name of McGraw's powerhouse team con-
noted a Goliath-size hubris or because the whole borough felt
overshadowed by their supposedly more enlightened island
neighbors to the west, Dodger fans savored their team's role
as National League underdogs and occasional spoilers.

In the years and decades that followed, little changed.
Brooklyn's curious mix of immigrant pride, guilt, inferiority,
and pessimism didn't lift. Even as they acquired Dixie Walker,
Pee Wee Reese, and Pete Reiser, and then Carl Furillo, Duke
Snider, and Gil Hodges; even as they integrated the majors
with Jack Robinson, then added Don Newcombe and Roy Campanella; even as they won pennants in 1941, 1947, 1949,
1952, and 1953 (each time dropping the World Series to the
Yankees, that other Manhattan rival); even as Ebbets Field

became the playground of the beloved "Boys of Summer," the Dodgers and their fans kept glancing apprehensively over their shoulders, never liked their chances, and never stopped hating the Giants. They expected the worst, and twice they experienced it. In 1951 and 1962, the Dodgers squandered enormous mid-August leads to finish in a tie with the late-charging Giants. On both occasions, a best-of-three play-off was required to determine which National League team would advance to play the Yankees for the world championship. In both play-offs, the Dodgers lost the first game, won the second, and took a comfortable lead into the ninth inning of the third before somehow managing to lose. Both times the Giants then lost to the Yankees in the World Series.

Although the Dodgers had won three NL pennants since coming to Los Angeles in 1958, and in each case had gone on to win the world championship, it was always a surprise to see the team on top. From the mid-1950s until the institution of divisional play in 1969, the National League experienced its feistiest phase. The roll call of rotating NL champs attests to the competitive balance: Milwaukee in 1958, Pittsburgh in 1960, Cincinnati in 1961. In 1959 the Braves ended the season in a tie with the Dodgers. In 1962 the Giants did the same. In 1964 the Cardinals took the pennant on the final day, with the Reds and Dodgers each one game back, the Giants three back, and the Braves five back. In 1965 the Dodgers gained the crown on the penultimate day, winning fourteen of their last fifteen games to outpace the Giants. Anyone could win in the National League — but anyone could lose too.

Fans of the Brooklyn Dodgers and New York Giants used to enjoy debating who was the better center fielder — Duke Snider or Willie Mays. A decade later, on the other side of the continent, the debate continued: Who had the better mound ace? Was the right-handed Marichal more dominating than the left-handed Koufax? Batters who had faced them both were split. Marichal's opinion? "Sandy Koufax is the greatest pitcher I've ever seen." Koufax's opinion? "I'm too busy worrying about Willie Mays to worry about Marichal."

Certainly, Koufax owned the more impressive records. He was the only pitcher in history to throw four no-hitters (including a perfect game) and the only person to be repeatedly voted professional athlete of the year by the country's sports editors (an award named the Hickok Belt). Koufax was older and more experienced. In the four seasons since Marichal had joined the major-league club, he had won more games than Koufax (86 to Koufax's 84), but he also had lost more (40 to 25). (Drysdale, over the same period, was 85–54.)

The two achieved comparable dominance through different techniques. Pitch after pitch, Koufax's motion was the same. It began gracefully, deceptive and easy. Then the right leg would descend. Suddenly, he was a very long, stretched-out man in a too-small uniform, about to pop his buttons. His back was so severely arched that it resembled a stringed instrument. As the left side of his body blurred forward, he'd deliver one of two overhand pitches, either a tumbling curve or a climbing fastball, with pinpoint accuracy. He always came over the top, but because of his crazy overextension, it sometimes looked as if he wasn't releasing so much as expelling the ball from his madly bent, out-thrust midsection.

Marichal was just as consistent, but batters found him less predictable, more capable of infuriating variations. He rarely seemed to be working very hard. With his straight right leg firmly set against the rubber, he would tilt back and kick out his free leg. The batter would watch in awe as the pitcher's left foot swiftly rose higher than his head. His throwing arm dropped straight down behind him, so low that the ball would nearly graze the mound, and then he'd rock forward. He could deliver the ball overhand, sidearm, or three-quarters with equal accuracy, so the batter had to guess on the release point. In addition, the high-kicking Dominican possessed at least five outstanding pitches — fastball, curve, slider, sinker, and screwball — and could effectively change speeds on each.

In the eighty-five times the two teams faced off after both Koufax and Marichal had become regulars, the two aces started against each other only three times. The Dodger left-hander won their first contest (June 3, 1961), while the Giant right-hander won their second (May 9, 1963). Their third and final meeting became a nightmare that would haunt Marichal forever. It took place on August 22, 1965, in San Francisco's Candlestick Park. Koufax lost, but Marichal was not around to earn the victory. He'd been ejected from the game in the third inning after hitting John Roseboro over the head with a bat, probably the single greatest expression ever of the Dodger-Giant rivalry.

It was a strange deed that defied not only the rules of the game but also the personalities of the participants. Simply put, the two players were not themselves that afternoon. Roseboro, facetiously called "Gabby" by his teammates because he spoke so rarely and exhibited such disciplined self-control, was edgy — anxious about the country's state of affairs, upset over the ugly things he was seeing on the nightly news, still fuming about the many blacks casually killed two weeks earlier on the streets of Watts. Marichal, a relaxed, affable man who dressed with such exceptional care that he was known as "the Dominican Dandy," was similarly distracted by reports that members of his own family, back home in the Dominican Republic, were being attacked and arrested in the wake of a recent military takeover.

There was more, of course. The two teams were at the end of a bitter four-game series, in the dog days of their annual pennant race, with their aces on the mound and bad blood in the air. There had been the usual dirty slides, shouted insults, controversial calls, and close plays. After Marichal threw at

Maury Wills and Ron Fairly, Roseboro demanded that Koufax retaliate. Sandy refused. (The umpire had already warned the dugouts, so any further beaning would have resulted in a Koufax suspension.) It was one of the very few disagreements between the like-minded, almost telepathically linked battery mates.

Few pitchers other than Walter Johnson have been as celebrated as Koufax for not throwing at batters. Few ballplayers, other than the famously upright Christy Mathewson, have been so highly esteemed for their ethics. But whether the characterization of Koufax as unwilling to pitch inside is accurate or not, Roseboro had no use that day for the diplomatic future Hall of Famer. He was pissed off, and he wanted Koufax to exact revenge. "If it had been Drysdale pitching," Roseboro would later assert, "he would've just knocked down Mays and McCovey, and that shit would've ended right there." But because of the velocity of his fastball, Koufax never liked throwing at batters. Roseboro, his patience wearing thin, took matters into his own hands. When Marichal came up to bat, the catcher deliberately dropped Koufax's third pitch. In picking it up, he scooted slightly to the left, then fired it back to the mound, alarmingly close to Marichal's head — so close, in fact, that it grazed the tip of his nose. The Giants' other star pitcher, Gaylord Perry, watched in shock from the dugout. "Of all things," Perry would say afterward, "it was a duster from the rear."

Nerves already frayed, Marichal spun on Roseboro. "Why'd you do that?" he hollered.

The catcher glared hotly from behind the bars of his mask. By way of answering, he balled his ungloved hand into a fist and jumped at Marichal. Roseboro was wearing a chest protector, shin guards, and cleats. He was heavier, stronger, and tougher. He was accomplished in both kung fu and karate.

Backing away, Marichal brought his bat down, a deplorable

act of instinct he would never be allowed to forget. *Jesus*, Rose-boro thought. *He creased the side of my head.* A two-inch gash opened in his forehead, and blood obscured his vision.

A sixty-man brawl ensued, fueled by three-quarters of a century of venom and vitriol. The San Francisco police were needed to restore order. After play finally resumed, Koufax was rattled. He couldn't concentrate. He surrendered a three-run homer to Willie Mays and lost. A half game now separated the second-place Giants from the Dodgers. National League president Warren Giles fined Marichal $1,750 and suspended him for eight playing dates. Marichal missed two starts, and the Giants lost the pennant by a game.

It took a year for Roseboro to forgive Marichal. In the meantime, he hit better than ever. His hands were bruised from receiving fastballs every day, his body banged up, but he was tough. "There were times," he would later disclose, "my hands hurt so bad it hurt terribly just to hold a bat, and times they were so numb I couldn't even feel the bat." He was a line drive hitter, usually low in the batting order, and would bat just .249 over his long career. Despite this, in 1966 Rosey would maintain a .300 batting average into August.

On Tuesday, May 17, Marichal started opposite Drysdale at Chavez Ravine. The Dominican was making his first appearance in Los Angeles since clobbering Big D's catcher the previous season. A total of 53,561 Dodger fans paid for the privilege of booing Marichal, who was undefeated on the season, with an ERA of 0.76. For eight innings, he shut out the home team. Thanks to a rare Dodger error, the Giants led 1–0 going into the ninth. Then LA rallied: a bunt by Maury Wills, a single by Jim Gilliam, a sacrifice fly by Willie Davis. (Such, at the time, constituted a Dodger rally.) Wills raced home. The score was tied. The game went into extra innings. An inning later, Marichal was gone. Three innings later, the Dodgers "exploded" with two singles (one from Wills) and scored on a wild throw from San Francisco right fielder Ollie Brown.

Wills seemed particularly pleased. He was coming off a muscle pull, having missed six games, five of which the Dodgers had lost. Now their captain was back, brimming with pride. "No club can stop the Dodgers in 1966," he enthused. Wills noticed players jumping up from the overcrowded bench to offer their seat to a teammate. He saw veterans happily helping out rookies. He perceived genuine harmony between the players and the coaching staff. LA's secret ingredient, he said, was "togetherness."[36]

This was true. The Dodgers of the mid-1960s possessed a team mentality, a selflessness that is extremely rare in professional sports. "It was such a special club," LA reliever Phil Regan remembered. "It didn't matter who got the win. It didn't matter who got the big hit. All it was was the Dodgers winning. And that was a total attitude."[37]

Backup catcher Jeff Torborg agreed. "It was a unique bunch of guys. Everybody looked out for the other guy."[38]

Even the opposition appreciated it. "Every club should learn to play like those Dodger clubs," Marichal would observe in the 1970s.[39] "They won so many games by one run, just because when one of their guys got on base, they tried to hit and run, squeeze play, bunt. They didn't care if they had the clean-up man at home plate — if they felt they could win with a bunt, they made that guy bunt. With the Giants it was different. Somebody would get on base, and that guy had to stay there until somebody hit a home run. If the home run didn't come, forget it." On this Roseboro agreed with Marichal. "San Francisco had the ability, but we pulled together as a team better."[40]

In every game, a new hero stepped up to the plate. On May 21, in the twelfth inning, it was Wes Parker running home to win the game on a single by Wills. On May 23, with two outs in the ninth and the score tied, it was Roseboro scoring from second on a squeeze. On May 24, it was the injured Ron Fairly homering to put the Dodgers on top. On May 25, again in the bottom of the ninth, again with the score tied, Willie Davis reached base on an error, advanced on a single by Lou Johnson, and scored on a single by Parker. On May 27, Osteen shut out the Mets. On May 30, Wills hit his first home run in two years. On June 2, Sutton shut out the Cards. On June 4, the injured Tommy Davis hit his first home run in two years. On June 7, Al Ferrara hit an inside-the-park home run in the tenth.

Los Angeles rolled on, sweeping Philadelphia, Atlanta, and St. Louis, winning fifteen of twenty-two. The team belonged to the little shortstop. Wills arrayed the defense in the field and sparked the offense at the plate. When he swiped his twentieth base in New York on May 28, it put him a game ahead of his record-setting pace of 1962.

But if Wills was their captain, Koufax was their inspiration. "We were a team and every player played a part in our victories but he was our top gun and we all knew it," Roseboro would later say. "The guts of that guy really got to us. We not only loved him, we really respected him." During those three weeks, Sandy had pitched six complete-game victories and struck out fifty-six while holding the opposition to less than a run a game. His record climbed to 10–1, with at least twenty-four starts remaining on the season.

Today Koufax remains a cipher, available to serve as an example in countless narratives. He was the baseball star who supposedly preferred basketball. He was the poster boy for traumatic arthritis, an early experiment in sports medicine. He was a gentleman competitor — hard on himself, easy on his teammates, intense but never angry. He was the Brooklyn-born Dodger who twice beat the team's ancient rivals the Yankees in the 1963 World Series. He was the exploited athlete who held out to get the money he knew he deserved. He was

the man who walked away at his peak. He was the youngest
player elected to the Hall of Fame. All this is true, but exam-
ining him outside the commonplace context of his career —
taking the mound every four or five days, working to retire
nine opponents, communicating silently with Roseboro before
each pitch, finding the strength, focusing, repeating over and
over his big windup, hitting the mitt — somehow seems to re-
duce the magic of his accomplishments.

It will always be debated just how much Koufax profited
from the twin expansions of the early 1960s: the addition of
new major-league franchises in 1961 and the commissioner's
enlargement of the strike zone in 1963. The former, it is believed, supplied Koufax with more naive strikeout victims,
while the latter is said to have helped him get high strikes on
his rising fastball. These and other factors, such as the fact
that his home field was such a great pitcher's park (whoever
took the mound, on whichever side, few batters got on base,
and even fewer scored), probably contributed to his success.
But that success still elevated him far above the other pitchers
of his time.[41]

By 1966 he had set a single-season strikeout record and
twice tied the record for most strikeouts in a single game. He
had won four consecutive ERA titles and two Cy Young
Awards. But he had never won thirty games.

Two and a half months into the season, he was on a pace to
do so, and with Wills determined to smash his own single-
season stolen base record, with a deep bench and small but
timely rallies, the Dodgers had tiptoed into first place. Their
manager, who possessed the pallor and personality of a tepid
potato, refused to get excited. "It doesn't mean a thing," Walter Alston said, "being a game in front or a game behind right
now. The entire league is tougher than last year, when we won
it the next-to-last day of the season." Two days later, on June
12, his club crept downward, out of first place, where they

stayed. When pressed about LA's pennant chances, Alston refused to guess. As always, he responded as if he were one step removed from the entire experience: "I'd rather surprise the fans than disappoint them." The Dodgers would stay in second or third place, behind Pittsburgh or San Francisco, until mid-September.

Despite the lack of spring training, Koufax wasn't the problem; he was pitching stupendously. So too was Claude Osteen, who had won twelve by mid-July. Drysdale was another story. After losing to the Mets on June 3, the tall, square-shouldered blond — "California large and California handsome," as Jane Leavy describes him — had compiled a 4.06 ERA, with only four victories against five losses. By this time, Koufax had completed ten games, Drysdale just three. Drysdale made a solemn vow with reliever Ron Perranoski, who was also struggling: each promised to win five straight.

In his next start, against the last-place Cubs, Drysdale surrendered eight runs and lost. He and Perranoski reevaluated. "We've decided," Drysdale announced, "we'd better postpone our pact a couple of days."[42] It was a smart move. In rapid succession, he lost to the Giants, Cubs, Astros, and Braves. When at last he beat the Reds on June 29 — thanks more to his ability with the bat than with the pitched ball — Drysdale's nine-hitter represented his first victory since May 30.

"Drysdale had worked hard for many years," Roseboro would later say, "and he was wearing down a little." Alston expressed confidence that the intimidating right-hander would turn the corner, but Alston's boss, Buzzie Bavasi, was less encouraging. The general manager claimed that Drysdale still wasn't in shape, and he blamed the holdout. But Drysdale, unlike Koufax, had been assiduously throwing in the off-season, and Dodger trainer Wayne Anderson disagreed. "Drysdale has never worked so hard," he protested. Bavasi also overlooked the fact that Drysdale had faced, in twelve of his first eighteen games, the ace of each opposing staff and had suffered from LA's lack of run support. In what was anything but a vote of confidence, Bavasi let it be known that Drysdale — who in 1961, at age twenty-four, had been the highest-paid pitcher in baseball — would be in for a pay cut next year. "He won twenty-three in 1965 and he demanded and got paid for it," the GM informed a reporter. "In the past, Don's performance wouldn't have had an effect on next year's salary, but he put it on a new basis this year."

In his comments to the press and the baseball establishment, as well as to his boss O'Malley, Bavasi still sought to counter the impression that he'd caved in to the salary demands of Koufax and Drysdale. Apparently, it wasn't enough that the two stars had received far less than their asking price; the perception lingered that they had somehow hijacked the organization. Bavasi trotted out excuses, one after the other. They had ganged up; they had shocked him. He had been too astonished to think clearly. "They took me by surprise," the defenseless Dodger executive whined to sportswriter Dick Young. Bavasi then claimed that his negotiating position had been undermined by the public's unwillingness to take the side of the owners. And yet he remained optimistic that such a thing would never happen again. He told Young that he sensed a change in the air: "I think the public was conditioned by that holdout to the point where now they'd be on baseball's side."[43] The fact that the public had sided with management all along failed to register with the GM.

Fortunately for the Dodgers, behind Koufax, Big D, and Osteen, they possessed, for the first time in many years, an impressively strong fourth starter: rookie Don Sutton. Like Drysdale, Sutton's approach to pitching was fierce and fearless. At any point in the count, he might drop down sidearm to throw a slider or brush back even the most seasoned veteran. Mature beyond his years (Koufax called him "21 going on 30"), he was four inches shorter and twenty pounds lighter than Drysdale, but every bit as intimidating a right-hander. They christened him "Little D," and he accepted the designation proudly. In deference to Drysdale, he even took to signing autographs without capitalizing his first name.[44]

Drysdale had a different nickname for Sutton: "Elmer Gantry," the name of the hypocritical fundamentalist minister in the eponymous novel by Sinclair Lewis.[45] Sutton — a devout Southern Baptist who read the Bible every morning, prayed during each game's national anthem, and was given to earnest pronouncements such as, "If I win 20 games this year but do not lead a completely Christian life I will consider myself a failure" — threw a good fastball, a great breaking ball, and an occasional spitball.[46]

Roseboro remembered how Sutton "came up with a way of doctoring the ball so he threw with his fingers off a rough spot that would cause the pitch to dip and be a guaranteed ground ball."[47] It was Sutton's sly use of this illegal pitch, and his disingenuous disavowals of the same, that brought Elmer Gantry to mind.

Drysdale, on the other hand, unapologetically threw a spitter, especially in times, such as now, when nothing else seemed to be working for him. In his early years on the mound, he had chewed slippery elm lozenges. "You had to mix them with gum," Drysdale remembered, "because they tasted so terrible."[48] The tablets stimulated the salivary glands, creating thick ropes of spit with which to work. Furtively brought to the ball with the index and middle fingers, then spread around with the thumb, the saliva reduced the friction of the release. The pitch, thrown without gripping the seams, behaved much like today's split-fingered fastball. "It had a funny lack of rotation," Torborg recalled. "It would come in hard and then the bottom would fall out of it."[49] In the mid-1960s, umpires began to enforce the ban on the spitball more seriously, looking out for pitchers who brought their fingers to their mouths and ejecting any whom they caught loading up the ball. In response, Drysdale, along with San Francisco's Gaylord Perry and a great many others, switched from saliva to grease.[50] Most would deposit a small glob of odorless K-Y jelly on their gloves or on the bills of their caps and then apply it to the ball in discreet amounts.

On occasion, pitchers were helped by teammates who would scuff up or "inadvertently" doctor the ball on their behalf. If Don Sutton was on the mound, Maury Wills, when tossing the baseball after a play, would apply a hidden emery board to the ball. Other infielders might "accidentally" dirty the ball or swiftly spike it, then toss it back to the pitcher. More often, the catcher would conspire. Torborg remembered wearing out his favorite catcher's mitt and asking Wilson, the glove's manufacturer, to replace only the facing rather than the whole glove. The mitt came back perfectly restored, except that, in the refacing, Wilson had thoroughly soaked the mitt's padding with grease. After a few hard fastballs from Koufax or Drysdale, Torborg's restored mitt would ooze grease through the holes in the stitched pocket. What he threw to the mound on those occasions was a well-lubricated ball. "Sandy couldn't stand it," Torborg recalled, "'cause Sandy didn't like anything slippery. He wanted it tacky. He liked pine tar, you know, for the grip that you need on a breaking ball." Consequently, whenever Torborg caught Koufax, he had to use a different glove. Drysdale, however, was grateful. "I love that glove!" he raved to the catcher. "Keep using that thing!"[51]

Unfortunately, even Torborg's magic mitt could help only so much. That year, for the first time since 1960, Drysdale was not named to the all-star team.

On July 5, 1966, the greatest fullback in the history of professional football sat down and dictated a letter to the owner of his team. "In the next few days, I will be announcing my retirement," thirty-year-old Jim Brown said.[52] "This decision is final and is made only because of the future that I desire for myself, my family, and — not to sound corny — my race." It was assumed to be a hoax, a publicity stunt, or perhaps an attempt to promote Brown's privately financed Negro Industrial and Economic Union.[53] It was not. Having set twenty NFL records, he left the game as he had run the field, head held high. He'd become a household name, but he wanted his life back.

Few legends ever left this way, still celebrated and successful. In film there was Greta Garbo, in literature J. D. Salinger. A few weeks after Brown's retirement, the young and madly popular Bob Dylan would embrace anonymity for many years. But sports observers recognized something else in Brown's retirement. What gifted athletes, after all, had quit in their prime, at the pinnacle of their physical prowess? The only comparison was heavyweight champion Rocky Marciano, who had retired in 1956, at age thirty-two, undefeated in forty-nine fights.

The idea of retirement was not unfamiliar to Sandy Koufax. Indeed, upon the completion of the 1960 season, he had thrown away his cleats. He had been walking almost one man per inning, losing more and more games, and setting team records for wild pitches. He had become just another left-handed flamethrower with control problems. This would scarcely have been noteworthy, except that the proud Koufax had endured his rite of passage in full view of the baseball world. At nineteen, essentially inexperienced with organized baseball, having pitched just sandlot contests and four college games (in high school, he'd played first base), he had debuted with one of the era's most popular sports teams. Alongside starters such as Don Newcombe, Carl Erskine, Johnny Podres, and Don Drysdale, Sandy had visibly struggled. After that, no matter how well he had performed, he could never seem to maintain Alston's trust.

After the 1960 season, Koufax had felt aggravated, disappointed, and overlooked. "I felt I wasn't going to get anywhere," he would later explain. "I felt I was getting to be a better pitcher and not getting results. I wasn't getting to pitch too regularly. . . . The toughest way to pitch is every ten days."[54] His control had been erratic, his record so-so, and his manager unsupportive. He'd come to camp in 1961 only grudgingly, willing to give it one last shot. He would try his hardest to succeed, but if he remained mediocre, he would quit. From that spring on, steered by a deep personal pride, he'd found the strike zone and turned himself into one of the best pitchers in baseball history. Unfortunately, during a game against the Mets in 1964, he'd hurt his left elbow diving back into second base on a pick-off play. Arthritis had set in. He had usually been a right-handed batter, but by 1966, no longer able to straighten his pitching arm, he was more and more often batting as a lefty. Noticing Sandy's willingness to bat from either side, wondering if this would increase his value on the bench, one reporter asked, "Are you a pinch hitter?" Koufax, probably the worst hitter in the majors, had to laugh. "No, I'm a pinch out."[55]

He had asked team physician Dr. Robert Kerlan to inform him when he might be risking permanent damage to the arm. During the grueling 1965 season, Kerlan had let Sandy know that the cartilage in his elbow was breaking down, causing ligament tears, aggravated swelling, and bone spurs. If he continued to pitch, he could become crippled. Resolved not to lose his arm to baseball, Koufax had gradually told a few select friends that 1966 would be his last season. Like a man putting his affairs in order, he'd worked in the off-season on his life story. *Koufax*, the autobiography, would be released by Viking Press in August 1966. Soon after, Koufax would follow Jim Brown's lead and take himself out of the story. His holdout with Drysdale, therefore, represented not just an attempt to be justly reimbursed for past accomplishments and to pave the way for other major leaguers to earn what they deserved, but also the desire to maximize his income for his final days on the job.

One week after Brown wrote to his team's owner, Koufax, accompanied by teammates Jim Lefebvre, Phil Regan, and Maury Wills, flew to St. Louis to compete in his last all-star game. He had been an all-star every year since 1961 and had pitched in three of the midsummer classics, but he had never taken the mound before the third inning. This time he was scheduled to start.

The outfield flags were limp, the air dead still. The temperature in the stands was 108 degrees. On the field, it was 115 degrees. Under the batting helmets, Brooks Robinson would say, "it felt like 200°."[56]

"What do you think of Busch Stadium?" a reporter asked Casey Stengel.

Stengel considered the question. "Well," he answered finally, "it certainly holds the heat very well."

NBC packed its television cameras in ice and rushed tons of air-conditioning equipment to the city in order to cool its mobile production trucks.

In the strange sterility of Busch Stadium's brand-new locker room, which did not yet reek of mildew or dirty socks, the other National League stars witnessed firsthand what Koufax went through to pitch. Despite the oppressively hot and humid day, Cardinal trainer Bob Bauman rubbed a fiery liniment called Capsolin into Sandy's body. The other players winced.

"You must be crazy," someone muttered.[57]

A small drop of Capsolin felt to most like the lick of a flame, pure torture, and there sat Koufax, calmly slathered in the stuff.

"How can you stand the smell of that," demanded Gaylord Perry, "much less the heat?"

Koufax gave a slight smile. "You get used to it." He heaved a sigh. "I have to use it to pitch."

Perry shook his head. "It makes my eyes water and my nose burn just standing here."

"Sometimes the pain on my skin keeps my mind off the pain in my elbow," Koufax replied.[58]

A masterful spitballer, Perry was enjoying the first of many exceptional seasons. He was always on the lookout for some new, more secretive way to doctor the ball. The sight of Koufax drenched with perspiration from his hot liniment rub gave Perry inspiration. He already knew that his spitball "was easier to load on humid days. With Sandy's Capsolin formula, I could be hot and humid even on freezing days. I became a convert. . . . I started out with half a tube of Capsolin a game and, over the years, worked my way up to three tubes of Capsolin a game."[59] Ultimately, Perry would win 314 games and become the first pitcher to win the Cy Young Award in both leagues. Twenty-five years later, thanks to Koufax and Capsolin, he would join Sandy in the Hall of Fame.

Atlanta's Joe Torre caught Koufax that broiling afternoon in St. Louis. Torre, a gritty plate blocker and a strong hitter for the Braves, was a fellow Brooklynite. Having an old friend behind the plate seemed at first to help Koufax. He required only five pitches to retire the side in the first. He appeared to have his stuff, but in truth his breaking pitch was misbehaving, and his control lacked its customary sharpness. In the second, he managed to retire Tony Oliva and George Scott only after taking each to a full count. He threw back-to-back balls to Brooks Robinson before giving up a line drive that Hank Aaron misplayed for a triple. He then attempted a curve on the first pitch to Detroit's Bill Freehan. The pitch never broke. As it sailed toward the backstop, Torre uncoiled his six-foot-two frame to its full extension and leapt. The ball bounced off his outstretched mitt and rolled to the screen. Robinson scored from third. A pitch later, Freehan lined out to Roberto Clemente in right field.

Torre blamed Koufax's wildness on the heat. He joked that

when the game started, he'd been hollering, "C'mon, Sanford," but as the second inning dragged on, his encouragement to Koufax shortened to "C'mon, Sandy." Soon he called out merely, "C'mon, Sand." And then, he admitted, "after a while, I didn't say anything."[60]

In the bottom of the next inning, Curt Flood batted for Koufax and grounded out to end the third. By this time, fans in the sun-drenched upper levels were being carried out on stretchers. Hundreds of others had abandoned their field-level boxes to drink up the shade around the concession stand. What was supposed to be a triumphant unveiling in one of America's greatest baseball towns had become instead a human barbecue of historic proportions. The umpires were taking turns behind home plate so as to share the equipment burden. In the American League dugout, the batboy had passed out.[61] Nearby, the president of the players' union, Marvin Miller, was so brutalized by the weather that he said he felt like Alec Guinness in *The Bridge on the River Kwai*.[62] He quit his seat and went below. He made his way into the home team's clubhouse, which seemed to be deserted and was deliciously air-conditioned. He was cooling off quite nicely there, in the bowels of Busch Stadium, when he suddenly realized that he was not alone.

Like Joe Torre, Miller too hailed from Brooklyn. When he looked over and saw how near he stood to the legendary Sandy Koufax, he was momentarily stunned. He was even more astonished at what he saw. Koufax was soaking his pitching arm in a tub of ice water, and "Koufax's upper left arm," Miller recalled, "was as big as my thigh."[63] Miller had never witnessed aggravated swelling like that before. He regained enough composure to introduce himself, but he could not wipe the look of alarm off his face.

"Don't worry, Mr. Miller," Koufax reassured him nonchalantly. "It always blows up like this after I pitch. This isn't bad at all. I only went three innings."[64]

Two pitchers — Sam McDowell and St. Louis's own Bob
Gibson — had refused to join the all-star squad that year.
Their arms needed rest. There is no indication that Koufax
ever considered not going to St. Louis in order to rest his own
obviously damaged arm.

Miller congratulated the lefty for standing up to Walter
O'Malley and Buzzie Bavasi. The pitcher's spring training
holdout with Drysdale had provided an important rallying
point for the players. Miller wished Koufax luck on the rest of
the season.

After the game, Miller boarded a flight to New York. "A
moment before the plane taxied out on the runway," he recalled, "a slender black man sat down in the seat next to
mine."[65] Having earlier stumbled onto Koufax quite by accident, Miller now found himself sitting next to another Dodger
marvel, Maury Wills.

Wills had appeared late in the all-star game, making a
splendid back-to-the-plate catch of a Frank Robinson pop fly
in short left-center, then winning the game for the National
League by slapping a single to right-center in the tenth to
score Tim McCarver. The hit had come in Maury's only at
bat.[66] "It seemed like I had been on the bench a week,"
grumbled Wills.[67] He should have started at shortstop instead
of Cincinnati's Chico Cardenas and had flatly declared as
much to sportswriters before the game. Wills was hitting and
fielding far better than Cardenas and owned twenty-five more
stolen bases.

Then again, nothing in Maury's life had ever gone the way
he'd wanted. The Dodgers had signed him as a pitcher at age
seventeen, then made him an infielder and bottled him up in
the minors for ten years. Thanks to Jack Robinson, the Dodgers,
more than most teams, had grasped the importance of the
stolen base. But in the 1950s, even they had been too caught
up in the slugging fad to recognize the value of a puny switch-

hitter with extraordinary baserunning skills and a keen memory for pitchers' motions.

Early in 1959, Don Zimmer, the Dodgers' starting short-stop, fractured a toe, a small crack that became a big break for Maury. At long last, Wills made the majors. He played superbly, but the Dodgers stubbornly withheld their approval. They continued to treat him as a temporary substitute until 1962, when he made his run at Ty Cobb's "unbreakable" record of ninety-six stolen bases, at which late time they acknowledged that he would be their starter at short. Fans flooded National League stadiums in 1962 to root for Wills, just as they'd packed American League parks a year earlier to cheer on Roger Maris's and Mickey Mantle's pursuit of Babe Ruth's single-season home run mark. Maury had become "Mousie," a pesky, wide-eyed pest to the opposition, a hoarder of stolen crumbs, a frantically scampering thief, a tiny frame with an ego to match, whose fleeting confidence too often resembled his fleet baserunning. Despite his considerable drawing power, Wills earned only moderate increases in salary. Roseboro felt that Wills had been cheated, that he deserved more money than Koufax. As an everyday player, the catalyst of their offense, and the captain of their championship teams, Wills contributed far more to the popularity and profitability of the Dodgers than any pitcher ever could.

"You were not the easiest little prick to manage," Alston would inform Wills late in his career, referring to Maury's passion and hardheadedness.[68] These same qualities, when called different things (determination, ambition, fire, drive), would lead Alston's boss Buzzie Bavasi to term Wills the most Brooklyn of the LA Dodgers.

Perhaps the Ebbets Field commoners would have embraced him, but lacking that, Maury had certainly made himself at home in Los Angeles. He loved hanging out with Hollywood celebs: he hobnobbed with Frank Sinatra and Sidney Poitier, taped television shows with Buddy Rich and Milton Berle, downed Dewar's with Mac Davis, recorded music with Glen Campbell, performed onstage with Sammy Davis Jr., and dated Doris Day.[69]

And when Koufax and Drysdale held out in March 1966, Maury did too. Paid $60,000 the year before, he'd delivered a stellar season, leading the majors in singles and stolen bases and batting nearly .400 in the postseason. He wanted to be paid $90,000 in 1966. Telephoning from Vero Beach, Bavasi offered Wills $85,000.[70] "I'm sorry, but that's not enough," Maury said. Bavasi hung up and notified the newspapers. "It looks like we won't have Maury Wills at shortstop this year because this is our final offer without any equivocation," the general manager declared. "He can take it or leave it." The next day, when a reporter called Wills, the star shortstop admitted forlornly, "I don't know what to do."[71] In later autobiographies, Wills would reveal himself to be a loner, frequently scared and miserable, plagued by recurring doubts regarding his own self-worth. He felt that the Dodgers always took him for granted. What caused this? Was it racism? What could he do?

Wills accepted Bavasi's terms. Four months later, flying to New York, seated alongside Marvin Miller, he was clearly still displeased. "He began talking about the special problems of blacks on teams training in Florida," Miller recalled. "He spoke about the time and money it took to hunt down decent, unsegregated housing and laundries, restaurants, and barber shops that would serve blacks."[72]

"The black and Latin ballplayers are especially eager to support this union," Wills told Miller. "Discrimination is not dead."[73]

They separated after landing, and Wills rejoined his team at the Roosevelt Hotel. In the series that followed, with the Mets leading 2–0 in the fifth inning of the second game, Wills dropped down a perfect bunt. As he spun from the batter's box and scampered to first, he felt something pop in his right knee.[74] He drew up abruptly and was thrown out. His knee began to fill with fluid. Nate Oliver was sent in to play short; Wills was sent to Los Angeles to have the knee drained. That was Sunday. He was back Wednesday, bandaged from his chest to his ankles. He hit safely nine times in the next four games and raised his average to an even .300.

Reluctantly, Wills had to admit that he would not be setting a new stolen base record in 1966.[75] In fact, he had been suspecting as much for some time. He had been playing professional baseball for sixteen years, and his banged-up legs were starting to bother him, reducing his momentum on the base paths. He now believed that it would be almost impossible for anyone else to steal 104 bases in a season. Maury's dramatic success in the early 1960s had forced the opposition to guard against the running game. "The pitchers have come up with some new moves," he admitted, "which make it more difficult to get a good jump." And more catchers, particularly Jerry Grote of the Mets and Randy Hundley of the Cubs, were throwing more accurately. "When they throw ten inches over the bag, I'm dead," he said.[76] Wills had led the National League in steals for six straight years, but never again. In 1966 Lou Brock won the first of four consecutive stolen base titles. Eight years later, Brock would steal 118 bases in a single season, not just proving Wills wrong but also effectively erasing him from the record books.

After the all-star break, Koufax had fallen off the pace too. Halfway through the 1966 season, he'd completed more games than the entire Baltimore Oriole pitching staff and amassed more victories than any Oriole pitcher would gain all year. Nonetheless, it now seemed unlikely that he would become the first pitcher since Dizzy Dean to win thirty games in a season. Due to the deteriorating condition of his elbow, he'd had to increase his pain medicine, and he won just three games in July.

"You all right, big guy?" Roseboro routinely asked.

"I'll get by, Rosey," was Koufax's weary reply.

"He got by," Roseboro would later observe, "but it hurt too much to go on much longer."

Koufax also was beginning to receive more frequent cortisone injections in his elbow.[77] "I lived on medication," he would say later. Although Sandy never complained, Roseboro reported that the shots themselves were agony. "They take the longest, thickest needle you ever saw, stick it deep, wriggle it around, and keep sticking it in and wriggling it around until they find the sore spot," Roseboro recounted. "It hurts like hell until they find it. When they do, it takes the pain away for a while, so you can play."[78]

The continuing competitiveness of the Dodgers was a miracle of modern medicine. In the second half of the season, they never fell more than four games out of first place, despite serious injuries not just to Wills and Koufax but also to Ron Fairly (badly bruised ribs), Jim Lefebvre (hairline fracture of the big toe on his left foot), Lou Johnson (aggravated back and sprained left hand), Willie Davis (injured elbow, pulled leg muscle), Claude Osteen (blisters on the index finger of his pitching hand), Tommy Davis (pulled thigh muscle [twice], strained Achilles tendon), and Nate Oliver (arthritic finger on his throwing hand). The one healthy infielder was Wes Parker, but the slender first baseman had played so long without a day off that he started slumping at the plate. "Players who deserve a rest haven't been able to get it," O'Malley acknowledged.[79] When substitute outfielder Al "the Bull" Ferrara (badly jammed ankle, lame leg) chased a fly ball straight through the right-field fence in Pittsburgh's Forbes Field, the Dodgers couldn't afford to replace him in the outfield. The trainers asked whether he wanted to be bandaged. "Nah," the big

man retorted. "Just patch up the fence. I'll give it one more chance."[80]

By Wednesday, July 27, the Dodgers were just a game and a half out of first place. That night in Los Angeles, Koufax went up against Jim Bunning and the Phillies for his eighteenth victory. In the second, Philadelphia's Richie Allen led off by driving a 2–2 pitch into the Dodger bull pen for his twenty-second home run, making the score 1–0.

Homering off Koufax was not the difficult part. Sandy's flaring fastball translated into a great many outfield flies, and one of every thirteen base hits he surrendered went over the fence. The greatness of Allen's feat was pounding a ball out of Dodger Stadium after the sun had gone down, when the cool summer nights turned damp and gravity, it seemed, increased. Whether this was due to California's coastal dew spreading fingers of fog down the gullies of Chavez Ravine or the stadium's air made heavy by the ghosts of displaced natives and the salty dampness of their tears, none could say. But in 1966, fewer home runs were hit in Dodger Stadium than in any other park in the league.

In the fifth, the Dodgers evened the score, countering Allen's muscular accomplishment with trademark wimpiness: they loaded the bases for Jeff Torborg, who hit a sacrifice fly. The game stayed tied at one run apiece for seven more innings. Bunning went on to strike out twelve Dodgers, while Koufax whiffed sixteen Phillies, a single-game record in the majors that season. After eleven innings, with the game still tied at one run apiece, Jim Lefebvre pinch-hit for Koufax. Bunning retired Lefebvre, and the game went into the twelfth.

Alston brought Phil Regan in from the bull pen. Roseboro called Regan "our salvation." Because of his herky-jerky short-arm delivery, the way he'd springboard off the pitching rubber, and the fact that he kept the ball down, Regan got a

lot of ground ball outs, and Alston liked that.[81] Anyone who could make a batter hit the ball on the ground would keep a game close.

Long ago, back in Detroit, Regan had been a teammate of Jim Bunning's. After being traded to Philadelphia, Bunning had insisted that every player should be traded at least once, because it gave him new incentives, showed him new faces, and kept him excited. At the time, it had seemed totally bogus, as if he'd just been trying to put a good face on a bad situation, but Bunning, Regan now saw, had been correct.[82]

Regan's story bore a striking resemblance to that of Baltimore's Moe Drabowsky. Like Moe, Phil had been a right-handed starter in the American League for many years. He had struggled in 1965, been sent down, and then been picked up by another team in an unnoticed deal after the season. Dodger fans had greeted him with low expectations. Against his will, he had been turned into a reliever, had found his groove, and was now having a career year, in a new city, on a new team.

In contrast to Drabo, the Polish-born prankster with the Harpo Marx hair, Regan was a teetotaling gent with a long melon of a head topped with a dark crew cut. By the time he relieved Koufax in the top of the twelfth, the right-handed reliever possessed the lowest earned run average (1.69) on the Dodgers — the team with the lowest ERA (2.60) in the majors.

Much of the credit, Regan insisted, went to fellow relievers Ron Perranoski and Bob Miller. Being as new to the bull pen as he was to the league, Regan needed a lot of guidance. Perranoski coached him through the warm-up routine, while Miller talked him through the opposing lineup. It helped that all three depended on sliders and fastballs. Regan didn't have a good off-speed pitch — no curve to speak of, no change-up. He threw a cross-seam fastball that he released with a twist, turning it over like a screwball so that it rose. And he threw a

Unfamiliar with both the bull pen and the league, Phil Regan received invaluable advice from teammates Ron Perranoski and Bob Miller. (Photo by Frank Worth, courtesy of the *Sporting News*)

hard sinker that broke down and in. His third pitch, as Jim Murray wrote, "is not only as illegal as spitting on the sidewalk but also somewhat resembles it."[83]

Regan faced three Phillies and retired them all.

In the bottom of the twelfth, the Dodgers' patented popgun offense came alive: Nate Oliver drew a walk, took second on a passed ball, and scored on a single. The game was over. Sixteen strikeouts, eleven innings, and no decision for Koufax. The victory went to Regan. The Dodgers now had eleven consecutive one-run wins.

Four nights later in Pittsburgh, Koufax again went for number eighteen. Again he fell behind early. Gene Alley walked in the first and scored when Roberto Clemente dribbled a high bouncer into right that hopped over Ron Fairly's head. Sandy struck out nine Pirates but remained behind by a run when he left for pinch hitter Jim Gilliam in the eighth.

The magnificent Dodger offense struck again: Gilliam walked and scored on, of course, a single. With the score tied, in came Regan. He had faced the Pirates on May 13, pitched two innings, and lost. He pitched two innings this night as well, but he shut out the Pirates. The Dodgers scored in the ninth, and the win was his. Regan now owned nine victories on the season, while Drysdale, who had pitched a hundred more innings, had just seven.

In two consecutive starts, Koufax had hurled 18 total innings, thrown more than 250 pitches, struck out 25, given up 2 runs, and earned neither decision. Regan had pitched a total of 3 innings and gained both victories. When the two pitchers met in the clubhouse after the game, Koufax said with a chuckle, "Regan, you're a real vulture, getting my wins like that."[84]

"Guess what he had for breakfast?" right fielder Ron Fairly asked with a smirk. "Two sparrows."[85]

The handle stuck. From then on, Regan would be known as "the Vulture." People from all over the world would send him rubber vultures, plastic vultures, articles and cartoons about vultures, postcards and snapshots of vultures. "It was unbelievable," Regan remembered with a laugh.

Regan would not post another loss in 1966. In fact, after having been beaten by Pittsburgh on May 13, the Vulture would pitch in seventy-one games before losing again. It would be the middle of 1967 by then, and he would be pitching with a practically unrecognizable Dodger team.

After trying for twelve days, Koufax finally earned his eighteenth victory on August 5 in the Astrodome. A week later, back home in Chavez Ravine, he got his nineteenth, striking out eleven Cubs while surrendering only three hits to beat Chicago 6–1. That day Sandy joyfully shared the victory circle with the resurgent Tommy Davis, who went four for four against the Cubs, including a two-run homer.

For all his preseason work, Tommy had seen frustratingly little playing time. He could sprint to first and swiftly round the bases, but he could accomplish this only in brief spurts, and then he'd have to work to hide his limp. Despite the pain, Davis begged to play, but Alston was wary of him reinjuring the ankle. Even though Tommy was hitting far better than anyone else on the team (he would be the only Dodger that year to hit over .300), he couldn't play every day.

Fortunately for the Dodgers, there was another Davis starting daily in the outfield. His first name was Willie, and although his batting average was a mere .277, he was quite prepared to make up for Tommy's absence. In the middle of August, Willie moved off the plate, widened his stance, borrowed a thirty-six-inch bat, and went on a tear. Over the next twenty games, he hit .395, at one point collecting eight consecutive hits and helping to keep the Dodgers always within a game or two of first place.

Willie was younger, smaller, lighter, and faster than Tommy, and the two looked nothing alike. Nonetheless, they were often confused for brothers. They were extremely close friends, even though baseball did not run in Willie's blood the way it did in Tommy's. Willie was simply fast and strong, blessed with good coordination and excellent vision. A basketball and track star at Roosevelt High School in Los Angeles, "he could," according to baseball scouts of the day, "neither hit nor throw."[86] Nonetheless, in 1959 the ever optimistic Dodgers had signed him. He'd been taught to hit left-handed and to play the outfield. Just as bats and gloves are manufactured, "Willie Davis," Vin Scully noted, "was a thoroughly manufactured baseball player." Following two years of intensive minor-league instruction, he had replaced Duke Snider as the centerpiece of a swift, new Dodger outfield in 1961. No one doubted his natural abilities, but his nonchalant attitude in the field, his inconsistencies at the plate, and his mental lapses on the base paths had sorely tested his manager. "Sure he's the fastest thing on earth and looks like money in the bank on a given day or play," Alston admitted, "but the next time you look up he is out, or throwing to the wrong base, and I don't know whether he'll ever hit."[87]

Willie Davis was both captivated by and clueless about hitting. It seemed as though he was concerned more about form than function, for he was never without a bat in his hands and was always gazing in the mirror, checking his swing. Once, after striking out, he returned to the bench and asked, "How did my stroke look?"

"Hey, Willie," a teammate answered, "you struck out."

"Yeah," acknowledged Davis, "but how did my stroke look? How was my stroke?"[88]

Between innings, when Dodger players debated a hitting strategy against particular pitchers — whether to move up in the box, go the other way, look high, look low, wait for off-speed stuff — Willie never joined in.[89] Although he usually batted second or third in the lineup, he was never looking to advance the runner. He was not a team player. He just went up and swung. He was notoriously impatient at the plate, almost always taking a cut at the pitcher's initial offering. His at bats seldom lasted long enough to become a base on balls. He walked just fifteen times in 1966. After Willie earned a rare free pass from Cincinnati right-hander Jim Maloney, an amazed Dodger official rushed into the Crosley Field press box and yelled, "Stop the game and give Maloney the ball!"[90]

Of particular frustration was Willie's indecisiveness regarding a batting stance. He would consistently mimic the style of the opposing team's star.[91] As the Dodgers' opponents changed, so would Willie's stance. Parodying a popular dance title of the time, sportswriters derided him as "the Man of a Thousand Stances."

"It was just a matter of adjusting until I got where I was comfortable," Davis explained during his late-August batting spree. "Now I don't think I'll ever change."[92] And indeed, he didn't change — at least not until he slapped a Gaylord Perry pitch into the pavilion seats of Dodger Stadium a couple of weeks later. His eighth home run of the year, it effectively killed his batting spree. "When Willie hit a home run," Wes Parker recalled, "everyone on the bench would go, 'Oh shit.' Because we knew he'd be swinging for the fences for the next two weeks, thinking he was a home run hitter."[93] After the homer, Davis did change his focus and characteristically fell into a slump. He hit only .219 for the rest of the season. He was unapologetic. "If I wanted to make myself a household word," he bragged, "I could. If I wanted to hit .400 I could. But over 162 games, that's not Willie Davis."[94]

"Willie was not the brightest guy," Parker observed. "He tried to hit home runs. That was basically his problem. If he'd just slapped the ball to the left side of the infield, with his speed he could've hit .350 every year, and he'd be in the Hall of Fame today easily."[95]

Davis regularly vowed to heed his coaches, to take more pitches, to lay down more bunts, to punch the ball to left field. At the plate, however, temptation overcame him. In desperation, Buzzie Bavasi promised Willie $15 every time he got a hit to the left of second base.[96] It didn't help. "He could have been a Hall of Famer," the Dodger GM succinctly put it, "but he had million-dollar legs and a ten-cent head."[97]

Those legs were indeed capable of truly exceptional feats. In high school, during a practice track meet, Davis once established an unofficial world record in the broad jump. He could run the 100-yard dash in 9.5 seconds, two-tenths off the national record. Due to his unusually long strides, he was the fastest baseball player of his generation. But his speed was just another disappointment for the Dodgers. "There was no way Maury Wills could run with Willie Davis," occasional Dodger third baseman John Kennedy remembered. "But Maury would steal a hundred bases, and Willie would steal twenty or thirty. If Willie made a study of it like Maury did, each season Willie would have stole a hundred bases easy — I mean, easy."[98] John Roseboro agreed. "Willie wasn't willing to work," the catcher later said.[99]

When Willie was aboard, third-base coach Preston Gomez drew the unenviable task of trying to get him to stop on a ball hit too shallow to allow him to advance from first to third or to score from second. Half the time, Willie would run through the coach's sign. His teammates would laugh uproariously as Gomez switched instantly from shouting, "Whoa, whoa, Willie!" to "Whatta go, Willie!" Ron Fairly didn't recall Willie, having made up his mind to take the extra base, ever being thrown out.[100] Nor did any of his former teammates. Instead, they recalled the blue blur of his batting helmet as he flew along the base path, and spoke of fantastic incidents, like the time at Dodger Stadium he outran a rundown between second and third, turned the corner, broke for home, and outran another rundown between third and home to score, or the time in Cincinnati Willie extended a grounder hit past first base into an inside-the-park home run, or the time in Houston he glided around from second base on a bunt hit down the third-base line, scoring before the fielder, Bob Aspromonte, had even picked up the ball.[101]

His speed gave him the ability to cover more ground in the outfield than most center fielders. It also gave him the ability to cover up his errors. He frequently broke the wrong way on a fly ball, but he could swiftly correct himself, leaving nobody but his teammates the wiser. He infuriated Maury Wills with his lack of fundamentals, drifting over at the last minute to snag a fly instead of charging over and properly setting himself.[102] For years he had been overthrowing the cutoff man, and for years he would continue to do so. Alston and his staff would just shake their heads in dismay. Frank Robinson's motto, and the title of his autobiography, was "My life is baseball." In contrast, Willie's stated creed was "Baseball ain't my life and it ain't my wife, so why worry about it?"[103] They were bound to face off at some point.

A small incident during the 1966 pennant race was an omen of ill to come. It was Sunday, August 28, and the Dodgers were battling the Giants in Candlestick Park. An easy pop fly was lifted to center. Willie called for it. The game was close, and there were two outs, with a runner in scoring position. Suddenly, the San Francisco sky seemed to swallow up the ball, and Willie lost sight of it. Jim Lefebvre and Maury Wills dropped back from the infield. Lou Johnson scampered over from left, as did Ron Fairly from right. Center was crowded with Willie's nervous teammates. At the last moment, as the pop fly fell from the stratosphere, Willie glimpsed it. Casually flipping his mitt, he snatched the ball as it dropped past his left hip, securing Don Sutton's eleventh victory.

"I called for it," Willie shrugged afterward, "so I had to do something."[104] But he wouldn't always be so fortunate.

While Willie Davis scanned the heavens above Candlestick for flies, others more celebrated were playing in center field down south at Dodger Stadium. They were the Beatles, and their concert on August 28, the first ever held in Chavez Ravine, would be their penultimate live performance.

Having heard that the Beatles might be planning a late-summer U.S. concert tour, remembering their highly profitable show at Shea Stadium a year earlier, and brooding over the wastefulness of his own park just sitting there empty whenever his club went on the road, Dodger owner Walter O'Malley had dispatched representatives early in 1966 to secure this chance for the Beatles to play Dodger Stadium. The negotiations went smoothly, the date was set, and all seemed cause for celebration. The mop-topped lads always packed the house, and this would help introduce a new type of youngster to the beautiful sunset skies — shades of lemon and peach smeared against the horizon — visible from Chavez Ravine.

By the time the Fab Four arrived in America, however, everything felt different. Baptists in the Bible Belt were busily burning their Beatle records in bonfires because of John Lennon's observation that "the Beatles are more popular than Jesus now." A popular psychic predicted that the group's plane would crash. If they survived that, the Ku Klux Klan had announced its intention to attack the entertainers.[105] Meanwhile, the youths of Southern California, heretofore presumed to be mainly surfers and Mouseketeers, were gathering nightly on the Sunset Strip to hear rock bands sing about death. "Beatnik boys with beards, and girls with long, stringy hair" was how disdainful newscasters characterized them.[106] They were smoking marijuana. They were impatient, angry, and defiant. And there were a lot of them.

By mid-August 1966, the Beatles as fresh-faced singers of sweet nothings; as funny, frolicsome crafters of pop candy; as well-dressed boys who wanted to please please you, hold your hand, yeah yeah yeah — and those delirious days of Beatlemania, of sobbing, shrieking fans and exuberant performances on *The Ed Sullivan Show* — seemed long gone.

The Beatles came in a hurry, sweeping across the continent in two and a half weeks. Their plane didn't crash. The KKK never materialized. Most cities lacked a proper venue for such large crowds, so the Beatles grew accustomed to playing in ballparks — D.C. Stadium, Crosley Field, Busch Stadium, Shea Stadium, Candlestick Park. The sold-out show at Dodger Stadium was the biggest of their tour. Afterward, the kids went wild. So did the police.[107] The Beatles witnessed the Los Angeles Police Department (LAPD) clubbing teenage girls and, disgusted, fled the chaos through the rear of the stadium in an armored car. A local reporter asked, "What do you think would happen to you four if you came to an appearance without the armored car or the police?" Positive that LA's cops had only exacerbated the riot, Ringo Starr made a face. "We'd get in a lot easier."

The Beatles were no longer saying things that parents wanted to hear. A week earlier, at a press conference in New York, they'd been asked to comment on the war in Vietnam. "We don't like it," John Lennon had replied. "We don't like war."

"It's just, war is wrong," George Harrison had elaborated. "And it's obvious it's wrong."[108]

Despite the applause accorded the Beatles in New York when they spoke up for peace, America's war, which had been fought by ground units in earnest for a little less than a year, was still popular. And the big hit of 1966 was not "Yellow Submarine," "We Can Work It Out," "Paperback Writer," or any number by the Beatles. Nor was it anything performed by Otis Redding, the Mamas and the Papas, the Rolling Stones, the Supremes, the Beach Boys, or Bob Dylan. The year's most popular song was "The Ballad of the Green Berets," penned and essentially narrated by a wounded Vietnam veteran named Sergeant Barry Sadler. Sergeant Sadler's resolutely patriotic chant held steady at number one for five straight weeks and ultimately sold upwards of eleven million copies. Its jingoistic sentiments attracted both ridicule and admiration, and even inspired a tribute by Phil Regan, who spent a few moments in the bull pen one evening adapting the hit into the pro-Dodger "Ballad of the Blue Berets":

> These are the men of the Blue Beret
> Waiting there for Alston's call
> They are ready to give their all
> Fighting Giants and the Reds
> Day and night until they're dead
> They are fighting for one thing
> They want to win the pennant ring

Game after game, throughout the year
Fans will come and they will cheer
They will watch and then they'll say
"These are men of the Blue Beret."[109]

The year 1966 saw the first B-52 raids on North Vietnam, the commencement and conclusion of Operations Masher and Hastings, the bombing of Hanoi, and 200,000 more U.S. troops optimistically dispatched to fight the communists in Southeast Asia. The soldiers commonly left from Southern California — "Dodger Country" — in troop transports. Every Thursday afternoon, the military released casualty figures. Seldom were more than a hundred or fewer than seventy Americans killed in any given week. Gradually, as the coffins mounted up and more boys came home without limbs, the numbers began to register. Battles would be announced as won or lost, but no progress would be reported. Instead, at suppertime televised scenes of chaotic carnage would bounce around the dining room. The desire to defend Saigon's corrupt regime would eventually dissipate, but by then it would be 1968, with more than half a million Americans "in country," and things in Vietnam, as well as in much of the rest of the world, would get a lot worse before they got any better.

Late in August 1966, as the Beatles quite happily left America, never to return, Secretary of Defense Robert McNamara announced plans to draft 40,000 men who had previously been exempted from military service because of a lack of education, good health, or nourishment. Thirty percent of those being reclassified were African Americans. Civil rights leaders were aghast. Harlem's congressman, Adam Clayton Powell Jr., called it "genocide." McNamara viewed it as reclamation. "We can salvage tens of thousands of these men each year, first for productive military careers, and later for productive roles in society," he said.

With the escalation of the Southeast Asian conflict, a dodger was now not only a professional baseball player in Los Angeles but also someone who fled to Canada to escape military service. One was reminded of how, during Senator Joseph McCarthy's reign of terror in the 1950s, the name Cincinnati Reds had so worried baseball officials that they'd briefly changed the club's name to the less commie-sounding Cincinnati Redlegs. Now it was the Dodgers who were suddenly unpatriotic.

No profession peddled its patriotism harder than baseball, whose every contest began with a paean to the Stars and Stripes. Major leaguers of the day, like the majority of Americans, enthusiastically supported the country's military. Most had to sign up for the reserves. Roseboro had played army ball in Germany; Koufax and Drysdale did time together at Fort Dix; Jim Lefebvre had served at Fort Ord and then put in several weeks drilling alongside Don Sutton at a camp in San Francisco.

Others found different ways to volunteer. Following the cue of Johnny Unitas and other professional football players, a group of baseball's all-stars — Brooks Robinson, Harmon Killebrew, Hank Aaron, and Joe Torre, along with sportscaster Mel Allen and Hall of Famer Stan Musial — announced their intention to go to Vietnam after the conclusion of the 1966 season to show their support for the troops. Overseeing arrangements for the goodwill tour was William Eckert, a retired lieutenant general in the air force who'd recently been named commissioner of baseball.

General Eckert would turn out to be the worst commissioner ever. Instead of just abolishing the office in late 1965, the owners had chosen a bland and clueless candidate over whom they could exert maximum control. He possessed a vague background in business and enjoyed baseball, but he had no particular knowledge of the sport. He had not been inside a ballpark in at least ten years. He'd heard of the Los Angeles Dodgers, but he did not know that they used to play in Brooklyn. Once General Eckert became the commissioner, he remained late in his office every night, reading baseball books and trying to master the history of the game over which he now presided. Despite his best efforts, he couldn't keep the teams straight. Speaking to the owners, he continually referred to the Cincinnati Cardinals. No one corrected him.[110]

Baseball felt familiar to General Eckert because it reminded him of the air force. "First, you have highly competitive units — the different teams, just as you have squadrons. Then you have rules and regulations in both, rules to be made and interpreted and changed. And third, you have franchises, like Air Force bases, being opened and moved to fill needs."[111]

It was true, to some extent, that baseball's regimentation and nomenclature owed a debt to the armed forces. This was not something that would prove to be very helpful in the coming years, however, as the youth of America shifted to the left, seeking fresh passions, exploring new liberties, and growing increasingly suspicious of a tradition-bound pastime that was overseen by a severe, white-haired former general who stood with ramrod posture, acclaiming order and conformity. As the 1960s wore on, baseball would begin to lose its appeal. By April 1968, when Eckert would not halt the games for a day of mourning after the murder of Dr. Martin Luther King Jr., baseball also would rapidly lose its relevance. Though elected for a six-year term, Eckert would be booted out of office after only three years of service and be replaced by baseball insider Bowie Kuhn.

The general's one meager contribution was the agreement he'd overseen in 1966 that every two years, a top major-league team would play a two-week exhibition in Japan following the World Series.[112] Such an arrangement had existed for more than a decade but had broken down in 1965 when

Major League Baseball had offered Japan the chance to host the Pittsburgh Pirates. Japanese officials had taken that as a slap in the face. The *Pirates?* They wanted to see stars!

The Japanese wanted the Yankees, of course, but they would accept the Dodgers, and welcome an opportunity to see Drysdale, Koufax, and Wills. O'Malley agreed — there was a good deal of money to be made — and the deal was struck: eighteen games against various Japanese teams starting October 18 in Tokyo. Eckert would accompany the players.

Los Angeles mayor Sam Yorty also agreed, at O'Malley's invitation, to go along.[113] ("Travelin' Sam" preferred to be anywhere other than the city he purportedly ran.) The only snag was that O'Malley hadn't bothered to discuss the tour with his players. They received it as a decree: You will be going to Japan. Your schedule now runs to November 16, for which you will be paid an extra $3,700. If you wish to take your wife, she will travel for free, but then you will earn only $1,500.[114]

The players were less than enthused.

"I can't blame them," Alston admitted. "By the time the boys get back, considering taxes and all, they'll have about $500 left of the money."[115]

Maury Wills bitterly recalled, "It was, we were given to understand, entirely voluntary." But O'Malley insisted that Wills come along. "You're the captain of the team," O'Malley told him. If he was too injured to play, he could pose for pictures and sign autographs. With reluctance, Maury consented.[116]

Not much later, Phil Regan was sitting on the team bus when Koufax plopped down beside him. They got to talking. Although Wills had been pressured into going, Don Drysdale, Jim Gilliam, and Wes Parker had already declared that they would skip the postseason trip. Sandy now revealed that he too would be staying home. Regan asked why.

"Because this'll be it," Koufax explained. "This is my last year."[117]

Regan wasn't surprised. He'd seen what Sandy had to en-
dure to get ready for a start: the steroids and cortisone shots,
the Empirin with codeine, the Butazolidin, the Capsolin rubs,
the whirlpools, the massages, the ice baths. With all the pain-
killers and anti-inflammatories Koufax took, he was, he would
later admit, "high half the time during a ballgame." Despite
all this, Koufax was the greatest pitcher Regan had ever
seen — simply unhittable, with a fastball that exploded, a
curveball that went straight down, and a pretty good change-
up. And yet Sandy apparently used to be even greater. There
had been a time when veteran umpire Mel Steiner, after calling the balls and strikes of a particular Koufax gem, turned in
bewilderment to his second-base field ump, shook his head,
and said, "If I hadn't been handing those baseballs to Roseboro, I would've sworn Koufax was throwing a Wiffle ball out
there."[118] Now, from behind the plate, the umpires could tell
it was no Wiffle ball. "I'll tell you," an umpire idly remarked
to Regan one day, "his pitches have lost a lot since last year. If
he keeps going, by next year Koufax will be an ordinary
pitcher."[119]

Two who agreed with this assessment were Jim Russo and
Al Kubski. Three weeks before the Baltimore Orioles had
clinched the pennant, they had already dispatched men to
scout probable postseason competitors. Don McShane and
Darrell Johnson had been sent to watch the Giants, Harry
Craft and Ray Scarborough to observe the Pirates, and Russo
and Kubski to scout the Dodgers. They sat as close as possible
to home plate and struck up conversations with their National
League counterparts. One laughed when Russo revealed his
assignment. "What could you possibly report about Koufax?"
he asked the Oriole scout. "Just write down, 'Great!' and you've
covered him."[120]

That was not what Russo and Kubski would write. "Has
been a great pitcher," their scouting report read, "but would

call him a very good one now. Has the standard assortment. Fastball is a 2 (good). Curve now lacks its former velocity and sharpness."[121]

By September 4, Koufax had posted twenty-two victories on the season. That same week, Osteen had won his fourteenth, Sutton had won his twelfth, and Drysdale had lost his sixteenth. All four were hurt. Osteen had injured his groin during Friday's game and hobbled off in the sixth. An exhausted Koufax had completed only six innings the next night (a very brief outing for him). Drysdale's left knee had popped out of place after two innings on Sunday. Sutton had quit the next game in the third after pulling a muscle in his right forearm.

As their third-place team flew home from Cincinnati, Dodger fans found themselves in a state of high crisis. Their club had played 135 games, of which Koufax, Drysdale, Osteen, and Sutton had started all but two. "The Big Four," as they were called, had held the opposition to two or fewer runs in almost half their games and had thrown fourteen shutouts. Their staff ERA was the lowest in the National League in twenty-three years. But if they hadn't managed to secure first place when the pitching staff was healthy, what hope did they have now?

Reporters began drafting obituaries. DODGERS IN TROUBLE confirmed a September 9 headline in the *Los Angeles Times*. Readers not only were treated to a woebegone catalog of the pitchers' various ailments but also were reminded that Maury Wills's right knee, taped tightly while his cartilage flopped around inside, was still "in considerable pain."[122]

Dread came easily to Southern Californians. Runaways were disappearing in 1966 like loose change, and anyone not employed by the entertainment industry helping to create escapist fantasies for the masses was probably a defense worker building bombs and rockets to safeguard those fantasies.

Angelenos lived with the high statistical probability of a huge seismic disturbance that would fell their buildings and rupture their boulevards. It was as if, through the wreckage of imminent disaster, they could see what lay ahead: Walt Disney and his California-inspired vision of a sunny future were both on their respective deathbeds. Flag-covered caskets were stacking up on the landing strips of California's air force bases. *Apollo I's* doomed astronauts were testing out the spacecraft that had been hurriedly constructed for them in a factory a few miles southeast of Los Angeles. Two riots in successive years had left thirty-seven dead in Watts. Come November, local teenagers would turn out en masse to defy a Sunset Strip curfew, and for almost a week the LAPD would brutalize them with scant restraint. In elections held across the country that same month, progressives would lose to conservatives, as the desire to address social ills gave way to nostalgia for easier, happier days.

Hollywood screenwriter Joan Didion perceived the "deterioration" of her personality at this time as a citywide phenomenon, a thoroughly appropriate response to the pervasive atmosphere of anxiety, the smoggy swirl of migratory inhabitants, the ominous convergences.[123] It was upon these flats of LA that another charismatic Kennedy soon would be sacrificed, and in the hills shortly after where Charles Manson would have his followers commit their infamous atrocities. Southern California no longer exemplified optimism and frivolity. It was alluring and deadly, a poisoned flower, the site where lovely things split apart. The banged-up Dodgers and the ailing Koufax — who, despite his agony, was admired by Didion's husband, John Gregory Dunne, as "the most beautiful ballplayer I ever saw" — were simply among the victims.[124]

Decades later, the rugged and intense Jim Lefebvre, by then a seasoned veteran of many tight pennant races, would pinpoint this particular September as "the most draining" of his life.[125] Day by day, often hour by hour, the Giants, Pirates, and Dodgers were shifting places, swapping percentage points in the NL standings. The pressure of the race began to exact a mental, as well as a physical, toll on the Los Angeles team. During a tense three-game home series against the Giants, which incredibly drew a total of 162,122 paying customers, Tommy Davis at last got fed up with the bossiness of Maury Wills. In the eighth inning of the final game, after Maury coached the infielders into the proper positions and then turned around to Tommy in left to convey that there were now two away, Davis responded by flipping off the team captain.

At the end of the inning, Wills waited for Davis in the dugout. "Let me tell you something, Tommy Davis —"

Before Maury could get out another word, Davis had thrown aside his glove and was punching the shortstop. Their teammates leapt in to intervene.

"Let me at that little son-of-a-bitch," screamed Davis, writhing angrily as his teammates tried to rein him in.

"Let him go!" hollered the much smaller Wills, adrenaline pumping. "Let him go!"

From down the bench, their phlegmatic, fog-skinned manager calmly watched. Alston didn't even bother to get up.[126]

The next day, the Dodger manager called a team meeting. Phil Regan remembered him telling the two would-be combatants, "Hey, if you guys want to fight, I'll tell you what we're going to do. We're gonna form a circle right here. And we'll put you guys in there. And you guys can fight." According to Regan, Wills declined after seeing the size of the proposed circle. "No, no," the tiny speedster said. "I'm gonna need more room than that if I'm fightin' Tommy."[127]

One person was elated to learn of the simmering brawl. "I think it's great," Walter O'Malley observed. "It's the sort of spirit you find in a family, and on a winning team."[128] In a way, Wills agreed. "There were a lot of fights on the Dodgers," he would later acknowledge. "People didn't fight in other clubhouses because nobody cared enough. We did, and the fights we had were usually something relating to the game."

Amid all this, on Friday, September 9, Houston arrived to play four games. A young, streaky, eighth-place team like the Astros should have stirred little concern, but given the worrisome state of the Dodger staff, the fraying tempers, the tight race, and the fact that Houston had won five out of six in Chavez Ravine that year, people were very nervous.

It proved unjustified. The Dodger pitchers not only won every game but also threw four successive shutouts. Particularly impressive was the oft-overlooked southpaw Claude Osteen, the one the Dodgers called "Gomer" (due to his squinting eyes, beaverish grin, and southern accent, which bore a startling resemblance to Jim Nabors, television's "Gomer Pyle"). Osteen, sore groin and all, started the weekend series with a complete-game performance. He threw eighty-nine pitches, sixty-two of which were strikes. He fell behind only one batter, on a 3–1 count. Except for three scattered infield singles, all hit weakly, Gomer pitched a perfect game. He also scored John Roseboro from second by driving a fourth-inning single through the pitcher's box. When added to the doubles hit by Wes Parker, Ron Fairly, Jim Lefebvre, and Willie Davis, it made the final score 7–0. The victory was Osteen's fifteenth of the season.

The next day, Drysdale — "the meanest, most intense competitor I've ever known," according to Roseboro — limped up the mound with his left leg encased in a long rubber bandage. Despite this restrictive encumbrance, Big D dominated Houston for eight and a third scoreless innings, looking every bit his old formidable self. Unfortunately, his own team required ten innings to push across a single run and gain the victory. (The 1–0 win went, of course, to Phil Regan.) A Sunday doubleheader followed. With Koufax starting the first game and spot starter Joe Moeller the second, the Dodger batters walked, blooped, dribbled, and stole their way to two more victories.

Jim Russo watched it all with incredulity. "How are you going to defense an attack like that?" the Oriole scout asked, of no one in particular. "Maybe the Dodgers don't have the long-ball threat of the Giants and Pirates — still they bunt, drag bunt, bunch singles, steal, take the extra base . . . and bingo, they've got two or three runs, and the pitching to protect their lead."[129]

In one weekend, Los Angeles jumped Pittsburgh and San Francisco in the standings. Suddenly, everything felt right again. The date was September 11, 1966. At long last, after a grueling five-month chase, the Dodgers were in sole possession of first place.

For nearly a century, the game's major-league clubs had been distributed unevenly about the nation, leaving sizable pockets of sports lovers with no home team to cheer for. Not surprisingly, many had adopted one of the two most visibly successful franchises — either the Dodgers or the Yankees — as their own. Each team had drawn superbly as a consequence, whether home or away.

By 1966, however, the Yankees were dead. Three years earlier, the Dodgers had been the focus of the most watched sporting events in history, Games Three and Four of the 1963 World Series. During the latter contest, on Sunday, October 6, nearly 40 percent of all television sets in the country had been tuned to NBC, as Sandy Koufax had outpitched Whitey Ford to complete the Dodgers' improbable sweep of the defending world champions. Now the same all-star lineup that had faced the Dodgers in 1963 and the Cardinals in 1964 — infielders Joe Pepitone, Bobby Richardson, and Clete Boyer; outfielders Tom Tresh, Roger Maris, and Mickey Mantle; pitchers Whitey

Ford, Al Downing, and Jim Bouton; catcher Elston Howard —
lost eighty-nine games. From 1947 to 1965, they'd won a
remarkable fifteen pennants. Now, like the mighty *Titanic*,
they settled to the bottom. For the first time in more than half
a century, the Yankees would finish in last place. Their attendance plummeted; one home game attracted only 413
customers.

The Dodgers, meanwhile, kept winning and continued to
draw well. In 1966 they became the first team in history to
bring in more than 2.5 million fans at home and 2 million on
the road. In sheer numbers, the 1966 Dodgers were baseball's
biggest attraction ever. Koufax, Regan & Company became as
emblematic of the era as a white Mustang GT 350 with side
scoops, a fashion magazine with Twiggy on the cover, a 45
of "Wild Thing" by the Troggs, or a Green Hornet lunch box
(with matching thermos).

For decades the Dodgers had meant Brooklyn — an insecure
borough, second-class, a place of grudges and character, across
the river from "the real New York." When they'd moved west
in 1957, the exile had been substantial. The team that had
stood for a community's soul became synonymous with its
owners, or its managers, or its star players — but it was a
mercenary affection. Eventually, only two things linked the
Dodgers with the Boys of Summer: their royal blue and
bleached-white uniforms, and their announcer.

To Vin Scully, every ballplayer showed up as a character in
a drawn-out sketch. "Hello there, ladies and gentlemen," his
broadcasts began, a welcome that was always sincere, never
saccharine, "and a very good day to you wherever you may
be." In 1966 he worked alone at the microphone, as he had
since arriving in Brooklyn in 1949 (and as he still does to this
day). Another announcer would occasionally relieve him, but
Scully considered it crucial that there be just one at a time, a
single narrative voice with which to generate a mood of

palpable intimacy: "If you're on by yourself, you're talking to the listeners. If you're on with somebody else, you wind up talking to your sidekick." Scully was spare in his images, simple in his words, never partisan, and always fair.

Both players and fans liked him. John Roseboro once paid Vinnie the ultimate compliment, noting that he "walked like an athlete."[130] During the 1950s and 1960s, tens of thousands of fans customarily brought handheld, battery-powered radios to the Dodger home games. They needed Scully there, needed his eyes even when they had their own. His relaxed, unhurried drawl helped them transcend the city setting. With lids closed, they could imagine themselves attending a casual contest in the country, in a sunlit pasture where no salaries or egos intruded.

Scully refused to accept any credit for this phenomenon of "transistor tune-ins." Instead, he attributed it to the gargantuan size of the Los Angeles Memorial Coliseum, where the Dodgers played from 1958 to 1961, while their new park was being built. "Some of those fans were 79 rows up, a half-mile from the action," he said. "It made sense to bring a radio."[131] The phenomenon only grew, however, when the more reasonably proportioned Dodger Stadium finally opened. Although the views were now unobstructed and the seats relatively close to the action, Scully's mellifluous tones continued to resound throughout the stadium. They echoed around to the broadcasting booth and washed back out to the fans, peppered here and there with the sound of applause, the crack of a hit, or the thud of a fastball in the catcher's mitt. In the dugout and on the field, the athletes themselves delighted in overhearing Vinnie's play-by-play. Ron Fairly termed Scully's accounts "great art," in possession of shading, color, even brushstrokes.[132] Koufax almost preferred listening to Scully call a game to pitching in one.

The voice may have belonged to the Dodgers, but the mad pennant stretches in the mid-1960s belonged to the voice.

During September 1965, as the Dodgers had fought their way back into first place at the last minute, Vin Scully's pleasant voice had been everywhere in Los Angeles, twinkling rhythmically from radios in supermarkets, drugstores, parking lots, restaurants, and bars. At the corner hamburger joint, astonished patrons had discovered teenagers listening to the Dodger game rather than rock and roll. The games had been high drama, and no one had wanted to miss a single inning. "Hey pal," one driver had been heard yelling to another as he pulled alongside, "would you turn up your radio and let me keep up with you for a few blocks until I get home?"[133]

On the next-to-last day of the 1965 regular season, Vinnie had provided narration as Koufax had beat Milwaukee's Tony Cloninger with a four-hitter to secure another photo finish NL title for the Dodgers.

Ron Fairly had gone out that night and gotten drunk. "I celebrated," he would bashfully admit, "maybe a little bit more than I would normally have."[134] Although one game yet remained in the season, manager Walter Alston had assured Fairly that he wouldn't be needed for it. This was a team, after all, that had won with their speed. The Dodgers had led the majors with 172 stolen bases. Of that total, the lead-footed Fairly had snatched just 2.

The next morning, Sunday, October 3, Fairly staggered into the clubhouse badly hungover. Fixing his bloodshot eyes on the lineup card, he groaned. His name had been written in the cleanup spot. He would be substituting for Wes Parker.

Annoyed, Fairly sought out his manager. Ron had already played in 157 games, despite being injured a fair amount of the year. The outcome of this particular game was meaningless. Hadn't he earned a day off?

"Parker didn't have a good night's rest," Alston explained. "You're starting at first base."

"Wes didn't have a good night's rest?" Fairly grumbled. "Hell, I haven't even been to bed yet!"

The manager shrugged.

With his pennant now clinched, Alston had decided to engage in a little Moe Drabowsky–style fun. Chatting before the game with Vin Scully, he had offered to let the Dodger broadcaster run the team from the booth for a while. Scully had agreed. It had been decided that whenever Vinnie wanted to put a sign on, he would signal Walter.

In his first at bat against Brave right-hander Bob Sadowski, Fairly drew a walk. Still buzzed and hazy-headed, he accepted his base on balls with reluctance. "He didn't trot to first base," Scully remembered. "He didn't really walk to first base. He sloshed to first base."[135]

It would be perversely twisted now to have Ron — the slowest runner on baseball's fastest team — attempt to steal.

Scully's smooth, effortless narration ran like an overturned beer over the park. Fairly could discern it spilling from the box seats. "I bet they wouldn't think Ron would try to steal a base in this situation," he heard Scully tell the fans over their crackling radios. Then, after a moment, "Maybe we can surprise them."[136]

As the number-five hitter, Lou Johnson, came to the plate and Sadowski peered in for the sign, Fairly glanced casually across at third-base coach Preston Gomez. To his astonishment, he saw Gomez flash him the steal sign. "I was not aware of this until later," Fairly recalled, "but in essence, Vinnie was announcing and managing the game at the same time."[137]

Sadowski delivered the pitch. Fairly took off. Sweet Lou swung at the ball, fouling it away. Strike one.

Jogging back to first, head down, Fairly heard Scully predict that he'd still be going: "You know, I bet they wouldn't think Ron would try that again."[138] Was he hearing things? Again Preston Gomez gave him the steal sign. Hearing things, possibly seeing things? What exactly was in those drinks last night? Again the pitcher threw, the runner went, and the batter swung. Again a foul ball. Strike two.

A little more slowly, Ron returned to first. The tiny bit of energy with which he'd started the day had now been fully expended. He stood on the base, bent at the waist, hands on his knees, fighting for air. At last he straightened up. Many in the stands were waving royal blue pennants. Several were tooting plastic horns. Warily, grudgingly, Fairly looked over at Gomez. Unbelievably, the steal sign remained on. Once more Ron obediently took off, and once more Lou Johnson fouled off Sadowski's pitch.

By now the crowd had begun to titter. This time, when Fairly came back to first, received the sign from Preston Gomez, and saw that he was still expected to steal, he just shook his head. No way. Impossible. Not going.

"And with that," Fairly remembered, "everyone in the stadium started laughing."[139]

"All right," Vinnie relented, addressing the manager over the air. "Walter, you're on your own now."[140]

And thus Vin Scully retired from managing the Dodgers.

Scully talked the fans through the breathless pennant race of 1966 as well.[141] "Vin Scully owns the town," an entertainment critic observed on September 17.[142] Experts at the time estimated that more than 40 percent of radios throughout Southern California were tuned constantly to KFI in order to catch the latest Dodger news. More than two million Angelenos were thought to be listening to Scully's broadcasts every day — not counting the transistor tune-ins in Chavez Ravine.[143]

On September 20, Koufax beat the Phillies at Dodger Stadium for his twenty-fifth victory of the season. It kept the Dodgers one and a half games ahead of the Pirates — and five in front of the Giants — with twelve to play. "The transistors in the bleachers were blaring so loudly that if Gabriel had been blowing his horn, it would have gone unheard," a reporter noted. "One gal had an enormous short wave set, which she turned on loud and clear. She could have picked up Vietnam with no difficulty; perhaps even the astronauts."[144]

LA's last eleven games were on the road. The home fans depended on Vinnie to describe them all. The team started in Chicago, splitting a four-game series with the Cubs, then proceeded south to St. Louis to take three out of four from the Cardinals.

By this time, opportunistic politicians had tracked down the Dodger bandwagon and slavishly jumped aboard. Insisting that the Dodgers would pull it out, Mayor Sam Yorty dashed off a telegram to Baltimore mayor Theodore McKeldin. Positive that the World Series would begin in Dodger Stadium, Yorty requested that McKeldin attend the first two games as his guest of honor.[145] The invitation went unaccepted; McKeldin would remain in Baltimore for the first two games.[146]

On September 30, as the Dodgers arrived in Philadelphia, the red-hot Giants flew into Pittsburgh. With the American League race long since decided, everything now converged on Pennsylvania — the contending NL teams, the nation's sportswriters, the attention of gamblers and fans everywhere, and a cold front crackling with dramatic weather. The National League standings now read like an open-ended algebra problem. The Dodgers were two in front of the Pirates with three still to play. San Francisco hung three and a half games back. Technically, however, the Giants had four games remaining in the season — three against the Pirates and one makeup game against the Reds, to be played in Cincinnati, if necessary, to determine the outcome of the pennant race.

Freezing rain entered from the west, pelting Pittsburgh first and washing out Friday night's Pirates-Giants game. The players sat in the clubhouse, playing cards and listening to the broadcast of the game from Philadelphia, where the Phillies' Chris Short (18–10) faced off against LA's Claude Osteen (17–13) under darkening skies. Osteen left early, down by two runs. Philadelphia added three more on a Bill White home run to right. They still led, 5–1, in the ninth, when Short walked two Dodger batters. Two outs later, the score was 5–3. Maury Wills stood on third. Willie Davis, representing the tying run, was on second. Lou Johnson, who had contributed many game-winning hits in the last month, stepped into the batter's box and took a mighty swing. He got enough of Short's pitch to send up a high pop fly. Wills and Davis raced home. Both crossed the plate before the ball came down, but it was caught, and the game was over. In both locker rooms at Pittsburgh's Forbes Field, the Giant and Pirate players breathed a sigh of relief. The Dodgers again led by just a game and a half.

The storm swept eastward. By Saturday Philadelphia was drenched, and the players didn't even show up at Connie Mack Stadium. The game was called, and the Dodgers spent the day in their hotel. Now it was their turn to watch.

A doubleheader was being played in Pittsburgh to make up for the previous night's washout. Of all things, the Dodger players found themselves rooting for the Giants. "I'd rather have the Pirates eliminated," Phil Regan explained. "Their hitting is just too much." Juan Marichal took the first game for his twenty-fifth victory of the season, and his teammate Bob Bolin won the second with a one-hitter. Ten days earlier, San Francisco had fallen five games back. Now they'd won five straight, and a plan for a National League play-off was quickly cobbled together. The World Series was supposed to start on Wednesday, but if the Giants beat the Pirates once more, the Dodgers dropped both games to the Phillies on Sunday, and the Giants then beat the Reds on Monday, a best-of-three Dodger-Giant series would begin Tuesday in Candlestick Park.

The Dodgers needed to win one of the two remaining games to clinch the pennant.

The manager of the Giants, Herman Franks, was optimistic.

"I've got a feeling the Phils are going to beat the Dodgers twice," he predicted.[147]

"It seems we're always involved in these Wild West finishes," sighed Sandy Koufax.[148]

In the first game of Sunday's doubleheader, Alston started Don Drysdale, who had straightened himself out after the worst pitching of his career and had handily won his last four starts. If Drysdale could give them a victory, the weary Koufax would be rested and ready to start the World Series Wednesday.

From the outset, it didn't look good. The irascible skipper of the Philadelphia team, Gene Mauch, had firmly declared, "We will play as hard as we know how."[149] The Phillies kept that promise, scoring twice in the first inning. The Dodgers appeared utterly puzzled by Philadelphia right-hander Larry Jackson. Drysdale, far from dominant, was gone by the third. Late in the sixth, a three-run blast by Ron Fairly seemed to turn the tide. Koufax jogged down to the bull pen in case he was needed to protect the lead. For the moment, Alston stayed with his long reliever Bob Miller.

Miller surrendered a single to Richie Allen to open the eighth, and Bill White followed by dropping down a bunt. The pitcher charged, grabbed it. Seeking two, Miller hastily spun, then hurled the ball over Maury Wills's head. It was the turning point of the game, the day, and the postseason. Instead of two away with the bases empty, there were no outs, with both Allen and White in scoring position. If Miller hadn't chucked an easy double-play ball into center field, Dick Groat would not have been intentionally walked to load the bases. The weak hits that followed — a blooper by Cookie Rojas and a dribbler by Clay Dalrymple — would not have scored two runs. Philadelphia would have lost the first game. Koufax would not have been called on to pitch the second game. Instead, he could have prepared to start Games One and Four of the World Series. (Koufax had never lost back-to-back starts in any postseason series.)

Philadelphia held on to win the first game 4–3, with Bob Miller absorbing the loss. Over in Pittsburgh, the Giants rallied to tie up the game in the ninth and scored four more in the eleventh to win their sixth straight. They showered, dressed hurriedly, and rode out to the airport, where they awaited the results from Philadelphia. If the Dodgers lost the second game, the Giants would board a flight to Cincinnati. Otherwise, they'd head home.

Koufax had won his twenty-sixth game just two days earlier in Busch Stadium, a masterpiece during which he'd held the Cardinals to four hits and one run. With typical candor (but atypical immodesty), he had afterward observed that his curveball had been better than it had been all year.[150] Its powerful plummet had helped strike out thirteen batters, upping his season total to 307. In addition to his many other record-setting accomplishments — he would, for example, remarkably retire 1,274 batters over 323 innings in 1966 without hitting one — he was now the first pitcher in history ever to have three 300-strikeout seasons. In St. Louis, per usual, he'd thrown all nine innings. "If this kid didn't have arthritis in his left elbow," a *Los Angeles Times* reporter drily noted, "there is no telling how good he might be." Despite the pain, the shots, the heat, and the ice, despite feeling more and more ill and disoriented from the medication each time he took the mound, Koufax led the majors in complete games, innings pitched, shutouts, strikeouts, wins, and ERA — even before starting the second game of the doubleheader in Philadelphia.

The test, as always, was his curveball. Whenever Koufax exhausted his pitching arm, he could not achieve the customary snap on his breaking ball. This had happened in Game Seven of the 1965 World Series, when he'd peered into his spent arsenal to find only a fastball after winning Game Five just two days earlier and leading the majors in every significant pitching category during the regular season. It also had happened in the 1966 all-star game, that feverish affair at Busch Stadium, when, again pitching on two days' rest, his attempt to throw a curve to Bill Freehan had gone wild, which had brought Brooks Robinson home from third.

And now, on the last day of the 1966 season, with the pennant on the line, it happened once more. In St. Louis on Thursday, his curveball may have been at its best, but by Sunday in Philadelphia, it was eminently hittable. With one out in the second inning and the ancient lights in decrepit Connie Mack Stadium just coming on, John Roseboro turned to home plate umpire Doug Harvey and said, "Sit back, kid."

"What do you mean?" Harvey asked.

"Koufax said he can't get his curve over," Roseboro explained. "He's gonna go with the heater, the fastball."[151]

One hundred miles to the south, the Baltimore Orioles waited. Wally Bunker had just completed five shutout innings against the Twins and earned the chance to start the third game of the World Series. Frank Robinson had just won the Triple Crown and was busily assuring his teammates that they would be able to put up the necessary numbers against LA's legendary pitching staff.

On the whole, despite the intimidating prospect of having to face Koufax and Drysdale, the Orioles preferred to play against the immensely popular Dodgers. Since gate receipts determined the size of the World Series bonus, and since Dodger Stadium seated more fans than either San Francisco's Candlestick Park or Pittsburgh's Forbes Field and also contained more box seats than any other park in the National League, playing Los Angeles would guarantee the most money for the Baltimore players.

Twenty-two-year-old occasional Oriole center fielder Paul

Blair had yet another, more personal reason for wanting to face the Dodgers. Paulie had grown up on Fifty-second Street, just a short distance from the Los Angeles Memorial Coliseum. The Dodgers had always been his favorite team, and he'd wanted to play professional ball for them. In 1961, after finishing high school, he had even attended a tryout camp in the Coliseum, auditioning for a spot on the Dodgers' Winter League roster. He had been a shortstop then. At his side, trying out for the second-base position, was another local kid, a former Dodger batboy — blue-eyed, big-jawed, deeply tanned Jim Lefebvre. Paulie had gathered three hits in five at bats, including a home run. His bat speed had amazed Lefebvre, but his glove work in the infield had left the scouts unimpressed. The Dodgers had never called him back, not even to say that he'd failed to make the team. It still hurt. He was just a utility outfielder now, and the least likely Oriole to smash any sort of decisive blow, but confronting the Dodgers in Dodger Stadium and beating them for the world championship had become his dream.

Opposing Koufax in Philadelphia was Jim Bunning. (It was a rematch from late July, when both had pitched eleven scoreless innings — after which Phil Regan, in relief of Koufax, had swooped down to earn both the victory and his nickname.) Bunning was an older, more experienced pitcher than Koufax. In 1966 he had appeared in more games (42 to Koufax's 40), thrown almost as many innings (309 to 314), and shown better control (54 to 76 walks), while winning but nineteen games. Three times in the past four years, Bunning had gotten caught on the edge of that threshold. He'd earned nineteen victories in 1962, 1964, and 1965. How maddening to continually fall one game short of a nice, fat, round number! Koufax may have dreamed of thirty victories; Bunning would settle for twenty. Here was his chance. He was pitching on three days' rest, hardly optimal but still more than Koufax had had.

Bunning lasted just five innings. When he left, he was down by four runs. Koufax took a shutout into the ninth, even though he had but one pitch and, during the fifth inning, something in his back had painfully popped. ("I felt like I knocked out a vertebra," Koufax would later explain.)[152] When Roseboro had started to the mound to find out what was wrong, Koufax had waved him back, worried that if he paused for too long, his back would tighten up and leave him unable to move.[153]

Though his body was giving way, Koufax's spirit held fast. Sandy gritted himself through the inning, scurried off the field and into the clubhouse, called for the trainers, tore off his uniform, and climbed on the table. They smeared his torso with yet more Capsolin ointment. Then three of them — Dodger trainers Wayne Anderson and Bill Buhler, joined by former Dodger Don Newcombe — took hold of Koufax and yanked him hard in opposite directions, trying to pop whatever it was back into place. After a time, unsure whether it had helped, Koufax wearily climbed down, put his jersey back on, and returned to the mound.

After every inning, Newcombe remembered, Koufax swallowed more pills.[154]

The Dodgers were ahead 6–0 in the ninth inning. Meanwhile, milling about the lounge at Greater Pittsburgh Airport, the Giants told themselves not to hope. "You guys don't even know where you're going, huh?" an airline employee asked Giant pitcher Ron Herbel.

"Oh, we know where we're going," Herbel said. *Home.* "Superman is not going to give them seven runs in the ninth inning."[155]

But after eight shutout innings, the Phillies could sense Koufax weakening, and they closed in to take advantage. A base on balls, a Jim Lefebvre error, two singles, and one double later, Philadelphia had scored three times. There were no outs.

Alston stepped out of the dugout and crossed to the mound, tentatively planting each foot before him as if tiptoeing across a hazardous, half-frozen lake. Here he was, a man who had seen one at bat in his big-league career — he'd ripped a long foul ball before striking out — coming out to converse with this guy who had struck out nearly two thousand batters since 1961, a kid who'd matured into an artist right before his eyes.

The pitcher and his skipper — both in pale flannel, both mild-mannered — came together in the middle of the diamond like a rendering in milk. No strain showed on their faces as they discussed the situation. They did not gesture. They stood stiffly, chatting in a war zone, surrounded by threats of a dynasty's looming downfall, and then abruptly Alston withdrew, leaving Koufax in.

The Philadelphia fans, some of the least courteous around, were in an elevated state of delirium. The visitors' bull pen was located out in center field. Surrounded by hostile natives, the nervous Dodger relievers tried to become invisible.

With a man on second, Philadelphia's backup catcher Bob Uecker stepped to the plate and struck out. One away.

At the airport, the Giants received the news with resignation. Hearing that Bobby Wine was being sent in to pinch-hit, Willie Mays shook his head. "Wine will probably hit into a double play," Mays said sadly.

Wine hit a grounder to Wills, who threw to Parker.

Two away.

Leadoff hitter Jackie Brandt came up next.

The stands could scarcely contain the hometown fans, who spilled in and out of their seats and periodically ran wild. The Dodger bull pen crew drew together and quickly devised a plan. Like riot police, they would array themselves in an arrowhead formation after the final out in order to muscle their way through the flood of patrons.

One man on, two out, Phillies down by three, Brandt at the plate.

Koufax stepped off the rubber, picked up the rosin bag, wiped his brow, gazed off abstractly, blew out a breath, and dropped down into his stretch. He was working on his 323rd inning of the year, pitching with a throbbing back, an excruciating elbow, and a dying fastball. Second baseman Lefebvre, watching in wide-eyed admiration, noticed that the pitcher had sweated through his blue-sleeved undershirt and gray travel uniform. He was reminded of the intensity Koufax had exhibited a year earlier when throwing his perfect game. The concentration, the endurance, the dignity of the man were phenomenal.[156]

Koufax was imagining, he would later tell Lefebvre, that Brandt represented the tying run. Briskly, with every ounce of energy he had left, he hurled three nearly invisible strikes past Brandt, who merely felt the wind of the fastballs as they zipped past, like a bracing blast of arctic air in the face. Brandt strode calmly back to the dugout.

Vin Scully summarized the news for the listeners back home: The race was over. The pennant belonged to the Dodgers. The fans in Philadelphia stormed the field. The Dodger staff burst from the bull pen with their battery mates.

"We had to get the heck outta there," Torborg recalled. "There was this one great big fat guy. Boy, he was all over us. He wanted to fight."[157]

"We formed a V," Osteen remembered. "We took off running. Whoever got in our way went flying. And they tried to get in our way. They tried to grab anything they could get — your hat, your glove, whatever. They were stealing the bases. They were taking everything that wasn't tied down. They would've taken anything they could get off us if they could've."[158]

Phil Regan's hat was snatched off his head and fluttered away, out of sight. Twenty-nine years later, when Regan was managing the Baltimore Orioles, he received a package. "I was in the service in 1966," read the accompanying letter. "I was the guy who grabbed your hat in Philadelphia. It's bothered me all these years." Regan opened the package. Inside, he found his long-lost Dodger cap. "An old Tim McAuliffe," Phil fondly remembered, "with the leather headband."[159]

The Giants boarded a flight for San Francisco. The Orioles bought tickets for Los Angeles.

PART THREE

Then Came Moe

aving captured the flag in the season's last light, the Dodgers
had scarcely enough time to wash the champagne and cigar
smoke from their clothes before the World Series was upon
them. They returned from Philadelphia early Monday morning to play the first game of the Series Wednesday afternoon.

"Rest." Koufax smiled. "Two whole days of it. How sweet
it is."[1]

They were spent, but they were home, and expected to win
the Series handily. They'd done it the previous year, riding the
momentum of another late-season charge to silence a slugging AL club in the postseason. Bookmakers made LA 8-to-5
favorites to repeat as world champions. Journalists debated
whether it could be accomplished in the minimum four games;
most assumed that it could, since Baltimore's starting pitchers
were so patently inferior and their players so woefully inexperienced. The only weakness in the Dodger squad seemed to be
the absence of Don Sutton, who had torn a muscle in his right
forearm against the Giants and would be unable to pitch until
the following season. But even without him, the Dodgers were
still impressive.

In the *Baltimore Sun*, sports editor Bob Maisel loyally
picked his Orioles to triumph, although he anticipated that

the effort would require at least six games. In his mind, however, Maisel secretly harbored grave doubts; even seven games
might not be enough.[2] Now that the Dodgers had disproved
all the doubters who'd picked them to finish fifth, everything
seemed to favor them. They had won all five World Series
games previously held in Chavez Ravine, a site in which the
Orioles had never performed particularly well. Baltimore had
played there often — it had been the home park for the American League Angels while the stadium in Anaheim was being
readied — and had never been able to take full advantage of
its vast and unforgiving foul territory, famously fast infield,
hard base paths of red clay, heavy air, distant fences, steep
mound. How could they now defeat Koufax, Drysdale, Wills,
and the rest when they couldn't even beat the lowly Angels
there?

Maisel was especially concerned about Baltimore's lack-
adaisical play as the regular season had wound down.[3] After
clinching the pennant, they'd grown even sloppier and weaker.
The team looked unfocused, uninterested. "What worries me,"
Maisel admitted, sharing a seat with Brooks Robinson on the
team bus immediately before the start of the Series, "is I don't
know whether you can turn these things on and off like a
faucet."

"Don't worry about it," Brooks assured him. "We can turn
it back on, no problem."[4]

The all-star third baseman owned a disposition that was
every bit as pleasant and sunny as Southern California. Even
sunnier perhaps — through the window of the bus, the smog
looked thick and the air hazy. The cloudless sky was bright
white — a buttermilk sky, it was called.

Proceeding to the stadium, the Orioles passed a large
sign that used to advertise real estate bargains: "Would you
believe . . . a four-bedroom duplex for only $24,000?" It had
been altered into a pro-Dodger billboard. "Would you believe . . .
four straight?"[5] A number of Baltimore players glimpsed it

from the bus with gritted teeth.[6] They were the underdogs; they could accept that. But a sweep? *That hurt.*

Brooks was too busy chatting with Maisel to notice the billboard. "The only things that worry me are things we don't know about now," he said. "Like background. We've never played here in the daytime, with the center field bleachers filled." Brooks had heard that it was sometimes difficult for a batter to follow the pitch against the sea of white-shirted patrons seated in the outfield stands. "That might complicate things some."[7]

Before the Series opener, Commissioner Eckert met with all the umpires, managers, and players. "After the introductions," barked the commissioner, "as you stand on the foul line for the National Anthem, you must stand at attention."

"Like a Marine?" Oriole manager Hank Bauer teased. Bauer himself had seen heavy combat with the U.S. Marine Corps in the Second World War and been decorated with a Purple Heart.

"Or like any good soldier," the retired air force general shot back.[8]

Eckert continued to have trouble distinguishing between the armed forces and the national pastime, also warning the two teams against "fraternization between enemy players."[9] As soon as the interminable meeting ended, the athletes poured onto the field for batting practice. Blatantly disregarding Eckert's instructions, Sandy Koufax strolled over to Frank Robinson and extended a hand. "Frank," Koufax said, "congratulations. You really went over there and showed them what you could do. A Triple Crown. That's great."[10]

Immediately, a photographer materialized to request a picture.

Frank pursed his lips, cocked an eyebrow, and suggested a deal. "If I pose with you," he proposed to the Golden Arm, "you're going to have to throw me all change-ups when you pitch."[11]

Koufax flashed his dimples, laughing, and shook his head.

Other newsmen with cameras photographed the game's opposing pitchers, Don Drysdale with Dave McNally, shoulder to shoulder, both facing the camera. The unshaven Big D loomed over the five-foot-eleven Baltimore southpaw. Despite being Series starters, neither pitcher was particularly proud of his stats for the season. Mac was 13–6, while Drysdale was 13–16. Even so, Drysdale was a 6-to-5 favorite. Feebly the two men shook hands, mouthing awkward smiles for the press, small-talking in forced bursts.

To take full advantage of McNally, Alston would be stocking his lineup with right-handers. The all-switch-hitting infield would bat from the right side of the plate. Left-handed Ron Fairly would sit; Tommy Davis would play instead. "The only way we can play them is the same way we played everyone else all year," Alston explained to the press. As always, the Dodger manager was unruffled to the point of being dull. "We'll peck away with singles and doubles and hope that our pitching can hold them."[12]

Hank Bauer also liked to platoon his outfielders to ensure a maximum of favorable lefty-righty matchups. Against Drysdale, Bauer would bench right-handed center fielder Paul Blair in favor of Russ Snyder.

Game time approached, and the city of Los Angeles braked to a halt. The freeways emptied as 55,491 people waded through the turnstiles, seeking seats, peanuts, popcorn, iced cokes, and Dodger dogs; purchasing souvenir programs for fifty cents, commemorative scorecard pens, plastic trumpets, and flat, imitation straw hats called boaters. Ballplayers jogged and stretched, talked with family, affably signed autographs. Forty employees of NBC prepared to beam the game around the globe. Forty million viewers were expected. Somebody wished good luck to Oriole owner Jerry Hoffberger. "We don't need the luck." Hoffberger grinned. "The Dodgers do. We're going to clean their clocks."[13]

During the mid-1960s, second baseman Jim Lefebvre recalled, he would often arrive at Dodger Stadium early, "just to sit in the stands and look at the field. It was that beautiful. No one would be there — only the birds chirping. And I'd see the sky and the grass. What a feeling! I think a baseball field must be the most beautiful thing in the world. It's so honest and precise. And we play on it. Every star gets humbled. Every mediocre player has a great moment. I smell the grass again and remember how I loved the smell, the way it came into my nostrils and filled me up. . . . After a while, things began to happen. The vendors would come in slowly. The place was beginning to come alive. It was like it had a heart, and it was beating slowly, softly — *boom, boom.* The fans started to arrive. *Boom, boom.* The visiting team arrived. You could see them in their dugout, and you'd look at them. *Boom, boom.* And the game was getting closer. And the heart was beating faster. *BOOM, BOOM!* It was loud now, crashing, beating wildly."[14]

Standing in his box, Eckert tossed out the first ball. Not far away, Dave McNally threw on the sidelines, warming up from a pitching rubber set in front of the Oriole bench, feeling so calm, he would say later, that he almost couldn't believe it. As he finished and ducked back into the visitors' dugout, he distantly heard the boom and rumble of John Ramsey making public-address announcements while Helen Dell played sprightly show tunes on the Conn organ.

John Roseboro sat in the dugout, snapping himself into shin guards. Drysdale was loosening up on the mound, throwing to backup catcher Jeff Torborg, one of only two Dodgers who would see no active play in the Series. Roseboro emerged, Torborg retreated. The clock struck one. The nation turned on its televisions. Drysdale completed his warm-up tosses, Roseboro threw down to Lefebvre, Luis Aparicio stepped up to the plate, and the sixty-third World Series got under way.

Drysdale's first pitch roared down the middle, a fastball.

The umpire called it a strike. The hometown Dodger rooters applauded approvingly. ("They did everything but say, 'Bravo!'" Dick Allen once observed, in deriding the politeness of LA's sports fans. "It was baseball as theater.")[15]

After that, Drysdale's game didn't go so well.

His second pitch was outside. Aparicio connected on the third for a long out to deep right; Russ Snyder, the next batter, walked on five pitches; and, with one on and one away, Brooks Robinson appeared on deck, Boog Powell waited in the hole, and Drysdale's old nemesis, Frank Robinson, stepped up to the plate.

The intimidating slugger known for crowding home plate was facing "the last of the angry pitchers" (as Ron Fairly described Big D), famous for throwing inside. Something was guaranteed to happen between these two. "They had a thing going," remembered Dick Williams, a teammate of Drysdale's in Brooklyn. "They would feud all the time."[16] When Robby was with Cincinnati, he'd hit few pitchers as hard as Drysdale, and in return few pitchers had hit him as often as Drysdale. "Frank and Drysdale had really had it out for many, many years," Brooks recalled. "Those two guys just didn't like each other."[17]

As Robby dug his cleats into the batter's box, Drysdale looked in at Roseboro, sneering like the King of Rock n' Roll, then threw over to Wes Parker at first. Snyder dove back. Safe. Drysdale mopped his brow and muttered; he was dreaming of a double play.[18] He needed a ball hit on the ground. Roseboro was thinking the same thing. He put down one finger and wiggled it: the sign for a spitball. Don nodded and delivered.[19] Robby didn't go for it. Ball one.

Roseboro again put down one finger. No wiggle this time. A fastball. Drysdale tried to come inside, to jam Frank, but he couldn't put the ball where he wanted it. Plus he was apparently still tired from his Sunday outing in Philadelphia, because his heater seemed to lack that extra zip. The pitch was too high, and Robby swung. The ball hit the bat halfway down, on the trademark.

The shot sailed deep into left field.

"Swung on," Chuck Thompson casually observed from his perch in the radio booth. (Vin Scully was handling the game's telecast, while Oriole announcer Thompson and Pirate announcer Bob Prince shared radio duties.) "Well hit." Thompson's steady inflection held while the ball arced 375 feet through the air. Tommy Davis scrambled back.

Thompson had watched Robby drive hundreds of balls deep to the outfield that year. Although most of them had been caught, a league best forty-nine had made it over the fence for home runs.

"Back goes the left fielder," Thompson noted, "on the warning track, leaps . . ." Thompson scooted forward to watch Tommy press against the field boxes and stab his glove into the crowd.

"He does not get it! It's in for a home run!"

Later, Frank could recall nothing after touching first base. Everything just went blank. "I think I floated around the bases."[20] The transcendent experience settled once he groped his way back to the dugout.

Meanwhile, Brooks was jumping around the on-deck circle in paroxysms of ecstasy. Seeing Robby hit a home run with Snyder on base to start the Orioles off in front — that felt great. The Robinson Boys had been strategizing beforehand, agreeing that their best chance to beat LA was to score early and force the Dodgers to play catch-up.[21]

Brooks, the cleanup batter, had been following Frank all year. He'd seen Robby hit so many home runs in front of him he joked that he was developing a complex.[22] Brooks felt humbled by Frank's ability to homer seemingly at will. It was true that this hadn't been one of Brooks's best years. He'd kept trying to hit the next pitch farther than Frank, but he'd wind up doing nothing. It was a hell of a competition when the hitter in front of you was the best at everything in the league. Still, Brooks was anything but bitter. As Frank scored, Brooks reached out to clasp his hand in congratulations.

Now Brooks stepped in against Drysdale. After a trademark Drysdale duster — high and inside — Big D followed with a good fastball. But it was right up where Brooks wanted it. And now this Robinson swung and, just like the previous Robinson, got more of it than Drysdale would have preferred. From the way the wood stung his hands and the severe jolt it gave his shoulders, Brooks knew that he'd gotten a good piece of it. Indeed, he mused in the split second, he couldn't hit a ball much better than this.

Again Tommy Davis retreated to lean against the field boxes in deep left, but he had no chance whatsoever to pull in this one either. "Davis looking up," called Chuck Thompson, voice rapidly tightening. "It's going, going, gone!"

The ball landed seven or eight rows up. The Orioles poured onto the field as if they'd just won the World Series. Prancing about the bases in a joyous flailing of limbs, Brooks slapped together his palms. He and Frank had done this before, he remembered, they'd hit back-to-back home runs in the — was it the first game of the season? — no, the second game, in Boston, but whatever, two games into the season, it was already obvious they were going to take the league, had been obvious since Frank had shown up at spring training.[23] That game hadn't mattered, given their destiny. But this one did.

In the Dodger clubhouse, Jeff Torborg sat stunned. After warming up Drysdale, he had sauntered back inside to switch shirts. Maybe eight minutes had passed. He rested there, bare-chested, a freshly laundered shirt in his hands. "I hadn't even gotten my shirt changed," he recalled, "and the two Robinsons had already hit home runs."[24]

Baltimore led 3–0. The previous year, in the three Series

games held in Chavez Ravine, Minnesota had managed to score just twice. In the two games played there during the 1963 World Series, New York had scored only once. In a third of an inning, the Orioles had scored as many runs in Dodger Stadium as the Twins and Yankees together had scored.

Boog Powell popped up to third baseman Jim Gilliam for the second out, Davey Johnson struck out swinging, and Drysdale finally escaped the first. But the Orioles padded their lead in the next inning, when Andy Etchebarren walked, then made it around the bases on a series of sacrifices and a Russ Snyder line drive into left field. "Since this made the score four to nothing," sportswriter Jim Murray joked in the next day's *Los Angeles Times*, "the game was immediately stopped to see whether the Dodgers wanted to forget this game and start the second one."[25]

Instead, the game dragged on. When Robby came up for the second time in two innings, it seemed to Drysdale a recurring nightmare. Frank took another good cut. The ball didn't travel as far this time. Tommy Davis gloved it for the third out. Frank felt just fine, aware that a 4–0 lead against the Dodgers was like a ten-run lead over any other club. "With their kind of attack, they can rally to make up two runs but if you lead by four, the Dodgers are in trouble."

Paying only partial attention was the man skulking about Dodger Stadium's executive chambers, cornering other major-league brass, offering almost anything to obtain more pitching. Bill DeWitt was close to desperate, Robby's homer yet another reminder of what a mistake the Reds had made.[26] The Indians wanted to dump Vic Davalillo, the Yankees were eager to unload Roger Maris and Clete Boyer, the Braves were willing to give up Eddie Mathews, and the Red Sox were entertaining bids for their team captain, Carl Yastrzemski, in exchange for a good-hitting catcher or a solid starting pitcher.[27] A few tempting deals were proposed for Yaz, but fortunately for Boston, they broke down, and he stayed in New England. The next season, Yastrzemski would astound the baseball world by repeating Frank Robinson's feat of 1966, winning the Triple Crown, carrying his team into the World Series, and earning Most Valuable Player honors. Failing to learn from history, the condemned Red Sox would narrowly escape repeating it. Meanwhile, DeWitt wandered the back rooms of Dodger Stadium with furrowed brow and the empty heart of a man whose blunders had been compounded by his big mouth.

Out in the sunlight, Dave McNally was having trouble of his own. The stocky, twenty-three-year-old left-hander, the pride of Billings, Montana, had been amply warned about the steep slope of Dodger Stadium's pitching mound. Still, for some reason, he couldn't adjust.[28] His arm kept coming through

Game One is scored on an antique truck parked outside Baltimore's City Hall. (Copyright © *Baltimore Sun*)

before his front foot hit the ground, and everything sailed high. He started the game by walking Maury Wills, a very bad sign. Wills didn't manage to score, but in the Dodger second, Lefebvre homered, then Parker doubled, and, on four straight pitches, Gilliam walked. Only a miraculous tumbling catch by Russ Snyder of John Roseboro's sinking line drive prevented further damage, holding the score at 4–1. The next inning, McNally's control deserted him. He issued consecutive bases on balls to Lou Johnson, Tommy Davis, and Jim Lefebvre. He had thrown sixty-three pitches in just two and a third innings. He'd managed only three strikes to the last four batters.

Drysdale was gone by this time, having been replaced by Joe Moeller. And so, with the bases loaded and one away in the Dodger third, with Wes Parker on deck and the Dodger fans on their feet, McNally watched Hank Bauer climb out of the dugout. The Oriole manager signaled for a reliever even before he'd reached the mound. The organ played as Mac departed.

In the Oriole bull pen out behind right field, Moe Drabowsky had already been tossing to Charlie Lau for an inning or so. Lau didn't think Drabo looked especially strong. There'd been occasions before when Moe had knocked off Lau's glove, but not now. His stuff was just so-so.[29] Relieving in an early-inning, bases-loaded situation in the opening game of the World Series required more poise than power, however, and by that measure, if Lau had to select someone from the bull pen to go first, it would be Moe. He'd been through the wringer. He'd been transferred and traded; he'd absorbed the blame for a ton of lost games; he'd seen too much to let the situation bother him.

There was another reason that the bull pen sentiment was to shove Moe out there first: now the rest of the relievers and the catchers in the pen could relax and settle down to enjoy the game. Drabo didn't confine his practical jokes just to hot-foots. Lately, he'd been doing a lot with white mice and snakes, mostly king snakes, sometimes boa constrictors.[30] You never knew where they'd pop up — inside lockers, luggage, shoes, showers. It was more than a little disconcerting.

So it was to the relief of all that the journeyman Moe Drabowsky journeyed through the bull pen gate as young McNally headed for the showers. Unaware that he was about to make World Series history, Moe tossed this comment over his shoulder: "They're bringing in The Machine early today."[31]

All season Robby and Drabo had helped to impel the team forward. Frank had made his contribution to this game already. It was time for Moe to show what he could do. As Wally Bunker would later point out, "Being funny wouldn't have mattered if Drabo couldn't have backed it up by being a good pitcher."[32] Although Moe's pitches had not impressed anyone in the Baltimore bull pen that day, by the time he had crossed the outfield and climbed the mound, he'd apparently loosened up. As Wes Parker watched Drabowsky warm up from the on-deck circle, he was thunderstruck. "I remember thinking, *Holy Good Lord Almighty, is this guy ever throwing hard.* I mean, he was really firing that day." Parker had faced Drabo before, but Moe had never displayed anything like this sort of sneaky velocity. "Oh my God, he had it that day. It was just one of those moments. He was throwing the living shit out of the ball, he really was. He was kinda coming sidearm, and normally you'd expect his ball to sink a little bit or something, but it wasn't. It was rising. Oh God, he threw hard! I remember watching him warm up and thinking, *Boy, I gotta turn it up a couple notches. I gotta really be ready because this guy is blowing it in there.* And even after I got to the plate, he threw it by me. Even though I knew he was throwing hard, I couldn't catch up to it."[33]

It took Drabowsky just four pitches to strike out Parker,

and then Jim Gilliam stepped in. Moe took Gilliam to a full count, then delivered a beautiful pitch on the inside corner, just where he intended. Plate umpire Bill Jackowski considered it, judged it a ball, and Gilliam went to first base, scoring Lou Johnson. It was the fourth walk of the inning issued by an Oriole pitcher. The score was now 4–2. The bases remained loaded, with two out and left-handed batter John Roseboro at the plate.

Once more, on a few very close pitches, Drabo fell behind in the count. The crowd was delirious, the whole park roaring. Moe could see Bauer standing on the top step of the dugout. He knew that another relief pitcher, Stu Miller, was already up in the bull pen, getting loose. If he walked Roseboro or gave up any kind of hit, he'd be gone.[34]

Theodore McKeldin watches Game One from his office in City Hall. (Copyright © *Baltimore Sun*)

Standing there in front of 55,941 delirious Dodger fans, in full view of Hollywood, America, God, even Mayor McKeldin (watching from Baltimore's City Hall, his small black-and-white television tuned to Channel 11, WBAL), Moe made up his mind. He would challenge Roseboro, pitch to his strength, fire it down the middle. If Roseboro hit it out of the park for a grand slam, so be it.

Moe fondled the rosin bag, dropped it. He toed the rubber, went into the stretch, delivered. Roseboro chopped at the pitch, getting only a small piece of it. The ball climbed high into the air behind home plate. Etchebarren pursued it, grabbed it to end the inning.

For the rest of his life, people would ask Moe about that particular Wednesday afternoon, his (quite literal) day in the sun, and how he'd felt as he'd retaken the mound in the bottom of the fourth. His answer: pretty good, not especially great. He was never one for grand anticipations. He'd fallen on his face too many times. He was just hoping to keep the score close. Like many athletes in the middle of an excellent performance, Moe was scarcely conscious of what took place. The first batter was Jim Barbieri, pinch-hitting for relief pitcher Joe Moeller. Fastball down and away. Fastball up and in. Slider down and away. Fastball at the knees. Barbieri drew a full count, then swung and missed. One away. Moe stymied Maury Wills with two quick strikes and got him swinging on the third. Two away.

"There was intense concentration on every pitch," Drabo remembered. "Tremendous focus."

The next batter was Willie Davis, who had homered in Philadelphia in the final game of the season. Three days later, as was his habit, Willie was still swinging for the fences. He'd been up twice already. Hacking at bad pitches, he had popped up weakly both times. In this at bat, he showed a similar lack of restraint. Moe fanned him. Three away.

The stadium moaned.

In the Dodger fifth, with the Orioles now leading 5–2, Moe reemerged to face Lou Johnson. Sweet Lou took a huge chop at a two-strike fastball but couldn't catch up. One away. Johnson staggered back to the dugout. His teammates pressed forward to ask what Drabowsky's pitches were doing. "They aren't hitting the bat," Sweet Lou reported with a mystified shake of his head.[35]

Tommy Davis followed, lifted a few foul balls, then took a cut that found only air. Two away.

Given the brightness of the day, fans were improvising sunshades out of empty food trays. They squinted at the field with expressions of confusion, as if trying to identify some unrecognizable creature. Out there on the mound — who was that guy? The stands grew quiet. Radios reverberated. Everyone, players and umpires included, could hear broadcaster Bob Prince barking out the park's measurements ("335 down both lines, then it goes right on out to 370, and ultimately 410 straight away") which might as well have been distances given in miles rather than feet, seeing how well this Drabowsky guy was throwing. For twelve years, Moe had been pitching in the major leagues. Hardly anybody had noticed him. In this season alone, he had twice struck out five straight batters, and yet he wasn't even considered Baltimore's strongest relief pitcher. Stu Miller had appeared in more games. John Miller had pitched more innings. Eddie Watt had garnered more strikeouts. Eddie Fisher possessed a lower earned run average. Dick Hall surrendered fewer walks. If anything, Drabo's virtual invisibility was an indication of just how much talent had been crowded into the Oriole bull pen, and how much credit the relief staff deserved for the team's pennant. Scouts, gamblers, opponents: all season they had looked at the Oriole pitching staff with blinders, searching for totals that would have accrued to a single hurler had the burden not been so expertly shared. They

had looked at the parts, not the sum. Searching for exclama-
tion points, they had overlooked the words.

Jim Lefebvre was next and had some trouble spotting the
ball.[36] As with Tommy Davis, he managed to connect for a
couple of fouls before he went down swinging. Three away.

The stadium gasped.

Moe had fanned the side in two consecutive innings — six
strikeouts in succession, a World Series record for a relief
pitcher. The only other Series pitcher to accomplish the feat
had achieved it forty-seven years earlier. He'd been a starter
with Cincinnati. His name was Hod Eller. "Never heard of the
fella," Drabowsky admitted afterward.

It was supposed to have been a day of few runs and overpow-
ering Dodger pitching. Instead, seven runs scored in the first
four innings, twelve walks were issued, both starters vanished
early, and Los Angeles quickly fell behind.

The final score remained 5–2, Baltimore.

After winning the first game of the World Series, Moe Drabowsky is congratulated by (left to right) infielders Brooks Robinson, Davey Johnson,
and Boog Powell. (*Sports Illustrated*)

Drabowsky ended up, over six and two-thirds innings, striking out eleven batters, all of whom went down swinging. In this, his longest outing of the season — entering the visitors' park with the bases loaded, pitching for the underdogs — he had displayed an unparalleled dominance. No reliever in World Series history had ever fanned so many. Simple contact had been managed in only ten at bats, just three Dodgers had moved the ball beyond the infield, and only Willie Davis had earned a base hit — a harmless, opposite-field single in the seventh. Otherwise, Moe had breezed along, setting them down in order, inning after inning. Over the same period, the Dodgers had required three relievers — Joe Moeller, Bob Miller, and Ron Perranoski. Although the Orioles had connected for five hits after the fourth, they too had been unable to advance a runner past second base.

Baltimore scout Jim Russo, whose full title was special assistant to the player personnel director, would later claim much of the credit for his team's surprisingly strong showing in Game One. After workouts a day earlier, Russo had passed around his sixteen-page report on the Dodgers. He had then spent two and a half hours talking the club through the thing. The pitchers had learned that Lou Johnson was tough in the clutch but could be gotten with a fastball in on the fists or a breaking ball down and in; that Maury Wills had a good eye but poor power and should be dealt with through low curves and high heaters down the middle; that Willie Davis could get fooled by straight change-ups and would bail out on sidearm fastballs; and that Jim Lefebvre liked the ball high when batting right-handed, down when batting left-handed. The fielders had heard that they should give Wills the right-field line when he was batting left-handed, should assume that Willie Davis would never bunt or drag, and should crowd the center of the diamond against Lefebvre. The batters had discovered that Koufax had a lousy move to first, Phil Regan a deceptive windup, and Drysdale two bad knees.

Due primarily to the thoroughness of this scouting report, Jim Russo built a reputation as a "superscout," a tag eventually so synonymous with the man that, in later years, it would become the title of his autobiography. It's debatable, however, how much Russo actually aided his team in the 1966 World Series. Frank Robinson had contributed a good many tips, not the least of which had been the repositioning of his fellow outfielders before each batter. As for Hank Bauer, he had found Russo's session far too long.[37] Bored, he'd left. Strolling about Dodger Stadium, the Oriole manager had bumped into Sam Mele, skipper of the Minnesota Twins. Deciding to capitalize on Mele's managerial experience in the 1965 World Series, Bauer had casually solicited his advice on how best to defeat the Dodgers.

Mele's advice had been as surprising as it was succinct. "Fastballs," he'd answered.[38] Most major leaguers had trouble with certain pitches, but most were considered capable of connecting with a ball that didn't bend, curve, or dive. For Mele to opine that any team as a whole — much less a championship ball club that had defeated his own — had difficulty swatting fastballs was more than just counterintuitive. It was extremely insulting. Nevertheless, it had been this brief recommendation, more than the tens of thousands of words typed and spoken by Jim Russo, that had led Bauer to insert Drabo into the first game. Although Moe was known for throwing spitters and hard sliders, he often mixed in a top-notch fastball, and that had been what Bauer had wanted. He'd passed the word to catcher Andy Etchebarren that if Moe's heater was working well, they should stick with that. They had. "Moe threw 85% fastballs," Etchebarren confirmed in the locker room afterward.

The successive first-inning shots by Frank and Brooks had certainly helped win the game, but Drabowsky was the bigger surprise. The heated scrum of reporters and photographers in the visitors' dressing room was at times so dense that the Orioles couldn't get to their lockers. After showering, Boog Powell, whose cubicle adjoined Moe's, had to wait for more than an hour to be reunited with his clothes. In the meantime, Boog sat patiently nearby, his immense waist wrapped in a too-small towel, as the hero of the day recounted the topsy-turvy story of his twisty life. "Go see the hitters," Moe would periodically urge. "I don't want to do all the talking."[39] This was the sort of attention Drabo (looking "stunned and slightly trampled," according to one account of the day) had always sought before through pranks and pratfalls; now it was wearing him out. "Moe deserves it all." Boog smiled. "What a job he did on those guys."[40] "I'd just like to thank the Dodger groundskeeper," Moe modestly told the nearly one hundred sportswriters who engulfed him after the victory, "for making the mound too steep for McNally." He then noted that the day's news wasn't all good. As a stockbroker, he'd just been alerted that the stock market had dropped to its lowest point of the year.[41]

Reporters who ventured into the losing clubhouse found an upbeat mood. Drysdale stood out amid the rampant horseplay and laughter. "I just made some bad pitches," he said with a shrug. "After that it was just trying to get back in the ball game. We had a couple of chances. Then came Moe. I haven't seen him pitch that good in eight years."[42]

Maury Wills was acting thoroughly unimpressed. "They had two big hits," the team captain sniffed. "After that, it was just a dead game." Like his teammates, Wills would have preferred to have opened the Series with a victory, but he knew that their history did not favor this. "We've had a bad start in every Series since I've been with the club," Maury reminded the press corps, "except when we won four straight from the Yankees in 1963." He ticked them off on his fingers. "We lost the first game to Chicago in 1959, eleven to zero, but won that series in six games. And last year, we lost the first two games to Minnesota, but won it in seven."[43]

Walter Alston leaned on a table in the Dodger training room, calmly answering questions. He wasn't terribly disappointed. They'd stranded five runners in the second and third innings, but it was just one game. There'd be other opportunities. They had Koufax going for them the next day, so things were bound to turn around.

Several LA players did acknowledge that their bench had been strangely lifeless, an alien planet rather than the dugout of the reigning champions. Alston was asked if the frantic pennant race had left his boys too tired to go on. "Well, I don't think so," he responded, "but I can't look inside them to see what they're thinking."[44]

Alston worked to change the subject. At the time, World Series games were played during the day, as they always had been. In its blind devotion to tradition, baseball was resisting a modernization that would both increase viewership and improve the quality of play. "During the season most games are played under the lights, so why change for the Series?" Alston asked rhetorically. "Playing conditions are better under the lights. You don't have those white-shirt batting backgrounds or the glare of the sun to contend with. In my opinion, they play better ball at night."[45]

Sportswriters assumed that Alston was bothered because of how well Drabo's pitches had vanished into the white shirts of the center pavilions, and they interpreted his gripes (like those of Maury Wills) to be sour grapes. But just then, across the way, in the Baltimore locker room, left fielder Curt Blefary and center fielder Russ Snyder were also complaining about how difficult it had been to follow the ball, both in the outfield and at the plate. Nonetheless, scant importance was attached to this consensus of opinion.

The following day, the daytime glare above Dodger Stadium would become national news.

PART FOUR

That's Not Sandy Koufax

That night, the Southland's warm air blew out over the Pacific, cooling quickly as usual, then growing thick with condensation. The next day dawned gray and foggy, like many mornings in Los Angeles. By noon, however, the sun had burned off much of the haze. The sky sparkled, not blue so much as white, like a worn seashell wet from the waves.

Before the game, Vin Scully discussed the ramifications of this with television viewers. "This might be one of the toughest ballparks in the big leagues to play the outfield in," he observed. "Most baseball parks are two decks, the lower and upper stands. Here you have six. It is extremely difficult to get a good jump on a ball when you are looking into six decks of color, on a bright day such as this." Scully then reminded everyone about Yankee first baseman Joe Pepitone, who, in the fourth and deciding game of the 1963 World Series, had been unable to pick up the throw from Clete Boyer at third because of all the white shirts in the Dodger Stadium crowd. Pepitone's error had cost New York the game.

At field level, settling into seats behind cages in the stadium's exclusive dugout boxes, were some of the biggest names in entertainment — Louis Armstrong, Doris Day, Milton Berle, Frank Sinatra, Cary Grant — all freshly coiffed, splendidly attired, and happy to cheer the hometown boys. But after the

teams were introduced, the anthem sung, and the Dodgers
took the field, it wasn't one of these famous pretty people who
threw out the first ball of the game. That honor went instead
to a shriveled and stooped man with a face permanently
leathered by thousands of innings of baseball. At age twenty-
two, this man had started in center field for the Dodgers.
Fifty-four years later, in 1966, Casey Stengel had at last
taken himself out of the game long enough to be elected to the
Hall of Fame.

Living now a few miles away from Dodger Stadium, just
over the hill in Glendale, Casey had been attending Dodger
home games throughout the season, marveling at Wes Parker's
glove work, Jim Lefebvre's range, Maury Wills's intensity,
and, in particular, the greatness of today's starting pitcher,
Sandy Koufax.[1] In his playing days, Stengel had faced most
of baseball's pitching greats — Christy Mathewson, Grover
Cleveland Alexander, Babe Ruth, Walter Johnson. He felt that
Koufax was better than any of them. "It takes almost a miracle
to beat him," Casey pointed out. "You try to put the whammy
on him. But when he's pitching, the whammy tends to go on
vacation."

A journalist waylaid Sandy before the game to find out
whether he could fathom Casey's trippingly surreal "Stengel-
ese." "When I was young and smart, I couldn't understand
him," Koufax acknowledged. "But now that I'm older and
dumber, he makes sense to me."[2]

At one P.M., the television cameras focused on Stengel as he
rose ceremonially before his seat. He shifted the baseball to
his left hand and, to much applause, fired it out of the stands
into the waiting mitt of John Roseboro. Casey's craggy face,
visible worldwide on tens of millions of television sets, creased
into a smile. "He had a little something on that one!" laughed
Vin Scully. "The great Charles Dillon Stengel!"

Casey couldn't have been happier. One of the first telegrams to reach Alston in the Philadelphia locker room the previous Sunday had been from Stengel, congratulating him on "expertly" managing the Dodgers. Anticipating this World Series, Casey felt no divided loyalties, even though he had managed most of Baltimore's coaching staff when, in more youthful days, they had played for the Yankees. "I'm a National League man," he firmly declared. But he gave the Orioles plenty of credit. Securing this year's world championship would not be easy for Los Angeles. "We all know," he allowed, "Frank Robinson is a tough man. They even know it now in Cincinnati." And the flawless play of Brooks Robinson astonished him. "From Kansas City to Kankakee and back again, I ain't never seen nothing like the guy on third. And then, when you see him, you don't believe it."[3]

Vegas held LA at 8-to-5 favorites to win Game Two.

One individual who felt differently was Jim Palmer, the Orioles' choice to start opposite Koufax. Palmer had been observing closely the previous afternoon when Drabo had closed down Los Angeles with his velocity. "You can beat the Dodgers with a fastball," Palmer had assured the press afterward. It was a naively arrogant disparagement for an erratic, inexperienced pitcher to pronounce against the current champs, and it made all the papers. In the morning Palmer awoke to roughly the same dilemma that Joe Namath later found himself in, on the day of Super Bowl III, against Baltimore's great 1969-1970 Colts. Like Namath, Palmer had to deliver an impossibly gutsy performance that could match his underdog braggartry. The scrawny, twenty-year-old righthander, with the overdrawn eyebrows and red crabapples for cheeks, now had to go out and beat the greatest southpaw in baseball history.

Ultimately, Jim Palmer would be an Oriole for nineteen years. He would pitch nearly four thousand major-league innings, post a career 2.86 ERA, and become the first pitcher to win as many Cy Young Awards as Sandy Koufax. But all that was in the future, vague and unknowable. On October 6, 1966, he was merely a kid who couldn't control his curveball, an orphan whose adoptive father had died, whose adoptive mother had remarried, whose family, though wealthy, kept moving, living on Madison Avenue in New York City, then in Beverly Hills, then in Scottsdale, Arizona. He was only seven years removed from the junior high schooler who had fallen asleep listening to Vin Scully recount Dodger games on KFI.

What made Palmer's comment of supreme self-confidence all the more astonishing was that he was injured. Throughout the 1966 season, after games and on off days, he had spent much of his time painting his new ranch house. "I would come home and get a fresh roller and mix up a gallon of Sherwin Williams. Again and again. That roller, heavy with paint, down the wall. Heavier and heavier. Roll after roll." This exercise was not, by any means, among those recommended for a pitcher, whose overtaxed arm was ideally limited to carefully monitored tosses between starts. "By the northeast wall of the second bedroom, my arm started to hurt a lot. I got introduced to cortisone injections."

Thus, by Game Two of the World Series, Palmer already had a tight shoulder. He would later admit, "In the back of my mind I was wondering, 'How's my arm going to hold up?'"

Palmer started off strong, retiring the side in the first, three up, three down. Ron Fairly led off the second. Palmer walked him. In stepped Jim Lefebvre, the number-five batter. The switch-hitting Lefebvre, like Wills and Gilliam before him, turned around to bat from the left side against the right-handed Palmer. It didn't matter; Palmer promptly struck him out. Next up was Lou Johnson.

Fairly, the least fleet Dodger, took a short lead at first. Without Scully at the helm, there was no chance that Fairly would be running. Nonetheless, Palmer checked him before throwing home. Sweet Lou swung weakly, slapping the ball off the end of his bat into right field. It was a single, the first Dodger hit of the day. As Robby ran up to catch it on the bounce, he lost his balance and fell down. Johnson rounded first and kept going; he made it into second standing up. The throw went home, holding Ron "Not-Be-Nimble" Fairly at third.

From the radios in the stands came the sound of broadcaster Bob Prince grousing. As in Game One, the "transistor tune-ins" had to make do with Chuck Thompson and Prince, "the Gunner," as he was called. "A very typical Dodger rally in the making," snorted Prince. "A base on balls and a bloop off the end of the bat. This is just a typical Dodger rally. They did it so many times over the season that . . . you know how they play for it." (This was what kept my guys from rightfully taking the league, the ever-partisan Pittsburgh announcer seemed to be saying, this piddling style of ball.)

Runners on second and third. One out. The batter Roseboro.

Palmer ran a fastball in on the handle. Roseboro, jammed, popped up to short. Runners held. Two down.

Wes Parker stood in, with Koufax on deck. Shortstop Luis Aparicio hustled in to talk with Palmer. They elected to walk Parker (.253 on the season) to get to Koufax (.076 on the season). As the crowd jeered and catcalled, Etchebarren hopped to his left four times to catch enough pitchouts to put the slight, erudite first baseman aboard.

The bases were loaded for number 32, who could hit off others about as well as others could hit off him. ("I can think of only one advantage I have in pitching against Sandy Koufax," Jim Palmer had informed reporters that morning. "Don Drysdale is a better hitter.")[4] In his entire career, Koufax had but two regular season home runs. In seventeen World Series games, he'd recorded only one hit. His arthritic elbow had eroded his swing of late, reducing it to a one-handed punch of the bat. The first pitch looked good enough. Sandy took a tremendous undercut and hit a high fly into shallow right. Davey Johnson dropped back to catch it for the third out.

Three Dodgers were stranded. Bob Prince was astonished. "The Baltimore Orioles are out of a jam!" he exclaimed. (His error-prone Pirates would have been down by a couple of runs by now.)

Returning to the Oriole dugout, Frank Robinson was mad at himself for falling while fielding Johnson's one-out blooper. "It's a high sky," Frank observed to young center fielder Paul Blair, "very bright. Tough to see the ball."

"It's brutal out there," Boog Powell agreed, hoping he didn't get any pop flies at first.[5]

Blair nodded. The fall sky throughout California had a distinctive glare: the sun dropping toward the sea, the clear western sky gleaming with refracted light. Robinson had seen a lot of it growing up in Oakland. Blair, a former Angeleno, was familiar with it too. He also knew that this park was worse than most.[6] The screen in back of home plate gave off a funny gold glare that made it difficult to locate the ball.

Paulie stopped. He had to think about hitting. He was due to lead off the inning.

Blair was nervous.[7] He deposited his glove and hat on the Baltimore bench, donned a helmet, took up a bat, stepped out onto the grass. His family was in the stands. "Paulie!" they called, waving. Meanwhile, sixty-plus feet away, the hero of Blair's teen years loosened up, throwing smoke. Koufax's warm-up pitches smacked Roseboro's glove with a characteristically wet pop, the splat of futility.

Paulie swung his bat in a circle of chalk. He knew well the fog that settled like a cough in the low San Gabriel Mountains, lingering even into early afternoon. It slowed fly balls, tugging at them slightly. This was why, among those great Dodger teams, only pitchers, never hitters, would find themselves inducted into the Baseball Hall of Fame. This was also primarily why the entire 1966 Dodger roster combined to hit only as many home runs as three Orioles (Robby, Brooks, and Boog).

When public-address announcer John Ramsey spoke Blair's name and the plate umpire motioned for him to stand in, Paulie was so lost in thought he didn't know where he was. He managed to locate the batter's box, but Koufax quickly rang up two strikes on him. Blair connected on the next one, flying out, somewhat respectably, to Ron Fairly in right field. Relieved, Paulie dashed back to the dugout while Etchebarren, the number-eight hitter, came to the plate.

Koufax started Etch off with a curve. Etchebarren checked his swing. "Ball!" the umpire bellowed. Another curve. This one came in about six inches over Etch's head, then fell like a wounded bird. Etch froze, his bat still cocked, watching as the pitch tumbled through the strike zone and Roseboro caught it on the ground.[8]

"Strike one!"

The 1–1 pitch was a fastball down the middle. Etch swung, came up empty.

"Strike two!"

Another fastball down the middle.

"Strike three!"

Etch went and sat down.

Representing the lineup's bottom was Jim Palmer. Koufax had retired the eight batters before him with supreme efficiency. Aparicio had outrun an infield grounder before being picked off first, then Blefary and Robby had popped out. Brooks had fouled out, then Boog, Johnson, and Blair had popped out. Now Etchebarren had struck out. In two-and-two-thirds innings, Koufax had thrown just twenty pitches. Eighteen had been strikes. What could Palmer possibly hope to achieve?

The Baltimore pitcher promptly popped the ball up. Gilliam

moved in to catch it on the infield grass. Palmer did not put his head down as he ran. Instead, he held his chin up proudly, content with having gotten at least some wood off the great man.

Back in Baltimore, the sun had sunk behind the facades of the stone buildings. The smokestacks, church steeples, and row house chimneys seemed to stretch toward the last light, while the emptying factories receded into the shadows. By five o'clock, Kirson's bar on Greenmount Avenue was packed. Not a stool was available, not even the one directly beneath the big color television set.[9]

There was a homey, congenial feel in the crowded tavern. The late-afternoon sun coming through the front window lit up lazy clouds of cigarette smoke and played off the creased faces of Kirson's stolid clientele — a steelworker, a mechanic, several factory workers, a retired sailor, a schoolteacher, a Bendix draftsman, a machine salesman, an operating room assistant. Many had been coming here since . . . well, since forever. Some of them even remembered the shoemaker's shop that had been on the spot before Al Kirson had taken it over.

Amid them, a *Baltimore Sun* reporter leaned on the glass of the Laguna Beach pinball machine, drinking, jotting in a notebook. The tavern fans let no Oriole action go by without a vigorous response. They'd cheer when a Baltimore batter paused to knock the dirt from his spikes. "With only three scoreless innings behind us," wrote the reporter, "the cast in the bar is like a light opera company about to break into song."[10]

To them, the game's color broadcast on NBC looked positively radiant. Most Americans did not yet own a color television, and only a few shows were broadcast in the broader spectrum. In every sense, the country was used to seeing things in black and white.

No African Americans were present at Kirson's because

Don Sutton admired the angry, aggressive competitiveness of Don Drysdale. In 1966 the twenty-year-old "Little D" joined "Big D" in the Dodger pitching rotation. Sutton became one of the few pitchers ever to strike out more than two hundred batters in his rookie year. He went on to join Drysdale in the Hall of Fame. *(National Baseball Hall of Fame Library, Cooperstown, New York)*

Brooklyn-born Dodger Tommy Davis was the best hitter in the majors until he broke his ankle in 1965. His stance and balance in the batter's box were ruined. Determined in 1966 to reclaim his rightful position, he drove himself hard, rushing his recovery. He would never again be great. *(National Baseball Hall of Fame Library, Cooperstown, New York)*

Maury Wills was the heart and soul of the great Dodger teams of the midsixties. Grandly promising that in 1966 he would break his single-season record of 104 stolen bases, he kept on pace for a few months, but injuries soon slowed him. That season, for the first time since his freshman year, he failed to lead the league in thefts. His worth as a player plummeted in the eyes of the Dodger brass, who increasingly viewed Wills as expendable. *(National Baseball Hall of Fame Library, Cooperstown, New York)*

Walter Alston began managing the Dodgers in 1954. He won his sixth pennant in 1966. "He was very quiet," Jeff Torborg remembered. "No big ego, no extra conversation. He was just a big, strong, silent type." *(National Baseball Hall of Fame Library, Cooperstown, New York)*

The Orioles acquired veteran Luis Aparicio from Chicago, where his graceful speed had ignited much of the fire in the famed "Go-Go Sox" of the 1950s. Positioned beside flawless third baseman Brooks Robinson, the Venezuelan shortstop made the left side of Baltimore's infield the best in the game. *(National Baseball Hall of Fame Library, Cooperstown, New York)*

Andy Etchebarren was Baltimore's third-string catcher, but after early-season injuries felled both Dick Brown and Charlie Lau, the rookie Etch settled in behind the plate. He brought immediate coherence to an erratic crew of knuckleballers, flamethrowers, sinker ballers, southpaws, and spitballers. *(National Baseball Hall of Fame Library, Cooperstown, New York)*

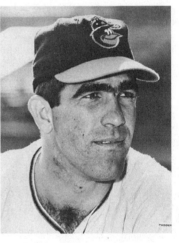

Hank Bauer began managing the Orioles in 1964. He won his only pennant in 1966. "He just wrote the same lineup, day in, day out," Brooks Robinson remembered. "He had a face that looked like the muzzle of an M1, but he had a marshmallow heart." *(National Baseball Hall of Fame Library, Cooperstown, New York)*

Phil Regan receives the call to get ready in the Dodger Stadium bull pen. The Dodgers had acquired Regan in an off-season deal noticed by few. Regan was a washed-up starter. The Dodgers made him a relief pitcher. *(Photo by Frank Worth, courtesy of the* Sporting News*)*

Regan's unusual delivery led to a large number of ground-ball outs. In 1966, to everyone's shock, Regan became the best reliever in the league. After dropping a game in May, he did not lose again all season. In sixty-five appearances, his record was 14–1, with twenty-one saves and an ERA of 1.62. Dodger catcher John Roseboro called him "our salvation." *(Photo by Frank Worth, courtesy of the* Sporting News*)*

The first-place Orioles disembarking in Minneapolis to play the Twins, last year's league champs, in early August. Paul Blair descends first. Behind him are Frank Robinson, Brooks Robinson, Sam Bowens, and Gene Brabender. Despite the formal dress, the ball club was open and loose on the road, loaded with funnymen and goofballs. No joke was off-limits, no topic taboo. *(Photo by John Croft, courtesy of the* Sporting News*)*

Baltimore's Curt Blefary drenches Boog Powell with beer after clinching the American League pennant in Kansas City. The bulk of the team's offense and run production came from the "Cannons at the Corners," including left fielder Blefary and first baseman Powell. The other "Cannons" were the Robinson boys—Frank in right and Brooks at third. *(AP / Wide World Photos)*

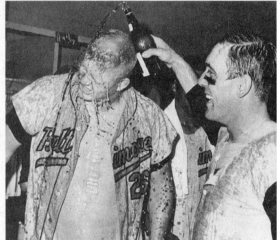

At the end of the 1966 regular season, city officials held an impromptu ceremony to honor their newest and greatest baseball star, Frank Robinson. The name of the street where Frank and his family lived was changed from Cedardale to Robinson Road. Here, Mayor McKeldin runs the ceremony from his microphone in the center of the crowd. Behind him stands Frank, holding his daughter, Nichelle, in his arms, with his wife, Barbara, at his side. *(Copyright © Baltimore Sun)*

Don Drysdale pitches in Game One. It had been a maddening season for Drysdale. He finally found his form in September, then lost it in the first game of the World Series. He gave up four runs in two innings and was gone. Starting a few days later in Game Four, however, he would deliver one of the strongest performances of his career. *(James Drake,* Sports Illustrated*)*

Frank Robinson homers off longtime rival Don Drysdale in the first inning of Game One. Brooks Robinson kneels in the background, watching from on deck. Before the game, he and Frank had agreed that the way to beat Los Angeles was to score first and make them try to catch up. Following Frank to the plate, Brooks also homered. After the top of the first, Baltimore was ahead 3–0. They wouldn't relinquish the lead for the rest of the Series. *(James Drake,* Sports Illustrated*)*

Moe Drabowsky pitches in relief of Dave McNally in Game One. Afterward, he recalled little. All he remembered, he would say, "was tremendous focus, fastball down and away, fastball up and in, slider down and away. And intense concentration on every pitch." *(James Drake,* Sports Illustrated*)*

A weary Sandy Koufax starts Game Two, the final appearance in his astonishing career. It was his fourth start in eleven days. That season, in agony from the strain on his pitching arm, Koufax had completed twenty-seven games, winning all of them. *(AP / Wide World Photos)*

Dodger center fielder Willie Davis drops Andy Etchebarren's soft fly in the fifth inning of Game Two. Davis had already botched a pop-up from the previous batter, Paul Blair. After dropping this one, Davis flung the ball wildly to third. It sailed high for his third error of the inning—a new World Series record. Two runs scored on the play. *(AP / Wide World Photos)*

Willie Davis and right fielder Ron Fairly admire a high fly ball—hit by Frank Robinson—as it falls between them in the sixth inning of Game Two. It was the fifth error committed that day by the Dodgers, who later added another to tie the World Series record for most errors by a team in one game. Robinson took third on this error and later scored. *(AP / Wide World Photos)*

Memorial Stadium was filled when the World Series came to Baltimore for Game Three. Sellouts were common when the Colts played there, but this was the largest crowd ever to attend an Orioles' home game. It had often been said that Baltimore was a football town. After 1966 baseball was every bit as popular. *(Copyright © Baltimore Sun)*

In 1966 Dodger pitchers Koufax, Drysdale, Osteen, and Sutton were the "Big Four," far and away baseball's best combination of starters. The overlooked one was Osteen. He had turned around the 1965 World Series, winning Game Three after the Twins beat both Drysdale and Koufax. A year later, he was asked for a repeat performance. *(National Baseball Hall of Fame Library, Cooperstown, New York)*

Luis Aparicio crawls safely back to first after Dodger pitcher Claude Osteen (out of frame) delivers a pick-off throw to Wes Parker in Game Three. One of the greatest base stealers in baseball history, the Venezuelan "Little Looie" stirred up little dust in the World Series against LA. He twice attempted to steal second and was thrown out both times. *(Copyright © Baltimore Sun)*

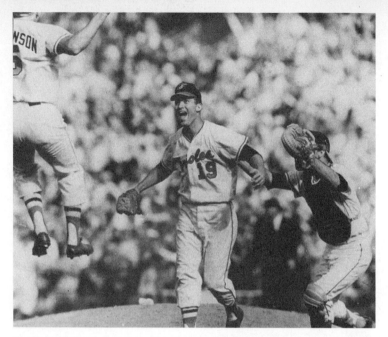

Ecstatic in the immediate wake of his Game Four victory, pitcher Dave McNally bellows as Brooks Robinson leaps at him and Andy Etchebarren thumps his back. At twenty-three, McNally was the oldest of Baltimore's World Series starters, and his dominating performance that day eased the memory of his horrific Game One outing. (Copyright © Baltimore Sun)

McNally leads a mob of triumphant Orioles off the field after Game Four, scurrying to stay ahead of the fans who were streaming onto the field. That evening, the city celebrated its first world championship with riotous pandemonium. (Copyright © Baltimore Sun)

Baltimore's bars had yet to be desegregated. The only blacks arrived there through the TV.

In the top of the fourth, with the game still tied at nothing apiece, Aparicio flied out to the infield. Blefary did the same. Sandy's pitches continued to display great movement. He'd given up just one ground ball. The game was another gem in the making.

Frank Robinson approached the plate for the second time.

Once again the game's top pitcher faced its best offensive player: the winner of pitching's Triple Crown (ERA, victories, strikeouts) versus the winner of batting's Triple Crown (average, RBIs, home runs).

There had been a time when Frank had handled this pitcher easily. "How do you hit Koufax?" Robby had once been asked. "Right-handed," he'd replied, with a sideways grin.[11] Over half a dozen seasons, from 1956 through 1961, he'd hit well over .300 against Sandy. That had ended in 1962, when impatient umpires had begun calling more strikes, the Dodgers had moved to Chavez Ravine, and Koufax had shed his wildness. After that, although Sandy had become an iconic presence, the most popular ballplayer in the land, and the foremost southpaw in the game's history, he'd never stopped feeling threatened by Frank's devastating power. Thinking back on the challenge Robby represented whenever he stepped into the box, Koufax had winced. "Like any other outstanding hitter, one year he might hit .500 against you, another year hardly anything." In fact, counting today, Frank had faced him forty-five times since 1962 and hit safely just four times. It was not, as the ever generous Koufax remembered of their matchups, "Sometimes yes, sometimes no."[12] During those years, it was almost always no.

Baltimore's scout Jim Russo had sat down with Robby and the other Orioles before the game to go over Koufax. "Bunt on him," Russo had recommended. "Steal on him. Don't swing at any high strikes or balls out of the high strike zone. Look for his big breaking curve to hang." He had recommended that they lay off of Sandy's high hummer, because of the bizarre way it seemed to rise. It would appear belt high and quite inviting as it approached, and then, at the last split second, the chagrined batter would find himself reaching for a pitch that floated around the bill of his batting helmet. By not swinging at these, Russo had said, they would force Sandy to pitch them low. The Oriole hitters had nodded at all this, then turned to Robby, who'd watched Koufax far more and from a far better angle than Russo, and asked his advice. "Go up there and bear down," Frank had encouraged his teammates, "and if you get a strike off this guy, take your cuts."

Frank had followed his own advice in Game Two, fouling off a couple in the first before flying out to Lou Johnson in left. In this at bat too, Frank wasn't shy about swinging at whatever looked good. The count went to 3–1. He fouled off the next pitch.

As the ball sailed out of play, Robby had an epiphany: Koufax was losing his rhythm.

Frank would later pinpoint this at bat as the moment he knew that Baltimore would win the game. Having to pitch the pennant clincher with only two days' rest was telling on Sandy. He'd gone 2–2 on Blefary; now the count was full on Frank. This wasn't the same Koufax that Robby had faced as a member of the Cincinnati Reds.

Koufax missed high with a 3–2 curve, and Frank took first. It was Sandy's first walk of the game, and he scuffled around the mound, disgusted with himself.

Brooks Robinson followed. He hit the 2–2 pitch on the ground toward the shortstop hole. Third baseman Gilliam cut across the diamond for the ball, but fumbled it for an error. Robby rounded second, saw nobody covering third, glanced at the infield, gathered the impression that the ball had gone through.[13] Impatient and eager to score, he took a couple of steps toward third. Gilliam came up with the ball, turned, and fired to Lefebvre at second. The crowd roared. Frank was trapped and tagged out.

Inning over.

Although his baserunning had been inadequate, Robby's assessment of Koufax's condition was accurate. In the fifth inning, Sandy threw four pitches before getting a single strike on Boog Powell. And then, with the count 3–1, Boog singled to shallow left for the Orioles' second hit. Davey Johnson tried to sacrifice but popped the ball high in the air down the first-base line. It was foul. Both Roseboro and Parker pursued it. They nearly collided, but the catcher reached high with one hand to snatch the ball from the first baseman. "The best steal the Dodgers have made yet," sportswriters scoffed.

The Baltimore rooters at Kirson's were distracted. A drunk man had pushed open the door, staggered inside. He wore a painter's outfit and an Oriole cap. The stub of a cigar was stuffed into his happy, screwed-up face. He shoved and gesticulated until he'd cleared some space for himself in the thick crowd. Al Kirson came around the bar, took the painter by the elbow, steered him outside onto the street. "Warm up and come back tomorrow," Kirson shouted, then shut the door. He glanced at the chalk scoreboard beside the bar.[14] The game remained scoreless. One away in the fifth, with "Boog the Behemoth" aboard at first.

Paul Blair was up. As in the third inning, Koufax quickly had him in the hole. But down two strikes and no balls, Paulie launched a towering fly to deep center. Willie Davis drifted to his right, looked up. The sun blazed into his eyes from above the five-tier grandstand.

Both Alston and Blair would agree that when a ball got directly in the sun, nothing could help. Tommy Davis, Ron Fairly, and Maury Wills would point out how much farther south the sun was at this time of year, which made it even tougher on the center fielder, and it was always especially harsh at this hour.

Something bad was due to occur. The vivid memory of Minnesota's Frank Quilici dropping an infield throw last year, Scully's prescient invocation of Joe Pepitone, Alston's remarks the day before about the difficulty of daytime ball games, fielders on both teams complaining to one another about the high sky and the white shirts — all foreshadowed disaster.

The tall, slender Davis could no longer see Blair's fly. He scoured the sky, looked into the sun. His vision was obscured by a pulsating afterimage. Still, he held his position.

And then suddenly — too suddenly for the Dodger outfielder — Blair's fly fell out of the sky. Davis spun, swiped at it. The ball trickled past him for an error.

In the press box, Jim Murray of the *Los Angeles Times* punched the keys of his manual typewriter. "Paul Blair," he typed, "hit what would have been a routine chance for anybody with fingers."[15]

Blair reached second. Powell stopped at third.

Murray pushed up his horn-rimmed glasses, drew on his cigarette, leaned back, looked at the field for a moment before continuing. "Sandy Koufax stands there like a guy who has caught his mother putting arsenic in his pablum."[16]

A scoreless game with one out and two on in the fifth. The young kid, the opposing pitcher, Palmer, was on deck. Alston and Wills convened at the mound to talk it over with Koufax. It was the same situation Baltimore had faced in the second inning: lumbering guy at third, poor hitter due up after this. Should they repeat Baltimore's strategy? Should they walk Etchebarren and load the bases to get to Palmer? They decided that Etchebarren himself was a pretty weak hitter; he'd looked bad striking out in his last at bat. They would just pitch to him.[17] The decision looked brilliant when Etchebarren proceeded to punch a soft fly to short center. Willie Davis appeared to have this particular pop-up handily under control. Catching an early glimpse of the ball, he raced in.

Watching from Baltimore's coaching box at third base, Billy Hunter recalled Jim Russo's scouting report on Davis. "When running laterally, his throws have nothing on them. He usually flips the ball side-arm and misses the cut-off man."[18]

Hunter ordered big, slow Boog Powell to tag up and prepare to break for home. Powell did so, directing his gaze toward the outfield to watch the fly descend.

But this time too Davis had lost the ball. It had climbed like the last fly, and then just vanished into the sun. He looked up at the sky imploringly, spread his arms wide, Job-like, beseeching. Willie recalled saying to himself right then, "Shit, here's that same kind of ball."[19]

The crowd held its breath. A few awful seconds passed, then the horror-struck fans saw the plummeting ball hit Davis in the heel of the glove and fall at his feet.

"I'll be honest with you, I wish both of them had been caught," Koufax would tell reporters afterward, "but they weren't. It's just one of those things." As always, the remarkable Koufax would be as forgiving of his teammates as he was unforgiving of himself. "I wasn't bothered by what happened out there . . . but it sure makes it tough on you."

Powell scored. Seeing Blair break for third, Davis snatched up the ball and flung it wildly to Gilliam. It sailed high over third base. While Koufax ran to retrieve it, Blair scored.

"The Baltimore dugout was stunned," Jim Palmer remembered.

The ballpark spectators complained loud and long, while the customers at Kirson's danced and cheered. A bartender snatched up a piece of chalk, skipped gaily across to the scoreboard, and put up 2 for Baltimore, 0 for Los Angeles.

The Dodger center fielder was charged with two errors on the play, a total of three errors in the inning. (A Drabo-worthy record, before yesterday.) Etchebarren was on third, and there was still only one out.

Vin Scully provided a literary perspective for those watching Willie's error-plagued play on NBC. "Brings to mind a line," Scully mused, "I think it might have been written by Jim Bishop, or perhaps he was quoting somebody when he wrote, 'Only saints want justice. The rest of us want mercy.' Well, I'll clue you, Willie Davis is on that mercy handout line right now."

Actually, most of the Dodgers agreed that Willie was the only one among them who would waste no time or effort seeking mercy or sympathy. "Willie, you know," Tommy Davis would say later, "he was cool."[20]

"If that was to happen to anyone on our team," Wes Parker agreed, "I would've picked him, because he probably could have handled it the best. He didn't have a real conscience about his play. He was a go-with-the-flow kind of guy. Whatever happened, happened. Anybody else who'd made three errors in one inning in a World Series would have been devastated. I know I would've been. It would've bothered me the rest of my life. But Willie, it just rolled right off him."[21]

Baltimore wasn't finished. After Jim Palmer struck out, Aparicio followed with a double down the left-field line, scoring Etchebarren from third. Blefary flew out to Fairly in shallow right to end the inning. Baltimore led 3–0.

As Davis trotted to the dugout, the fans on the third-base side roared their displeasure. About ten feet from the dugout, he tipped his cap. Later, Willie would explain to a reporter, "I was just sort of telling the crowd — you *assholes.*"[22]

Davis found Koufax in the dugout and immediately apologized for misplaying both pop-ups. "They both came out on the same angle."

Sandy put an arm around the outfielder's shoulders and shook his head. "Don't let it get you down." He smiled. "These things happen. There's nothing you can do."

Don Drysdale piped up, "Hell, forget it. You save a lot of games for me with great catches."[23]

When Willie was late to emerge from the dugout after the inning, one reporter in the press box asked another, "Do you suppose he may be about to commit suicide?"

"Hope not. He might miss and kill an usher."

"Koufax," another newsman recommended, "ought to soak Willie's head with ice today instead of his own elbow."

"I wonder if Davis will be able to catch the plane to Baltimore," a third joked.[24]

And Willie's reputation was about to take another hit. Frank Robinson led off the sixth inning with a high fly ball toward right-center. Davis and right fielder Ron Fairly converged on the warning track. Fairly was cautious, assuming that Willie would want to glove this easy fly just to show the fans that he still knew how. But "as it turned out," Fairly would say later, "he'd already made three errors, he was afraid of making four. That might have been going through his mind."[25] Too late, Willie called for Fairly to make the catch. The ball fell between them and bounced to the wall.

Robby dug around second, kept going. He ran like a guy hurting. He slid into third, his uniform taking on a great deal of dirt. Fairly's throw was relayed home. The crowd booed madly.

Frank, tired and noticeably hobbled, instantly leapt up and began brushing off his pants. When he'd fallen down in the second inning and missed picking up Lou Johnson's single to right, and then when he'd been picked off second base to end the fourth inning, he'd been worried that he would be the goat. But thanks to Willie Davis, Frank's miscues would go completely unnoticed.

Brooks Robinson fouled to Parker for the sixth inning's first out. Then Boog singled, and Frank, using his arms to do most of the work, jogged home to clamorous cheers in a far-off bar: 4–0, Baltimore. Davey Johnson followed with another single, this one off a rare Koufax forkball. It scooted speedily past Parker into right field, rolling into the record books as the last hit Sandy Koufax would ever surrender. ("That's why I knew I was washed up," Koufax would tease Davey afterward.)[26] To memorialize it further, Ron Fairly scooped up the ball and hurled it frantically toward third. It bounced past Gilliam for the fifth error of the game.

Koufax intentionally walked the next batter to load the bases for Andy Etchebarren, who kindly sent a grounder to third. Gilliam snagged it, fired it to Roseboro ahead of Boog Powell. Roseboro wheeled, fired it to Wes Parker ahead of Etch. A double play. The Dodgers were out of the inning.

Vin Scully had been keeping the patrons at Kirson's — along with the rest of the estimated twenty-five million people watching on television — abreast of Koufax's condition. The redheaded broadcaster had seen every pitch Sandy had thrown in his major-league career, had watched him since he was skinnier even than young Jim Palmer — just a nineteen-year-old recruit in a baggy Brooklyn uniform. He could pinpoint the signs of a fatigued Koufax, and he shared them with the viewers: the extremely long stride, the stumble after releasing a pitch, the arching of his back instead of following through. The exceptional elegance of the southpaw's windup; the splendor of his uncoiled, full-bodied, bow-backed delivery; the beauty, the grace, and the poise — all were in complete contrast to the grimace of utter agony Scully saw, more and more clearly, clouding Koufax's countenance. By the end of the Baltimore sixth — the 330th inning Sandy had pitched that season — he felt the weight of every pitch as his body began to tire. The baseball grew as heavy as a brick. He was drenched with perspiration. His game face had become a shifting series of death masks — a rotation of agonized expressions, reminiscent of a saint preparing for martyrdom. He was so clearly struggling that it surprised no one when Ron

Perranoski walked in from the bull pen (to the stadium organist's accompaniment of "Hello, Dolly!") to start the seventh.

Koufax had allowed just one earned run, but he left the game behind by four.

Some loud person at Kirson's shared the opinion that God was involved, that he was punishing Koufax for pitching on October 6, a Jewish holiday.[27] His bar mates nodded, warmed by mugs of draft beer and the notion that here the Lord was, at last taking pity on Baltimore, finally siding with those less fortunate. It sounded right. Hadn't Koufax refused to pitch the opening game of the World Series against Minnesota on October 6 of the previous year, on account of it being Yom Kippur? Everybody knew the story.

Koufax had not played out of respect for the Jewish Day of Atonement, his religion's holiest day. And the Dodgers had lost. He'd pitched the next day, but his team had lost again. He'd gained another chance in Game Five and shut out the Twins, and he'd pitched in Game Seven and shut them out one last time. It was the stuff of legend, a religious miracle. In one week, he'd gone from sitting to losing to winning to earning, on two days' rest, the world championship.

And now here he stood, pitching on October 6. What, did he think the Lord was no longer watching?

Not exactly. On the lunar calendar observed by the Hebrews, Yom Kippur always occurs on the 197th day of the year (the tenth day of the seventh month). In 1965 the Jewish calendar had begun on April 3, so Yom Kippur had been celebrated on October 6. But in 1966, the Jewish year had begun on March 22, and Yom Kippur had fallen on September 24. The Dodgers had been in Chicago, and indeed Sandy had not pitched.

Something about Koufax's delivery seemed guaranteed to

ensure that he would leave behind disputed memories, stories swirling in mythic mists. No photo of him in action was without a blur somewhere. Even after Koufax tired that afternoon, he continued to throw so fluidly that by contrast, Palmer's delivery appeared to be jerky, a shuddering series of still lifes. The young right-hander would lift his hands and left knee; he'd bend his right knee, rear back, peer over his shoulder; he'd point his index finger and fall; he'd twist, come over the top. After walking two in the second inning and escaping unscathed, Palmer promptly settled down. With hard fastballs and a couple of sliders, he calmly retired the side in order in the third and fourth, gave up a meaningless single in the fifth, retired the side in the sixth.

In the Dodger seventh, he fanned Jim Lefebvre for a second time. Lou Johnson followed by drilling a sharp grounder to third. Despite charging down the first-base line, Sweet Lou was thrown out. Palmer had completed six and two-thirds shutout innings, duplicating Drabo's feat of the day before.

Over two championship seasons, Johnson had been the team's buzzing dynamo. His electric presence and timely hitting had opened holes, created possibilities. Now, jogging across the diamond to make his way back to the home dugout, his shoulders drooped. Head down, he grew pensive, slowed to a stroll. The home plate umpire stood, as did Etchebarren. Palmer stepped off the rubber to stare. The game was momentarily held up while this morose spectacle ambled past.

Nothing could have better communicated how lost the home team felt at that moment. The great Koufax was already in the clubhouse, elbow packed in ice, and Baltimore had just broken Sweet Lou's spirit. Registering all this from the Oriole bench, another Johnson, reserve infielder Bob Johnson, nodded with satisfaction. "I think we have them now."[28]

And indeed they did. But first, with two on and one out in the eighth, relief pitcher Ron Perranoski threw away a ground ball for the sixth Dodger error of the day, making the score

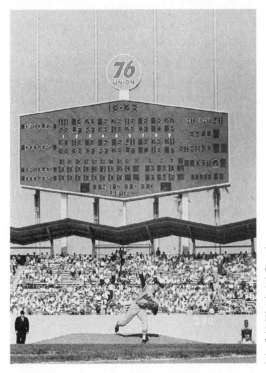

With two out and one on in the ninth, Baltimore's twenty-year-old Jim Palmer prepares to retire his final Dodger in Game Two. (AP / Wide World Photos)

6–0. Appearing as a pinch hitter in the bottom of the eighth, Tommy Davis singled and moved to second base on a wild pitch. It would constitute the last Dodger threat of the day. Though stadium organist Helen Dell tried to rally the home-town boys by playing "Bye Bye Blues," "With a Little Bit of Luck," "Beyond the Blue Horizon," and "Great Day," it was all to no avail. Tommy was stranded at second, and after Roseboro popped up to Aparicio in the ninth, it was over.

After the game, a reporter asked Palmer, "Having won the first two, where do you see the Series going from here?"

"To Baltimore," the kid replied.[29]

Los Angeles mayor Sam Yorty, a sudden but fervent Dodger booster, turned away from the game in revulsion, as if person-ally implicated in the loss. The mayor's life would never again be so blessed. He would be narrowly reelected three years later, but only by running what his opponent's campaign manager would term "the most racist campaign in the history of California." It would be the last election ever won by the perennial candidate. Ultimately, a survey of civic experts, urban historians, and political scientists would judge "the Little Giant" to be one of the most callous officials of the turbulent 1960s and one of the eight worst American big-city mayors since 1820.

Jim Palmer, however, was a winner. Somehow, despite the sour pitching arm, he had done it. He'd announced that he could beat the Dodgers with a fastball, and indeed he had. In so doing, he had delivered not only the first shutout of his career — and in the World Series, no less — but also his last good outing for quite a while. His arm would take a long time to recover, and Palmer would spend most of the next year in the minors, just trying to throw half as well as he had that Thursday afternoon against Los Angeles.

The game was also the last one Sandy Koufax would ever pitch. It was his fourth start in eleven days and only his third start since mid-August that he didn't finish. He lost by his biggest margin of the season. "What did he get, two strikeouts in six innings?" Robby asked afterward, having gotten the better of their historic matchup by walking, tripling, and scoring twice. "That's not Sandy Koufax."[30] Lacking the ability to strike men out, Sandy had relied on his teammates to play their usual sterling defense. Instead, Jim Gilliam had bobbled grounders, Willie Davis had lost balls in the sun, and Ron Fairly had pulled up short. Balls had missed gloves and cutoff throws had sailed high. And so he had lost.

Boarding the airplane to Baltimore immediately after the game, Sandy was flagged down for one last TV interview. "Were you disappointed by the play behind you?" asked the interviewer.

Koufax had done little but quash that question for an hour. This time he said nothing, just glared at the reporter.

"I mean specifically Willie Davis."

Sandy studied the man icily, color rising in his cheeks. He held his tongue.

"I can stand here as long as you can," the reporter challenged.

Finally, Koufax lost his composure. "What are you trying to get me to say?! No! I wasn't disappointed! Without Willie Davis we couldn't be here in the World Series! We never would have won the pennant without Willie!"[31]

That may have been an overstatement, but it was indeed true that Willie's homer in the season's final game had cushioned their lead over Philadelphia. Unfortunately for Los Angeles, as a consequence of that blast, Davis now perceived himself to be a home run hitter and would spend the postseason working without success to prove it. Batting near the top of the lineup in every game, he would hit just .063 in the 1966 World Series.

Having given the reporter a piece of his mind, Koufax spun on his heels to join the others on the plane.

By the time Vin Scully and Bob Prince signed off on their respective broadcasts, the record 55,947 fans had filed numbly out. Even the knowledge that they had helped shatter previous attendance records meant nothing. (Although all Series games played at Dodger Stadium were sellouts, somehow, conveniently, this particular sellout crowd had been declared the biggest in stadium history.) Their mood was as limp as the pennants that drooped like wilting sunflowers from their hands. The aftertaste of peanuts and Cracker Jack was like ashes in the mouth. Prior to one P.M. yesterday, their boys had never dropped a World Series game at home. Now, appallingly, they'd lost two, back-to-back. Among the departing spectators shuffled Casey Stengel and a slew of frowning Tinseltown celebrities. But in the expiring light over Chavez Ravine, neither Stengel's muttering disgust nor the disappointment clouding the lovely faces of Hollywood's cinema stars would prove the fitting symbol for this, the West Coast's final championship baseball game of the decade, the last game of the country's most popular athlete, the end of an era.

In the crowd that day were three men who sat ramrod straight in the commissioner's box, watching as guests of baseball's number-one military man. In the bottom of the second inning, the three were introduced to great fanfare. They were to be the first Apollo astronauts, and one among them, their legendary leader, Gus Grissom, had been assured privately by NASA that he would be the first man on the moon.[32] A few months later, however, during a simulated launch, all three men — Grissom, Ed White, and Roger Chaffee — would die in a fire aboard their Apollo spacecraft.

Soldiers, astronauts, and baseball players — uncomplicated heroes; fit, short-haired, clean-cut, steady-eyed, and mostly white — appeared to be natural extensions of one another for the last time on that day in early October. That game was over, too.

Koufax departed, and night fell.

PART FIVE

Bunker's Just Not That Good

Baltimore mayor Theodore McKeldin was praying that this Series would indeed signal an era's end, accomplishing not just the conclusion of the Dodgers' postseason dominance but also the elimination of something far more pernicious — segregation in Maryland's drinking establishments. The World Series was about to bring national attention to, and scrutiny of, his precious city of Baltimore. McKeldin urged the city's white tavern owners to begin serving blacks, to take this opportunity to distance themselves from the prejudices of the past. "I find it a distasteful piece of irony," he said before the Series, "that I must make this plea in light of the fact that without Frank Robinson, a person who could be excluded by such businesses, we would probably have no World Series."[1]

Such an exclusion had already been tested by one of the city's most admired African American athletes, Claude "Buddy" Young, the diminutive star halfback of the beloved Colts. While hosting a banquet for the team, a Baltimore hotel had adamantly refused to serve cocktails to Young.[2] Aghast, Colt owner Carroll Rosenbloom had shifted future events to a more open-minded downtown establishment. Beyond that protest, however, the owner's response had been limited. Rosenbloom's muted call for racial equality in Baltimore had achieved as little as would that of McKeldin in the fall of 1966. Anyone who hoped that, in returning triumphant from Los Angeles, the mighty Orioles would bring with them all the powers of integration was disappointed.

Undaunted, the mayor met the team as they arrived home in the early, dark hours of Friday morning.[3] He was too excited (or too cold) to wait for the unrolling of the traditional red carpet. As the plane taxied to a stop, McKeldin bounded up the motorized stairway even before it had been secured in place. Despite a biting wind and surprisingly frigid temperatures, thousands of enthusiastic well-wishers had been patiently standing all night behind a chain-link fence. The plane door swung open, and Hank Bauer emerged. McKeldin snatched the manager's hand and raised it in triumph. A waiting brass band broke into a wobbly, off-key version of "When the Saints Go Marching In." The night air filled with throaty hurrahs. Flashbulbs popped. Scarves twirled. Whistles blew. Bells rang. Placards shook.

Surveying this burst of activity from the stairway's top step, Bauer, the blunt-featured former marine, beamed with pleasure. He had managed Baltimore's club to just two postseason victories, but that was enough to make the city eternally grateful. Even if Bauer lost the Series, he'd still be hailed for having lent Baltimore some much-needed credibility. For generations, the people had fought for the return of a major-league franchise, an explicit acknowledgment that Baltimore was a big-league city that deserved a big-league team. It had taken half a century for that to occur, and then another decade to make the Orioles competitive, but now, thanks to Bauer and his boys, Baltimore at last was earning some respect.

No sooner had the Orioles clinched the AL pennant than a luncheon had been held at the Sheraton Belvedere by McKeldin and the Chamber of Commerce. There they unveiled a civic war cry — "Bomb 'Em, Birds" — as well as a number of additional mottoes, such as "Act Positive — Think Big — Talk Championship."[4] Immediately thereafter, flags, pennants, armbands, T-shirts, and plastic ball caps bearing the official "Bomb 'Em, Birds" slogan had gone on sale. Radio commercials and TV spots had joined in, as did hundreds of store windows and newspaper advertisements for everything from appliances to groceries.

After tickets for Games Three through Five had become available through a mail lottery system, the local post offices had been deluged. Lines of eager fans outside Baltimore's main post office began at the downtown intersection of North Calvert and East Fayette streets and stretched for thirty blocks, with 84,000 requests for tickets mailed in less than three hours. Police had to learn to deal with something completely new: the scalping of Baltimore baseball tickets. Eight-dollar obstructed-view seats were fetching between $35 and $50 on the black market. PLEASE DON'T SWEEP THEM beseeched the hand-lettered sign of one fan who greeted the Orioles at the airport on the night of their return. I HAVE TICKETS TO GAME 5.[5]

Claude Osteen had a bad case of déjà vu.

Gomer's debut season in Los Angeles, 1965, had turned out perfectly. His sinking fastball, deceptively timed curve, and splendid control had served him well. He had especially loved the camaraderie, the way that all the pitchers — relievers and starters, little guys and big guys — would huddle around a table after dinner and talk hitters. His fifteen victories that year had helped his new club take the NL pennant. Osteen was intimately familiar with the Dodgers' opponent in the World Series, the Minnesota Twins, a team he'd never lost to when he was pitching for the Washington Senators. Koufax and Drysdale had even come to him for advice on how to pitch to Bob Allison, Tony Oliva, Harmon Killebrew, Zoilo Versalles.[6]

Not that it had helped much. By the time Osteen's turn had rolled around in Game Three, the Dodgers were already two games down to the Twins. Only four teams in baseball history had ever come back from such a two-game deficit to win the Series.

He had responded with a complete-game shutout that had turned the tide. He hadn't just silenced the thunderous bats of Minnesota; he'd made a fifth game necessary, which gave Koufax one more chance. That's all Sandy had needed; they wouldn't beat him again.

A year later, Gomer was again in the position of stopper. But this time there was a difference. The Dodgers had played the previous year's Game Three at home. This one would be played on the road. Even so, Osteen had always pitched well in Baltimore when he was a Senator. "It's the same old thing," he shrugged to a reporter.[7] The question was never whether he could do his job. The question was whether his team could shake off its lethargy and score some runs.

Since Moe Drabowsky had entered the first game in the bottom of the third and walked Jim Gilliam with the bases loaded, no Dodger had crossed home plate. Sixteen Dodgers had struck out, and the team had collected five hits in fifteen innings, only one for extra bases. In some regards, this wasn't too surprising. The 1966 Dodgers had been shut out seventeen times in the regular season, a record number for a team that won the NL pennant. Still, as Walter Alston admitted after the second game, "I can't think of many games this season when we've looked worse than we have in these two." In addition to Game Two's embarrassing six errors, the Dodgers were exhausting their bull pen, having deployed six pitchers in the first two games. Despite all that, their manager remained hopeful: "One thing about this club, it is liable to reverse itself at any time."[8]

The gamblers in Las Vegas were not so sure. The Orioles were now 5-to-2 favorites to win the Series. Baltimore's subdued, rangy right-hander Wally Bunker, however, was given little chance of beating the more experienced left-hander Osteen in the third game. A lot of bases had been stolen behind Bunker's back because he did not possess a good move to first, which was a severe shortcoming against a team as swift as the Dodgers. Bunker also put a backward spin on the ball, and many Dodgers — especially Lefebvre, Fairly, Parker, Roseboro, and Willie Davis — were known to be good low-ball hitters.

And the oddsmakers didn't know the half of it. During pregame practice tosses in the bull pen, Wally's arm hurt like hell. The pain was like a toothache, a nasty throbbing that never let up.[9] He revealed nothing, but catcher Andy Etchebarren and pitching coach Harry Brecheen could tell there was something wrong. At first Wally was so stiff that he could not even attempt a breaking ball, and Brecheen briefly considered inserting a different starter; Bunker was just in too much pain to be effective.[10] Brecheen weighed his options, then decided to let Bunker start the game. He didn't have much hope and expected Bunker to tire early.

Beneath a blue sky, on a brisk autumn afternoon, the two teams left their dugouts to stand on the base lines. One by one, the players were introduced. The loudest applause went to Willie Davis, whom one Baltimore fan thanked on a banner as OUR TENTH ORIOLE.[11]

After the introductions, a solemn voice over the loudspeaker instructed the crowd to remove their hats for a moment of silence. After all, this stadium was also a war memorial, and more war dead now required memorializing. Dutifully, the ballplayers, umpires, and fans dipped their heads in honor of the 6,543 American soldiers who had been killed, as of October 8, 1966, in the Southeast Asian conflict. As the Vietnam War dragged on, the death total would increase to nearly nine and a half times that number, more than could fill Memorial Stadium.

At 1:01 P.M., Wally Bunker strode from the cool, dark dugout into the sunlight. As he proceeded to the mound, he felt as if he were entering the center ring of a giant circus, with flags fluttering, airplanes circling overhead, poles and railings garlanded with bunting, and the crowd going crazy. There were people everywhere he looked — high in the corners, back in the flanks, even minuscule, droplet-sized spectators stuck out against the sky on the stadium wings in deep right and left. The wooden bleachers in center, which hadn't even been open during the regular season, were now packed to capacity with enthusiastic men in crisp white shirts, thin dark ties, and shiny dress shoes. They were sipping National beer from plastic cups, their heads shaded by Styrofoam skimmers festooned with CHARGE! ribbons, and their wives sat beside them, wearing mink stoles and orange dresses, with stuffed orioles perched on their hats and shoulders. This was not just the largest crowd Wally had ever pitched before; it was also the largest ever to attend an Oriole home game: 54,445.

The first batter Wally faced was Maury Wills, who arrived at the plate and left the bat on his shoulder to watch the first pitch. The umpire called it a strike, then called time. The ball was taken out of play and mailed to Cooperstown: the first baseball used in Baltimore's first World Series game. One pitch into the game, Wally Bunker was already in the Hall of Fame.[12]

Out on the mound, with his cap pulled low over his dark flaring eyebrows, his long narrow face shortened by the brim, Bunker appeared less shy, more comfortable: relaxed, calm, in charge. Baseball had always been his game. Early on, he had made an asset out of restraint, becoming a control pitcher with an exceptionally smooth delivery. Neither he nor his fastball ever screamed — would that really be necessary?

Because Bunker was a righty, Wills came in attacking him from the left side of the plate. Maury preferred this. He seemed to get aboard more frequently when he had that extra step toward first. And he needed an advantage; he'd gone oh for seven so far in the Series.

Baltimore's infielders figured that Maury would lay one down. Bunker was not a fantastic fielder, so Brooks crept toward the infield grass, while Boog tiptoed up, subtle as an earthquake.

Bunker fired two more fastballs. Wills no more bunted than homered. Instead, he went down swinging for the first out.

Behind Wills was another switch-hitting Dodger infielder, Wes Parker. He too turned around to bat from the left. He fouled off the first pitch, saw a sinker nail the inside corner for strike two, watched a curve cut through for strike three, then returned to the dugout.

Six consecutive pitches, two strikeouts, and up came Willie Davis. As always, he swung hard on the first pitch, a curve. Reaching for it, he just managed to slap it off the end of his bat. It sliced high down the left-field line.

The Baltimore left fielder, Curt Blefary, bolted toward the grandstand. He hadn't been positioned there at all; he'd been over toward center. Blefary was a slugger, not known for being particularly adroit with the glove. Now he turned, following the ball with his eyes, pursuing it with his entire essence. He had to go a considerable distance. Blefary knew the retaining wall was approaching, but he wasn't thinking about running into it.[13] He was thinking about quick Willie, who already was almost to second. The ball wasn't much more than a foot fair, and Blefary couldn't stop. He met the ball perfectly, making a fine running catch for the third out. Then he disappeared from the view of the TV audience, crashed into the edge of the grandstand, and rolled off. The wall was wood; he had hit plenty of harder things. It was easily the best defensive play of Blefary's career.

The sound of rapturous applause rose to a deafening crescendo before subsiding slowly, a retreating wave on a pebble-strewn shore. As it did so, Willie Davis snatched off his batting helmet and spun it underhand toward the bench. The Orioles jogged happily into the dugout, where Andy

Etchebarren took a seat beside Harry Brecheen. As Etch shed his gear, the catcher assured the coach that Wally was really starting to pop the ball. Despite Bunker having retired the side on seven pitches, Brecheen had misgivings. The kid had looked so lousy warming up and hadn't had a very long outing in quite some time.

Claude Osteen also retired the first two Orioles he faced. Then Frank Robinson, his former teammate, stepped in.

Osteen's relationship with Robby was entirely different from Drysdale's vindictive rivalry or Koufax's dispassionate, thoroughly professional admiration. Osteen had been a star high school athlete in Cincinnati in the mid-1950s. A hopeful fan of the hometown team, he had been there when the Reds had brought Robby up from the minors in 1956. The Dodgers had offered Osteen a professional contract out of high school, but he'd signed instead with Cincinnati, because they promised to clear a spot for him on their roster. He'd arrived in the major leagues immediately. At age seventeen, Osteen shared a locker room with some of his baseball heroes — Ted Kluszewski, Smoky Burgess, Vada Pinson — admiring close-up the beautiful thing that was Frank Robinson. "I knew Frank as well as anybody," Osteen remembered. "Great base runner, one of the best base runners I've ever seen."[14]

In 1961 Cincinnati dispatched Osteen to the Washington Senators. He'd had a lot of opportunity to observe Robby at the plate, but not much experience in getting him out. Now, in the first inning of the third game of the 1966 World Series, Osteen had yet another chance to measure himself against one of the game's all-time greats.

"Pitching against him was always very difficult, a real challenge," Gomer remembered. "You had to almost be perfect."[15] Frank was three for eight in the Series, with a single, a triple, a home run, two runs batted in, and three runs scored. Osteen started him off with a hard fastball in on the hands, a strike.

Before the 1961 World Series, the pitchers of the New York Yankees had met to go over Cincinnati's batting order. They'd gone briskly through the first three Reds, then halted when they'd arrived at the cleanup hitter, Robinson. "It was decided," Jim Bouton would later deadpan, "we would pitch him underground."

Osteen had his own strategy for pitching to Frank. "He stood right on top of the plate, and you only had a li'l small window that was right up under his hands. You could almost knock him down with a strike. He was so close to the plate that anything on the outside corner was pretty much in the meat part of his bat."[16] If a single pitch caught too much of home, Gomer knew that he could lose this game in the first inning, just like Drysdale in Game One.

He wasted a pitch in the dirt, then rode the outside corner with another fastball. Strike two.

He followed with a pitch high and inside for a ball, then one low and outside for another ball. Now the count was full, and Robby perched hungrily at the plate, impatiently pumping the wood back and forth, while Osteen stared at the pitching rubber and contemplatively toed his rosin bag, mulling it over.

Roseboro was recalling how Robby would occasionally pull away from an inside pitch, if he'd been set up correctly by alternating brushbacks with pitches off the plate. (The Dodgers' approach to Frank Robinson, Roseboro would later reveal, was "to spin him like a top.")[17] Rosey called for an inside fastball. Osteen nodded. Robby wasn't knocked down. Instead, he swung hard, foul-tipping it in and out of the catcher's glove. The count held at 3–2. Next, Gomer delivered a breaking ball. Again Robby swung. This time he missed. Inning over.

That afternoon, for the first time in a very long while, the heart of the Oriole lineup — Blefary, Snyder, and both Robinsons — would go hitless.

Much of Osteen's advantage was often thought to derive from the stylistic differences of the number-three starter as compared to numbers one and two, Koufax and Drysdale. Starting games in the wake of the other two, Gomer used altogether dissimilar weapons. As he pointed out, "Don would throw his stuff out there, Sandy would throw buzz bombs, and then here I'd come, pitching on the corners, turning it over. I'll have to admit it helped me."[18] Osteen was also a strong fielder and a good hitter. Serving a team that knew how to use their bats better, he would almost certainly have accrued more victories. His fourteen losses in 1966, for example, came when his LA teammates provided him with a total of just sixteen runs.

As a Dodger for nine years, he would accrue a 3.09 earned run average, fourth on the club's all-time list behind Koufax, Drysdale, and Sutton. Osteen felt that the credit for much of his, and the Dodgers', success in the 1960s belonged to the tough, crafty guy behind the plate, John Roseboro.

"Rosey was great," Osteen reflected. "He knew the strike zone of every one of us, knew our strengths and how to call the game for us." This seemed like a basic thing, but it was a rare expertise that was greatly appreciated. "It meant an awful lot. Once you got a catcher back there and you were on the same wavelength, you didn't have to shake off a lot of signs. It was a huge advantage.

"What used to mess me up was that if I had to shake off a lot to get to the pitch I wanted, the hitter would step out on me. And then, when he got back in the box, he was a different hitter. You might have had him in an offensive mood where you wanted him to pull. . . . Well, if you were having to shake signs off to get to the pitch that you wanted, now all of a sudden you've changed the hitter's mind-set. Where he once had been a pull hitter, and you were gonna beat him with a location pitch, well, after he gets out of the box and gets back in, all of a sudden he's a defensive hitter, a lot more apt to go to the opposite field on you. That in itself can affect your game quite a lot." Being in sync means keeping the advantage. Roseboro watched and learned, frantic for tiny details at the same time he was as calm as a boulder.

"I threw him a backdoor slider one day, comin' in the back door, where you start it outside, and it comes in and catches the outside corner," Osteen recalled. "A hitter will give up on that. Rosey didn't know I could throw it. He fell in love with that pitch. He used to come out and he'd say, 'Os, don't forget that backup slider. That's a great pitch.' "[19]

A great catcher is a combination of matchmaker and elephant. The Orioles had no such genius. Certainly, Andy Etchebarren, their rookie catcher, had handled the pitchers surprisingly well through the regular season. But in the postseason pressure cooker, Etch's inexperience, as well as that of Baltimore's starting pitchers, was certain to show through eventually. The Orioles possessed only one advantage: the Dodgers continued to have trouble with heat. And so with Drabowsky, Palmer, and now Bunker, Etch followed one basic rule: batter after batter, he put down a finger and called for the fastball, varying it occasionally with an off-speed pitch, then following it up with another fastball. Exerting all the temerity and fortitude he could summon, Wally obliged.

As the game proceeded, Bauer and Brecheen debated which reliever they'd fetch first — perhaps Fisher, perhaps Watt — while down the bench, between innings, trainer Eddie Weidner tenderly ministered to Wally.

Wearing surgical gloves to avoid any contact with his own skin, Weidner continually rubbed Bunker's right arm with Capsolin. The trainer's eyes watered from the spicy fumes. Perspiration drenched his shirt.

For Wally it was agony, but they'd already tried everything else on him this season: pills, shots, hot packs, water treatments.[20] This stuff seemed to work, seemed to keep him loose. At the top of each inning, he put aside the pain, marched out to the mound, recorded three outs to great applause, and then came back to the dugout. He stared stoically at the Dodger infielders while Weidner massaged more fiery oil into his elbow.[21] Trembling, Wally lit a Marlboro and held it in the shaking fingers of his left hand.[22] He smoked one cigarette after another, tried to concentrate on the task at hand — getting through the Dodger lineup: Maury Wills, Wes Parker, Willie Davis, Ron Fairly, Jim Lefebvre, Lou Johnson, John Roseboro, John Kennedy, Claude Osteen.

In the suspenseful duel that unfolded that afternoon, both Bunker and Osteen were aided greatly by fabulous fielding. The Orioles had committed no errors in the first two games of the Series, and they continued to handle the ball flawlessly, while the Dodgers showed themselves fully recovered from the mistakes of the second game. On the rare occasion that an opponent made it to first, each starter relied on the gloves of the sure-handed men in back of him and were never disappointed. There was the broken-bat grounder from Lou Johnson, with Ron Fairly on first base, which Aparicio scooped up and fired to Davey Johnson. Though sent reeling by Fairly, Johnson completed the double play to Powell. There was the hard one-bouncer up the middle, slapped by LA's John Kennedy, a sure hit, which Little Looie speared blindly and threw to Boog in time. Then there was the ground ball hit by Davey Johnson, with Boog Powell aboard at first. Wills snatched it up and snapped it across to second. Lefebvre stepped on the bag and pivoted, only to find himself confronting Boog. Jim flung the ball in the general direction of first base before disappearing beneath the big man, pressed like a decal into the dirt behind second. The throw to Parker was wide, and Davey Johnson wasn't slow, but anchoring his left toe on the bag, stretching his legs flat against the infield, the Dodger first baseman nonetheless gloved it for the last out of the inning.

A third of a century later, Davey Johnson — by then a successful manager who had just steered the Baltimore Orioles into the postseason — would be appointed skipper of the Los Angeles Dodgers. He'd name Osteen as his pitching coach.

"When I joined him in 1999," Osteen would later relate, "the first thing Davey said to me was, he brought up that he hit into a double play off of me in the 1966 World Series."[23]

As for Willie Davis, he received his first shot at redemption when Brooks Robinson popped a fly to shallow left-center in his initial at bat. With a rising note of suspense in the stands, Willie settled comfortably beneath the pop-up. Spectators and listeners alike edged forward in their seats. For excitable Lou Johnson, it was just too much to take. Dashing over from left field, Lou cut in front of Willie and snatched the ball out of the air for an out. As he did so, his glove almost slapped Willie in the face, nearly making the metaphorical insult real. The crowd laughed uproariously. ("Lou came and caught a ball that was not only in dead center but two cab rides and a shuttle bus from where Lou plays," Jim Murray would write. "It was so far that Lou didn't get back to left field till the fourth inning.")[24] Davis was livid, and he gave Johnson hell. Baltimore would launch only two more fly balls into center that day. Willie would easily catch both.

With one out in the fourth and neither side yet to score, Wes Parker belted a long liner to right-center. He didn't think he'd hit it hard enough for a home run, but he wasn't going to stop running until he knew differently. Loping past second, Parker was halfway to third before he heard the umpire calling him back. His drive had hit the cinder track 395 feet away and bounced over the short fence for a ground rule double. Wes stood at second as Willie Davis came to bat and drew a count of three balls and one strike.

A reporter roaming the stands overheard a local man

speaking to his small son. "Every game has its psychological breaking point," the man explained. "This may be the pitch that decides the game."[25]

Bunker delivered a fastball. Davis hit it in the air toward center. Paul Blair caught it for the second out.

The boy in the stands could now be heard scoffing. "You," he spoke, belittling his father, "and your psychological breaking point."[26]

In the Dodger dugout, Alston was kicking the dirt. If the ball hadn't bounced over the fence, Parker would have made it to third, would have made it home on Davis's long fly. He grew weary of their situation, for something similar had happened early in Wednesday's Game One, when an LA fan had leaned over to touch the ball in play, limiting Parker to a ground rule double. The Dodger skipper spread his hands in despair. "It seems we just can't score any runs," he grumbled to a nearby player. "We've had trouble scoring all year, never anything this bad."[27]

With two outs, Ron Fairly came up. Bunker pitched the left-hander cautiously, fearful of coming inside with a fastball, instead throwing off-speed breaking balls and low fastballs. The count climbed to 3–1, and on the next pitch, a breaking ball that missed the inside corner, Fairly earned a base on balls.

Etch was displeased by the call. After the game, he would go out of his way to compliment the eye of Chris Pelekoudas, the home plate umpire. "He called a great ball game," the Baltimore catcher would declare. "I can think of only one pitch that he might've missed, that three-and-one curve to Fairly in the fourth inning. I'm not saying he was wrong either. I might be wrong. But it was the only pitch he called on which there could've been a question."[28]

Now two Dodgers were aboard. Jim Lefebvre stepped into the box. LA's Hollywood-handsome second baseman was not just the team leader in RBIs and home runs this season, but, with his home run off Dave McNally Wednesday, he was also the only Dodger in the Series to have a hit of any true consequence. Bunker delivered a couple of pitches, and Lefebvre ripped a few long fouls into the second deck. The pitcher's nervousness then momentarily overcame him, and he delivered three bad pitches that Etch barely caught.

A full count now, two outs, and as Bunker set and threw home, the runners on first and second took off running.

Lefebvre swung and missed. Three away.

Bunker would later call it "the best pitch I ever threw in my life."

Etchebarren was inclined to agree. "That's about the best sinker Wally's ever thrown. It must have dropped a foot. It went down so far and so fast, you might have thought it was a spitter, but Wally's never thrown one in his life."[29]

Osteen was keeping pace with Bunker. He had the benefit of having faced most of these Baltimore players before, in his years pitching for the Senators. The ones he did not know were the young guys — Andy Etchebarren, Davey Johnson, and Paul Blair. But he pitched well even against these Oriole youths, leaving Etch and Johnson hitless for the day. Blair was a different story. In the Oriole fifth, with two out, none on, and the score still knotted at nothing apiece, Blair strolled to the plate. Paulie was hitless in the Series, Willie's botched catch of his fly having been scored an error. Observing how they had pitched him in his four previous at bats, he went up expecting a fastball and was determined to swing at the first pitch.

Because of how Blair crowded home plate, Osteen tried to pitch him outside. He threw the ball precisely where he wanted to. It was the same fastball with which he'd earlier retired both Robinsons. Osteen believed it to be a good pitch that Blair would pop up. "I have no regrets whatsoever about that pitch," Gomer insisted afterward.[30]

Paulie quickly opened his shoulder on the swing, got out in front of the ball, and pulled it. There was no uncertainty about the destination of his blast. It was hit with such authority that everyone in the park knew it would go out as soon as it was struck. With the benefit of a mild tailwind, it stayed aloft, sailing high over deep left field. Lou Johnson disdained to give chase; he simply waved it good-bye.

Blair's ball cleared the Baltimore bull pen, landing in the bleachers, 430 feet from home plate. The score was 1–0, Baltimore. The stadium roared with happy huzzahs.

Watching from the mound, Osteen sagged a bit. When he later ruminated on it, he said that he wasn't all that surprised. Although Paulie was but a .277 hitter with a measly half-dozen home runs, Osteen had seen him display some power in spring training in Miami.[31] And he had heard that Robby had been helping Blair with his hitting.

Paulie, though, was thunderstruck. It was the farthest he

Paul Blair steps on home after his fifth-inning home run in Game Three.
(Copyright © *Baltimore Sun*)

had ever hit a baseball. Even in batting practice, he had never driven one over the bull pen. He bounded about the bases like a joyful boy crunching through a carpet of autumn leaves. Circling back around to home, he remembered, "I was in another world."

"If the Oriole centerfielder's grin had been any broader," one reporter noted afterward, "he would have swallowed his own ears."

When Blair finally got back to the dugout, he whooped and hollered, trembling like a puppy. He was so keyed up that he kept chattering and leaping around.[32]

"Careful," cackled Robby. "You'll jump straight through the roof."

"If I do I won't feel a thing!" hollered Paulie. "Man that has to be the best thrill in my life right there!"[33]

Hooting raucously in praise of young Blair, Mayor McKeldin settled back down into his box in Section 3, hunching with characteristic intensity over the low railing, chin on his hands. Only a year earlier, Tony Oliva and Jim "Mudcat" Grant had become just the third and fourth black American Leaguers to homer in the World Series. Now Frank Robinson had become the fifth and Paul Blair the sixth. Nothing could have pleased McKeldin more.

The mayor understood this game very differently than most of the Oriole rooters. He believed devoutly in "the brotherhood of man," a credo he'd cited while desegregating the state's beaches, parks, and buses. He could appreciate how the National League's swift integration eased Walter Alston's job, so that the Dodgers now essentially had three autonomous player-managers on the field — Roseboro, Wills, and Gilliam — all incidentally of African American descent, whereas the Orioles had but three black players on their entire roster, and only one who played regularly.

The mayor's wife, son, and daughter-in-law sat beside him,

joined by Baltimore County Executive Spiro T. Agnew and his wife. Asking the Agnews to share his box would be the first of McKeldin's many open endorsements, as Agnew was running for governor of Maryland that year against George Mahoney, a southern Democrat opposed to open housing. McKeldin, conceiving of Agnew as a decent man intent on quieting social tensions, would work hard to help defeat Mahoney in November. But to McKeldin's horror, Agnew would scarcely be sworn in before gaining national prominence and endearing himself to right-wing ultraconservatives by mocking war protesters and lambasting black leaders. He would ultimately be driven from elected office after evidence emerged that he had accepted kickbacks on construction contracts while still the Baltimore County Executive.

Another opening emerged for Los Angeles in the seventh, after Lou Johnson chopped a one-out single into shallow center. It was the fifth base hit off Bunker, but Baltimore still clung to a 1–0 lead.

Hank Bauer saw LA's number-eight batter, John Kennedy (playing in place of Gilliam), climb the dugout steps and cross to the Dodger on-deck circle. Figuring that, with the tying run aboard, Alston would call back his soft-hitting third baseman for a pinch hitter (Tommy Davis probably, or Dick Stuart), Bauer phoned his bull pen. Bunker's dominating performance had surprised everyone, especially his own manager. Despite Wally's injured elbow and pitiful warm-up session, he'd been firing the ball, moving it around, keeping it low for the most part, throwing almost all fastballs and sinkers, and mixing in a few curves. Although Bauer was impressed, he was also cautious. These were the world champions, after all. Veteran reliever Stu Miller began loosening up.

Roseboro stepped in. The left-hand-hitting catcher cut on the first pitch, hit a pop-up to shallow center. Paul Blair dashed in, losing his cap but catching the ball. Unable to advance, Lou Johnson jogged back to first.

Two away.

Alston now did something that baffled Bauer. He allowed Kennedy to come to the plate even though, in two previous at bats against Bunker, the third baseman hadn't hit the ball out of the infield.

Etch dropped into a crouch as Kennedy planted himself in the box. Johnson took his lead. Bunker heaved a sigh and slid his foot against the rubber. His pitching arm was scorched red from the Capsolin, an angry rash on his right forearm was blistering, and his fastball was beginning to climb.

Bauer rang the bull pen a second time. Eddie Watt got up to throw alongside Miller.

Wally looked over at Sweet Lou, exchanged a glance with Boog, and delivered to Etch.

Johnson broke for second. He had the base stolen, except that Bunker's sinker had thoroughly confounded Kennedy.[34] Misreading the pitch, Kennedy had unshouldered his bat. The ball had broken sharply down, and trying valiantly to pull his bat back, Kennedy had instead tapped a check-swing grounder right back to Bunker. The pitcher fielded the soft roller easily and threw to Powell for the third out. Johnson's steal was erased.

Bauer phoned his bull pen a third time. In a tight, raw voice that sounded as if he'd been gargling with gravel, he ordered everybody out there to sit their asses back down. He couldn't believe his good fortune. He hadn't been expecting shutout pitching from either Palmer or Bunker. How could he? Palmer had never shut out anyone before — he couldn't usually pinpoint his pitches like Bunker — and it had been ages since Wally had been able to balance his control with any power. This looked a lot like the Wally of 1964. Bauer had figured he'd be using his bull pen quite a bit, but the way it looked to him now, Eddie Fisher and Stu Miller might just as well have gone on vacation.

Bunker casually entered the dugout, lit another Marlboro, and handed his arm back over to Weidner.

The Dodgers closed out the Oriole seventh with another crisp double play, performed with such rapidity and assurance that it temporarily stirred the team's flagging spirits. The players began to pep up, and at the top of the eighth, Alston finally decided to go to his bench in place of his powerful pitcher. He sat Osteen down and sent Tommy Davis up to bat in his stead. In batting practice, Tommy had driven one clear out of the stadium, à la Frank Robinson. "We're going to get you a couple of runs," the team assured Gomer.[35] They didn't. After Davis got aboard on a single, he could not advance past second. The Dodgers quietly went down in order in the ninth.

The third game was complete, a Baltimore victory by the slimmest of margins. Blair's solo shot had been the difference.

As the Orioles recorded the game's last putout — Aparicio to Powell to erase Lou Johnson — a huge billboard was unveiled on Thirty-third Street opposite the stadium. WOULD YOU BE-LIEVE FOUR STRAIGHT? the billboard cheekily asked as happy fans filed past.[36] The individual who had been placed in charge of the city's "Bomb 'Em, Birds" campaign, Frederick L. Wehr, enthusiastically stamped his feet on the slanted dirt of the Memorial Stadium parking lot. A bright melody played in his heart. "That was a wonderful thing to watch," Wehr raved. "Those bunch of punks come in and think they are so good."

Now the punks were three games in the hole.

The members of Wehr's favorite team had quietly retired to their lockers. No Oriole spoke a word about having the Series locked up. They hardly felt victorious. Three hits! Their whole lineup had managed just three hits off Osteen. The Dodgers had collected six, the Orioles had gotten half that many. Shouldn't they have lost? The Dodger lefty had pitched a game that was every bit as brainy as his memorable Game Three performance the previous year. This one too should have turned the tide of the competition. If not for the defensive support of Brooks and Little Looie, if not for the unlikely heroics of Paul Blair and Wally Bunker, this Series would have been running at least five games in length. Such a fate would have been awful to consider. The guarantee of a fifth game would have meant they'd go up against Drysdale in Game Four knowing for certain that they'd be facing the greatest left-hander in the history of the game in Game Five.

Baltimore's Boog Powell and other teammates congratulate pitcher Wally Bunker after an astounding Game Three victory. (Copyright © *Baltimore Sun*)

It would have meant they'd have to find a way to beat Koufax a second straight time — and it was highly doubtful that Willie Davis would again aid their cause quite so much.

Much later, Bunker would chuckle at his team's good fortune. "How many times you gonna beat Koufax that way?" he'd ask rhetorically. "I mean, c'mon now, let's get serious."[37]

Blair, Bunker, and Bauer were shuttled from their clubhouse and guided to a conference room, where waiting newsmen stuck a mike under Blair's nose and asked him how it felt to become the third man in Series history to win a 1–0 battle with a homer — Casey Stengel had done it for the Giants in 1923 and Tommy Henrich for the Yankees in 1949.

Paulie beamed. "That's fantastic company," he said. He had so much to say, about how he used to love the Dodgers madly, about how he had cheered them, home and away, every game, they hadn't signed him, his heart had been broken.[38] Now — impossibly! — he'd just beaten them with a 430-foot home run. In the World Series. "I'm just . . . I'm still in another world." It was like a dream, that's what it was. "I can't believe it," he repeated over and over. "I can't believe it. I can't believe it."[39]

Turning to Bauer, a journalist reminded him that no team had ever won the best-of-seven World Series after losing the first three. "Have you got the momentum now?" the sportswriter inquired.

"I still don't know what that word means." The Oriole manager frowned. "Momentum. I mean, when you win, that's momentum."[40]

Other newsmen were urging Bunker to take some of the credit, but he appeared constitutionally incapable of such a feat. "The Dodgers are better than they've shown," the right-hander pointed out. "They must be, or they wouldn't have won the pennant. They're not even running. We thought they'd be running."[41]

"This is the best pitching I've seen," interjected Bauer, "since the 1950 Series." That was when the Yankees (with Bauer in center) had set down Philadelphia's famed Whiz Kids. "We beat the Phillies 1–0, 2–1, 3–2, and 5–2. Along the way we beat Konstanty, Roberts, Heintzelman, and Miller. That was a pitching Series; so is this one."

It had also been, one writer noted, the last time an American League team had swept the World Series. Bauer simply nodded and grinned.

The press needed a picture of Blair and Bunker together, the game's astonishing double whammy. Blair glowed, scratching his head in delighted bewilderment. His mouth was naturally wide-open; they called him "Motormouth" for a reason. Wally's chin was out-thrust, his nose long and thick. Controlling his emotions as he controlled his pitches, Bunker put his aching twenty-one-year-old arm around the trim center fielder's twenty-two-year-old shoulders and gave a small, embarrassed smile.

Up and down Wally's crazy, Drabo-esque, roller-coaster career had gone. He'd been a star in high school, but professional scouts had become suspicious of his poise; they'd derided him as docile, not competitive enough. He'd grown up outside San Francisco, imagining himself penciled into the Giants' rotation — Marichal, Digger, Sanford, and Bunker. It had a nice rhythm. But after word spread that Wally lacked zeal, only the farseeing, hardworking Baltimore scouts had maintained an interest. They'd brought him to the bigs just three months after he'd signed an Oriole contract, on the last day of the 1963 season, but he'd given up ten hits in four innings to lose his first major-league appearance. The next year, he'd won nineteen and lost five and been named Rookie Pitcher of the Year by the *Sporting News*, but that proved to be his last healthy season. After that, his arm was always acting up — either his shoulder or his elbow or his wrist; even, occasionally, a finger. He seemed to be laboring in the shadow of Barber, McNally, Pappas, and Palmer. He hadn't thrown a complete game since June 10 of this year, against Boston. His last shutout had occurred on June 5, 1965, against California.

Now he, of all people, was the second youngest man in history to pitch a World Series shutout, following on the heels of Jim Palmer's outing Thursday. And the entire time, Wally's arm had been killing him. Later, remembering the anguish of Game Three, Bunker would quietly admit, "No one knows how hard that game was." Etchebarren would insist, "What Wally did that day was one of the greatest performances I've ever seen for a guy with a sore arm."[42]

It would remain the high point of Bunker's big-league career. His worsening arm would permit him to win just twenty-one games over the next five seasons, and then he'd retire. He would go unrecognized everywhere in the country except Baltimore, where still, forty years later, people would approach him in restaurants and offer to buy him a plate of crab cakes in gratitude for what he'd achieved on October 8, 1966, at Memorial Stadium.

Following the conclusion of the game, Steve Barber wandered into the Oriole dressing room. Barber had been put on the disabled list on the season's final day. The people's choice for Game Three starter, Barber had instead been watching the Series from the stands, dressed as a civilian, the twenty-sixth man on a twenty-five man roster. Wally's complete-game shutout had Barber flabbergasted. Bunker had used only ninety-one pitches. He had walked only one Dodger — Ron Fairly, in the fourth inning, on that 3–2 breaking ball that Etch had disputed. It had been simply the best-pitched game Barber had ever witnessed. He found Wally and congratulated him. "Great job," Steve said drily, "but you're not that fucking good, and you know it."[43]

Wally swallowed. "Yeah." He grinned sheepishly. "Thanks."[44]

Throughout 1965, Barber had been clamoring to be traded. During the 1967 season, the Orioles would oblige him. Although he would go on to pitch for six other clubs, he would never again wind up so close to postseason play. Like Wally Bunker, he would look back on 1966 as a high point. "The biggest thrill of my career was being part of that team," he would divulge later, a bit ruefully. "Also the biggest disappointment."[45]

PART SIX

We Regret to Announce . . .

Sixteen years, eight months, three weeks, and three days after starting his last postseason game for Los Angeles, Don Drysdale checked into a hotel with the Dodgers for the final time. He was fifty-six years of age, his high head of blond hair graying on the sides. For six years, he had performed broad-casting duties for the Dodgers, a former starter relieving Vin Scully during the middle innings. He'd flown with the team to Montreal, chatted up first baseman Eric Karros in a postgame interview, and then disappeared into his hotel room.

Scully, by this time, was certainly a veteran of misfortune. He had described many cheerless events to Dodger fans: the night in 1959 when young Roy Campanella was wheeled onto the field by Pee Wee Reese, and each of the 93,103 spectators sitting in the darkened Coliseum had struck a match in tribute; Yankee championships at the expense of the Dodgers in 1953, 1956, 1977, and 1978; Don Larsen's perfect game; the agonizing collapse of the Dodgers in the ninth inning of the third game of the 1962 National League play-off.

But the toughest broadcast of his life, he would admit after-ward, took place on July 3, 1993.[1] Although he had noticed that Drysdale wasn't on the team bus, he had assumed they'd meet up at Olympic Stadium. They did not. Instead, Montreal police, using a passkey, pushed their way into Big D's room. They discovered him in bed, skin cold to the touch. He was dead.

Scully was handed the news during the game. In the Dodger eighth, grief-stricken, he addressed his loyal listeners from the broadcasting booth. "Friends, we've known each other a long time," he said, his sonorous voice choked with emotion, "and I've had to make a lot of announcements, some more painful than others. But never have I ever been asked to make an announcement that hurts me as much as this one. And I say it to you as best I can with a broken heart. Don Drysdale, who had a history of heart trouble — you may remember a couple of years ago he had angioplasty — was found dead in his hotel room, obviously a victim of a heart attack, and had passed away during his sleep."[2]

He managed a few words of condolence, paused for twelve seconds, and then, ever the professional, returned to the game, with Dodger center fielder Brett Butler at the plate, the count one ball and one strike.

Reporters immediately phoned Claude Osteen, now a pitching coach with the Texas Rangers. Gomer's first thoughts were of the final stages of the 1966 race.[3] Late one September night, Drysdale had isolated Osteen and Ron Fairly, seeking to invigorate them with the belief that they could yet snatch the pennant away from the Giants and Pirates. Galvanized by Drysdale's speechifying, not to mention the indisputable weight of the combative pitcher's credibility, Osteen and Fairly had zealously gone out to exhort the others. "Many of us may not have really believed we had that kind of team," Gomer recalled, "but we came back to steal that pennant."

When tracked down for a reaction, Fairly too immediately flashed on Dodger successes of the mid-1960s. When playing behind Drysdale and Koufax, the ex–right fielder remembered, "we knew we were going to win, we just knew no other team could stop us."[4]

Such, at least, had been their conceit until the fall of 1966. By the time Sunday, October 9, rolled around, bringing Game Four and, with it, Drysdale's second Series start, the veteran squad had been shut out twice in succession by callow, sore-armed pitchers. The charm of a baseball game was supposed to be the comfortable, clock-free way it unfolded, with no regard for schedules or deadlines, without undue haste, but so far the Series had sped past, each contest swifter than the last, with Saturday's game dropped by the Dodgers in less than an hour and fifty-five minutes.

The statistics from the Series so far sent LA's fans reeling. In dropping the first three games, the Dodgers had left twenty-one men on base, with Wes Parker and Tommy Davis tied for most abandoned, having each found their way on base four times and four times dying there. Swinging at the plate with mad, mounting futility and connecting rarely, the Dodgers had now struck out twenty-four times. "A couple of days ago, we told you the Dodgers looked dead," wrote one Southland sportswriter, by way of breaking the bad news to their fans. "We regret to announce at this time that their condition has deteriorated."[5] Their team batting average had plummeted to .141. The New Hampshire Forestry Division sarcastically telegrammed the National League champions to note that so few Dodger bats had seen any real use that Los Angeles should be acclaimed as the club "which has done the most to conserve wood — one of our most important natural resources."[6] Oriole fans, out of mock concern for the opposition's anemic hitting, displayed signs that read SUPPORT THE DODGERS — GIVE BLOOD.[7]

The Dodgers had not scored a run in twenty-four innings. No drought of this magnitude had occurred in a championship series since early in the century. In the scandal-plagued 1919 "Black Sox" Series, Cincinnati had held Chicago scoreless over twenty-six innings, but those games had been fixed. The record had occurred in 1905, during the second World Series held, when the New York Giants had blanked the Philadelphia A's for twenty-eight innings. It was a strange, pathetic mark that had seemed eternally out of reach in the modern age of baseball. New York no longer even had any Giants, nor did Philadelphia have any A's, but the record books still listed their historic string of goose eggs. Unbelievably, the favored 1966 Dodgers had been so turned around that they now stood not just a game from being toppled as the reigning champions but only five shutout innings — a measly fifteen outs — shy of absolute ignominy.

The unlikely suddenly seemed the inevitable. News leaked out that the Dodger brass had instructed the players to pack their bags Sunday morning in preparation for departure after Game Four. Pressed about this, a team official grew defensive. "That's realism, not pessimism," he snapped. "You just can't check out at the last minute."

Although Dodger executives may have abandoned hope, there remained optimism among the athletes in the visitors' clubhouse. "Can the Dodgers rally from a three-game deficit to win the Series?" a reporter asked Maury Wills before the game. With unhesitating sincerity, the team captain fired back, "I'm sure we can."[8] The fact remained that Don Drysdale would be pitching the fourth game, and, as Ron Fairly would later point out, "right to the end, Drysdale believed that the 'Dodgers' across your shirt means winners."[9] Even better, Big D would again be opposed by Dave McNally. In their previous matchup on Wednesday afternoon, Baltimore's rattled lefty had lasted just two and a third innings, walking five and giving up two earned runs.

Oddsmakers, flabbergasted by the unexpected shape this Series had taken, simply could not conceive of a Baltimore sweep and so picked Drysdale to prevail over McNally on Sunday.

Some watchers wondered whether Koufax could be persuaded to pitch in place of Drysdale. After all, he had won the previous year's Game Seven — which was supposed to have been a Drysdale start — after having scant time for replenishment. Few knew that it had been the fiercely competitive Drysdale who had (with difficulty) swallowed his pride, privately lobbying Alston to go with Koufax in that last, decisive game of the 1965 postseason. A year later, Sandy returned the favor, expressing a defiant faith in Big D and shaking off those Drysdale doubters who thought the southpaw might be a better choice for the starting assignment in the fourth game against Baltimore. Big D had won nearly a hundred games over the previous five years, never missing a start. "We are going with our best," Koufax insisted, his gaze steady, his jaw clenched with determination. "Do you think I can do a better job than Drysdale? With only two days' rest? I've only done that once this season, and that was the last game against Philadelphia."

When reporters speculated that he and his teammates were playing poorly because they were distracted, too anxious to embark on their goodwill trip to the Far East, Koufax silenced the talk with a dismissive wave of his hand. He wouldn't be accompanying the team on their trip, he pointed out. Besides, he added portentously, "I'm barely getting through this season."

Not surprisingly, the sole Dodger still looking forward to the Japan trip was Walter O'Malley. This burly dealmaker was the pioneering owner who had succeeded in stretching Major League Baseball's previously rigid body to the very edges of the country. He knew the value of opening new markets, knew that professional baseball needed to continue to spread, to spill far beyond the confines of the continental United States. Over the horizon somewhere, growing up in the inconceivably distant villages of Asia and Latin America, were tomorrow's paying customers, as well as the star players of the future. O'Malley could smell the globalization trend from far away, and toward that end Sunday's game was being aired in Guam, Taiwan, and the Philippine Islands; throughout Canada and Latin America; and even in Great Britain, where British Broadcasting Corporation (BBC) commentators struggled valiantly to explain the appeal of this odd, ritualized pageant to a novice audience. It was not easy. As Etchebarren crouched behind the plate at 2:05 P.M. to signal for McNally's first pitch, a Brit in a pub in a far-off time zone raised his pint toward the television. "Why," the man asked, eyeing the catcher's getup suspiciously, "is that man wearing a fencing mask?"[10]

Dave McNally had informed sportswriters of his game plan for Sunday: "I'm gonna go out and throw a few strikes." He'd made it sound simple, even though he'd looked incorrigibly wild on Wednesday. As Game Four got under way, the Dodgers gave Mac little opportunity to reveal just how few strikes he could go out and throw. Instead, consistently, rashly, they jumped on the first pitch, as their manager looked on forgivingly. "In a game this close," Alston would say afterward, "you go after anything that looks good."[11] Mac threw eight pitches in the first inning; the Dodgers swung at seven. The other was a called strike. In the blink of an eye, Maury Wills popped up, Willie Davis grounded out, and Lou Johnson fouled out.

NBC broke for a Plymouth commercial, then Drysdale sauntered in to face Aparicio, Snyder, and Robby. In Big D's last outing, he had allowed four runs and four hits in two innings. Now his team was in a must-win situation. On the heels of the worst season of his career, eight months after seriously contemplating retirement alongside Koufax, he had inherited the role of Dodger stopper.

As he had the previous Wednesday, Drysdale started Aparicio off with a fastball for a called strike. He followed with
another fastball. Little Looie swiveled around to bunt and
popped it high behind home plate. It soared straight back,
homing in on the announcers' booth. Bob Prince stopped
talking long enough to duck. There was laughter in the background. "That one was out to get the ol' Gunner," Prince said
shakily as he reemerged. "Strike two, foul came right back,
yessir, I wasn't gonna try 'n' catch it."

Aparicio popped up the next fastball. This time Roseboro
saved Prince further embarrassment by snagging it in foul
territory. One away. Now Russ Snyder, the left-handed center
fielder who batted only against right-handers, came to the
plate for the first time since Game One.

Like Aparicio, Snyder tried to bunt, but he chipped the
ball into the air. Colliding with his own pop-up in fair territory as he ran to first, he was called out. Two away.

Frank Robinson entered the batter's box, swung hard at
Drysdale's first pitch, a slider, hitting it off the end of his bat.
Tommy Davis drifted over, hauled it in on the left-field warn-
ing track. Three up, three down.

After the Dodgers went quietly in the second, Brooks
Robinson led off the Oriole second by slapping a knee-high
fastball into center for a single. It was the game's first hit.

Boog Powell followed with a couple of good foul balls and
then struck out on an inside curve. One down.

Brooks remained at first while Curt Blefary came to the
plate, drew a full count, and walked. Two on, one out, no score,
second inning. Next up, Davey Johnson hit a chopper down
toward second. Jim Lefebvre grabbed it. Ignoring Brooks (who
was sliding into third), the second baseman flipped the ball
across to Wills for one out. Maury pivoted and confronted Curt
Blefary, barreling into second. The Oriole scouts had made sure
that the big right fielder knew all about Maury's bad knee.

The National League had always been thought of as the

rougher league, the one that went in for brushbacks and beanballs and full-body slides. That was before Robby had traveled south to teach the Orioles his style of play. "I believe that when the other guy is wearing a uniform that doesn't read 'Baltimore' across the front," Frank had said, "I should do whatever I can to beat him and win the ball game."[12]

Blefary threw a vicious rolling block at Wills.

"Fifteen yards, Blefary!" an Oriole jokingly shouted, borrowing from football for an apt penalty.[13] The terminology felt right: not only had Blefary been an all-state gridiron star in high school, but Baltimore itself was routinely described as a football town — at least until Robby's Orioles ignited such a fierce regional pride. Fantastically large crowds would gather on Friday nights all over Baltimore for high school football games. They'd turn out on Saturdays for clashes of helmets and shoulder pads hosted by Johns Hopkins, Navy, Western Maryland, or the University of Baltimore, and religiously reserve their time after church on Sundays to watch the Colts. In the 1950s and 1960s, even with sideline seats added and capacity expanded to 62,000 spectators, every home game the Colts played was sold out.

And indeed, on this particular Sunday, the city's sports fans sat close by their TV sets, flipping frequently between McNally against the Dodgers on Channel 11 and the favored Colts playing the Bears on Channel 2. The football game soon became the harder of the two to witness, as Johnny Unitas and his blue and white squad stumbled up and down Wrigley Field, on the way to their second loss in four outings. Better they stumbled there than at the home park they shared with the Orioles. During the second half of the regular baseball season, the Colts would regularly tear up the field during scrimmages and practices. "They'd play a couple exhibitions there and just leave the field in horrible shape," recalled Brooks Robinson, the Gold Glover who was always meticulously attentive to the conditions of dirt and grass. "It was atrocious."[14]

At other times during the baseball season, the Colts' young head coach, Don Shula, would drop by Memorial Stadium. Coming simply to watch the Orioles play, he would dream of poaching their nimble, red-haired first baseman to buttress his own offensive line. "Shula used to drool over Boog," sportswriter Bob Maisel remembered. "He used to say, 'I'd love to make that big son-of-a-bitch an offensive tackle! Here he is, weighs 270, and never lifted a weight in his life. You could get him to weigh probably 280 or 90. He's nifty. Ah, he'd make a hell of an offensive tackle!' "[15]

The previous year, the Colts had played a title game against Green Bay on the day after Christmas. All of Baltimore had tuned in to watch. The Colts had narrowly lost in overtime, due largely to a Packer field goal, which subsequent frame-by-frame photo sequences showed to have missed the uprights. The bad refereeing and unfair nature of the Colts' last-minute defeat that icy afternoon had strengthened calls for wider use of the latest technological breakthrough, which many were terming "instant replay." In 1966 *ABC's Wide World of Sports* had begun to use an instant replay videodisc recorder. NBC used the technology for the first time in a World Series when Baltimore met Los Angeles.

Now, in the bottom of the second inning of the fourth game, NBC leaned heavily on it. Over and over again, they showed Blefary charging fiercely into second and Wills somehow escaping, getting the ball off to Parker in time for an inning-ending double play, then glancing over darkly at Blefary.

Every Dodger keenly shared the predicament of Maury Wills in that moment. The second inning had been their twenty-sixth straight without a run, tying the mark set by the Black Sox forty-seven years earlier. Like the blurring approach of Blefary in endless instant replay, the men on LA's bench could sense disaster unfolding in very slow motion. Had it been at all possible, they would have covered their eyes. The notably languid pace of baseball was being translated, pitch by pitch, out by out, inning by inning, into an un-hurried demonstration of torture. McNally had only to add two more shutout innings, and the 1966 Los Angeles Dodgers would match the sixty-one-year-old World Series record for all-time scoring futility.

LA's John Kennedy came to the plate in the Dodger third, lifting a towering fly into left. The visitors' bench emptied, the players crowding forward, watching, applauding, cheering. Memorial Stadium fell silent. Kennedy's long drive suddenly curved foul, just a long strike into the upper deck. Bird fans sighed in relief. Stricken, the Dodgers retreated into both their dugout and an overarching sense of melancholy. Kennedy weakly popped up a curveball to the right side of the infield. Davey Johnson dropped back to get it. One away.

Don Drysdale stepped up. Ordinarily strong at the plate, he had been hitting as poorly as he had been pitching and fielding. McNally threw his opponent two pitches, a ball and a strike. On the third pitch, a breaking ball, Drysdale took a monstrous cut, hitting it to Aparicio, who threw to Boog. Two away.

Mac had now faced everyone in the LA lineup, and the Dodgers were still looking for their first hit of the game. The ominous voice of stadium announcer Bill LeFevre intoned the name of the next batter: "Maury . . . Wills." As if to taunt the Dodger captain, the Oriole outfielders — Snyder, Blefary, and Robby — came in and stood just behind the infield. Wills couldn't get it even that far. He popped up behind home plate. Etch spun around, mask off, and caught it. Three away.

Before breaking for a shaving cream commercial, Bob Prince recited the mantra of the Series: "No runs, no hits, no errors, score remains Los Angeles nothing, Baltimore nothing."

The Dodgers had now gone through twenty-seven innings without scoring. Over three and a third games, Baltimore pitchers had an incredible ERA of 0.60 against the defending world champions. Of course, the Orioles were hardly hitting or scoring either. Only one thing in this Series had happened as expected: Dodger pitching had remained masterful. But Baltimore's "Baby Birds" had been better. The 1966 World Series was fast becoming one of the best-pitched baseball championships in history.

The vice president of the United States — sharp-eyed, pale-faced Hubert Humphrey — sat jovially in the owner's box behind the Oriole dugout, resting his arm after throwing out the first ball. Humphrey was a former senator from Minnesota and a baseball nut. The previous year, he had been thrilled by the dominance of his Twins. And on this occasion, although he had diplomatically declared himself to be impartial — "I'm the vice-president of both leagues" — he would not much mind seeing the Dodgers get humbled, to avenge what they had done to his boys the previous October.[16]

In the Oriole fourth, with both McNally and Drysdale still throwing magnificent shutouts, Frank Robinson came to bat for the second time. The owner of the Orioles, Jerry Hoffberger, leaned over to Humphrey. "Home run," Hoffberger predicted.

The vice president raised his dark eyebrows. "Really?"

Hoffberger nodded. "Just watch."[17]

Robby stepped into the box. He had anticipated a pitch inside. Figuring that Roseboro knew this, however, Frank now wondered if they just might start him off by going the other way. He went up determined to protect both sides of the plate.[18]

The Dodger outfield shifted around to the left.

On the mound, under a hazy sky, Drysdale was considering how best to keep the ball out of Robby's reach. He had no desire to repeat what had happened the previous Wednesday. He received the sign and the target from Roseboro: fastball, low and away. Good idea. He wound up. He delivered.

Decades later, Roseboro would be asked to differentiate between those two Hall of Famers, Koufax and Drysdale.

Rosey considered the question, then said, "Sandy seldom grooved the ball, gave up a home run or other big hit, but Don did. And a home run or big hit often beats you in a big game."[19]

This particular fastball failed to obey Drysdale's exact wishes. With a mind of its own, it dove for the middle of the plate, in and up, just below the belt. It was precisely the pitch Robby had dispatched into the left-field boxes four days earlier in Los Angeles. Frank pounced. His hips pressed forward, then his shoulders. The bat lashed through.

Vice President Humphrey jumped to his feet. The rest of the stadium followed his cue. All eyes strained to follow the flight of the ball.

All eyes but two. Drysdale dropped his head and kicked the pitching rubber. "I knew the moment Frank hit the ball," he would say afterward, "that it would take a guy with a ticket to catch it."[20]

The guy, in fact, turned out to be a twenty-one-year-old university student sitting more than four hundred feet away, in Seat 15, Row 32, Section 13.[21] As the fans roared, the student held the ball aloft, the very same ball Drysdale had been holding just moments before. It signified the eighth home run Drysdale had surrendered in World Series competition, as well as Robby's fifty-first round-tripper of the year. It had come within ten rows of clearing the bleacher railing and leaving the park altogether.

A happy fan in the upper deck snatched off his straw skimmer and sailed it into the air. The hat descended — a spinning flicker of white, a celebratory blossom — falling in front of the backstop screen to rest behind Roseboro.

As Robby jogged around the bases, Drysdale flicked his glove at Roseboro, called for a new ball, and stood angrily rubbing it down. As he headed home, Frank considered how well McNally was pitching and how poorly the Dodgers were hitting. He said to himself, "This may be enough to win."[22]

Outside the stadium, a group of women from Thirty-seventh

Street set down a small black coffin with a sign that read: HERE
LIES THE LA DODGERS. PUT TO REST OCTOBER 9, 1966.

Across the Atlantic, British observers grappled with the
greater significance of Robby's home run. "A most colossal
blow," one BBC analyst explained. "After all," he reminded
the audience, "he was using a round bat."[23]

Brooks followed by grounding out to third, then Boog
Powell crushed Drysdale's two-out, 2–0 pitch deep to dead
center, a towering blast. Willie Davis scurried to the fence. He
coiled and prepared to leap, then a gust of wind blew the ball
six feet to the right. Willie hurried over, leapt, and, twisting
spectacularly, made a one-handed grab to prevent the ball
from going over the fence for a home run.

Watching from the home dugout, Paul Blair, a great outfielder in his own right, couldn't believe what he'd just seen.
He rubbed his eyes, looked around in wonder at his teammates, and then dashed down the runway to watch the replay
on television. (NBC was glad once again to show off its slow-
motion replay capabilities.) "I still can't get over Willie Davis
taking a homer away from Boog," Blair would say later. "I
was there and I saw it, but I still don't believe it."[24]

Hank Bauer felt that it was the best defensive play of the
Series.[25]

The British especially admired Willie's leaping catch. "If
that had been done at Lords," said one BBC commentator, referring to the leading cricket ground, "why even the members
would be running out to kiss the chap!"[26]

"I think one nice thing about it," Vin Scully reminded listeners, "is it's the same man. It's the same man who was
called a little-league outfielder by some for dropping two fly
balls. And from one human being to another, I'm sure glad he
got off the hook."

The fourth inning complete, the jubilant Dodgers ran in
from the field. Ignoring the fact that they were behind, having

momentarily shed the gloomy knowledge that they had now been shut out for twenty-eight consecutive innings and that they stood poised, in this inning, to set a new record, they were revived. The mood in the dugout was lively. Willie's miraculous catch had lifted their spirits considerably, providing a tiny kernel of hope from which a giant triumph could yet sprout. When Powell had swung, Walter Alston had fearfully imagined the score at 2–0. He hadn't believed that Davis had a chance to pulling in Boog's booming drive. To a man, the Dodgers felt that such a thing could reverse the momentum of the Series. *Now we have a chance*, Alston was thinking. *An epic turnaround, from the brink of elimination. The greatest comeback in baseball history. One catch like that changes everything. It gives us a light.*

That light lasted precisely one batter and then was doused. Jim Lefebvre led off the fifth with a single up the middle. Wes Parker followed with a bouncer into the hole right of Aparicio. Brooks Robinson stumbled, and the hearts of the Dodger faithful leapt. But somehow Brooks stabbed it, spun, and delivered a perfect, chest-high throw to Davey Johnson. ("The throwing," a BBC analyst commented, "was in a single rationalized flick of the wrist.")[27] The second baseman danced across the bag and sent the ball to Boog. It was Baltimore's fourth double play of the Series. Roseboro was up next and did not take his bat off his shoulder. He watched four pitches: two strikes, one ball, and another strike. Three away.

The young lefty from Montana had just extended LA's streak of shutout innings to twenty-nine, a new and truly pitiable World Series record. McNally strode from the mound, feeling good. Both he and Drysdale had struck out two and walked one, both teams had two hits and no errors, and yet his side led.

McNally guessed that the Dodgers had been anticipating a lot of free-swinging Orioles. Probably they had assumed that if they could keep the games tight and the score close, they would win. But they had failed to properly register the fantastic fielding of Brooks and Little Looie, and they had overlooked the fact that Baltimore had led the league in defense during the regular season.

Eventually, decades later, McNally would acknowledge that he deserved some of the credit for Game Four. He was moving the ball in and out, throwing hard, getting strikes. Certainly, the movement on his fastball was sufficient, plus he possessed a pretty fair curveball and change-up. Not a cocky man and always a realist, Mac later would come to admit that he was "throwing pretty good that day."[28]

In the sixth inning, another double play erased two Dodgers, and then Wills grounded out. In the seventh, Willie Davis and Tommy Davis flied out, and Lou Johnson fouled out. "We just couldn't do anything right," Jim Lefebvre remembered. "We'd try to bunt and we'd pop up. We'd hit the ball well and it would be right at somebody. And the other guys, they couldn't make a mistake."[29]

Lefebvre earned his own chance to test the opposition in the top of the eighth. To protect Baltimore's meager one-run advantage, Oriole manager Bauer had just made a defensive swap in the field, benching butterfingered Blefary, moving Russ Snyder to left, and dispatching Saturday's hero, Paul Blair, to center.

Immediately, as if to challenge the new center fielder, Lefebvre drove a long fly ball to the fence at the 410 mark in left-center. Paulie could see that it was headed over the fence. He turned. He ran. He came to the dirt of the warning track and raced on, watching over his shoulder, gauging the ball's arc and descent. Their lead would be lost if he did not catch it. He arrived at the chain-link fence, took a deep breath, and leapt as high as he possibly could, several feet above the top of the fence. He stretched out his left arm, flung out his glove, and grabbed the ball as it sailed over.

Parker and Roseboro followed by grounding out.

"The fielding on the boundary," remarked one BBC commentator in rapt appreciation, "is quite superb."[30]

Thirty-two scoreless innings.

In the stands, an Oriole fan with a plastic trumpet began to play "Taps" for the Dodgers.

What turned out to be Don Drysdale's last postseason game was also his finest. He held Snyder, Blefary, Etchebarren, Johnson, and McNally hitless all afternoon. He struck out more batters than McNally, including, most gratifyingly, Robby in the seventh, on three curveballs. When Aparicio singled to get aboard, Drysdale pitched out to Roseboro, who threw down to Wills, who nailed Little Looie trying to take second. He retired the Orioles in order in the bottom of the eighth.

The score held at 1–0.

The Dodgers came to bat for the final time.

The enormity of the situation slowly dawned on Russ Snyder, Baltimore's number 9. As the big Nebraskan jogged to left field in the Dodger ninth, an anxious tingling suffused his limbs, which satisfied him immensely. The previous week in Los Angeles, Russ hadn't been at all nervous. Truth to tell, he hadn't even been that excited.[31] He kept wondering when the thrill would kick in and how he would respond. Now, at long last, he grasped it: three more outs, and they would have 'em. He began to shiver with anticipation.

With the number-eight and number-nine hitters due up, Alston predictably inserted two pinch hitters. Dick Stuart hit for John Kennedy. Al Ferrara appeared on deck to bat for Drysdale.

Stuart swung at a fastball and missed, swung at a second one and fouled it off. Etch called for a slow curve, but what Mac delivered instead was a terrifying mistake. The pitch hung. "It sat up there," the Oriole catcher recalled, "just begging to

be hit out of the park."[32] A former American Leaguer, Stuart
had plenty of experience hitting home runs in Memorial Stadium. He had been counting on another fastball, however.
McNally's pitch, terrible though it was, completely fooled
him. He swung, didn't get his bat on the ball, and struck out.
One away.

Al Ferrara stepped in, promptly swung at the first pitch,
and lined it to center for a single. The lumbering Ferrara was
replaced at first base by a pinch runner, the speedy Nate
Oliver.

McNally now confronted the top of the order. Maury Wills
stood in. Mac threw a fastball. Dodger desperation was such
that even tiny Wills, the master of little ball, had become in-
toxicated with home run fever, convinced that he could win
the game with one swing.[33] Maury swung with everything he
had and missed. Oh and one.

McNally then threw three balls out of the strike zone,
opening a decisive moment. He was just one ball away from
having two fleet Dodgers aboard. Luis Aparicio jogged to the
mound to offer his expert counsel. To the many millions
watching and listening, this appeared to be a consultation of
considerable import. It was not. Aparicio wanted to get Mc-
Nally to relax. As the shortstop well knew, in circumstances of
this sort, you don't have to tell anybody much of anything.

"Hey," Little Looie said.

The pitcher squinted at him. "Yeah?"

"Just make the guy hit into a double play."

Mac nodded. "Okay." He wasn't really listening. Afterward, he would admit that he had no idea what his shortstop
was saying.[34]

Aparicio jogged back to his position. McNally wound up,
delivered. Ball four. Wills walked. Nate Oliver took second,
the first Dodger all day to make it that far. With one out in the
ninth, LA had at last moved a man into scoring position.

Bauer phoned his bull pen. Drabo and Stu Miller rose stiffly and began to throw. McNally observed this without concern. Baltimore had only right-handed relievers. He figured that Bauer would leave him in to pitch to the next Dodger, Willie Davis — left-hander against left-hander.

Bauer did. Willie Davis came to the plate, and Etchebarren requested another slow curve from McNally. Unlike the near disaster he had thrown moments earlier to Stuart, this one did not hang. Willie did manage to land his bat on the ball, but only to send a fly to Frank Robinson in right. The runners held. Two away.

It was Lou Johnson's turn. Although Sweet Lou, at .267, possessed the best Series average of any Dodger, the prospect of pitching to him didn't exactly worry Harry Brecheen. In truth, ever since Wally Bunker had found his groove the previous afternoon, the pitching coach had been calm. "Nervous?" Brecheen would later say with a laugh. "I sat in one little crack out there and spat tobacco juice for two days." Nonetheless, Brecheen stirred, stood, and strolled out to chat with McNally, buying some time for his righties in the bull pen to get warm. He climbed the mound, shifted the wad of chew in his mouth, and greeted the pitcher. "I just came out to give you a breather."

McNally nodded. "Okay."[35]

"So this guy" — the coach indicated Johnson — "is a first-ball fastball hitter."

"Right, yeah."

"Just take a deep breath and relax."

"Okay."

"And be careful where you throw the first pitch."[36]

Brecheen patted him on the butt, walked back to the bench, and took a seat beside Bauer. The manager, meanwhile, was asking himself, "So what happens if McNally issues a two-out walk to Lou Johnson and loads the bases for Tommy Davis? What then?" For the first time all Series, Bauer felt as if he might have a tough decision to make.[37] *Although it would in-*

deed be a positive thing for McNally to earn this complete game, Bauer thought, *if he walks Johnson, I bring in Stu Miller.*

The sky had been overcast, but as Johnson came to the plate, the sun suddenly broke out and sharp shadows fell, doubtless an omen of something. Sweet Lou dug in and awaited a breaking ball. Brecheen may have thought that Johnson was a first-ball fastball hitter, but his favorite pitch in this situation was actually a curve down and in. And he knew that McNally was proud of his breaking ball today, that he was getting it over. If it came, Johnson planned to knock it out of the park.[38]

Nate Oliver stepped off second base, taking his lead. Davey Johnson wasn't even holding him on the bag. The second baseman seemed lost in another world, muttering to himself, "No dying quails. No dying quails."[39] Davey wanted the ball hit to him, but he feared a broken-bat blooper, a weak flare, a duck fart — a dying quail. He wanted the ball up in the air or on the ground. If it was squarely hit, he was confident it wouldn't get through their infield. And if it came at him, he swore, he would stop it one way or another.

Mac delivered two breaking balls.

"Beautiful curves," Etch remembered.

Sweet Lou swung hard and missed them both.

The plate umpire, John Rice, stepped forward, providing another dramatic pause. Rice withdrew a whisk broom from his belt, stooped, and meticulously swept home plate. He then returned to crouch behind Etchebarren.

Two on, two out, LA down to its last strike. McNally attempted another curve but got it up a little too high. Again Johnson swung. Lou made good contact, driving it to center. He felt, as he broke from the batter's box, that it might be a home run.[40]

Paul Blair felt differently. He walked in a few steps and stood there. He was impatient. It seemed to be a routine fly, but it was moving so slowly. He began urging it on, calling for it. *Hurry up!* "I felt like I was waiting a whole season," he remembered.[41]

At 3:47 P.M., the ball finally descended. It landed in Paulie's glove for the final out. McNally looked into one of NBC's television cameras, gave a happy, hearty wave to the folks back home, and then disappeared from view as his teammates mobbed him. Pandemonium erupted. Thousands of elated Baltimoreans poured onto the playing field. Two youngsters raced out, unfurled a big sign: HOW SWEET IT IS!

For the first time in the twentieth century, their Orioles were champions, the first non–New York American Leaguers to win the World Series since 1948.

And the Dodgers were the most shut-out team in Series history.

The vice president was taken first for a visit to the umpires' underground dressing room. Plate umpire John Rice was just inside, shedding his dark garments. As Humphrey entered, the umpire spun to greet him, delighted. They shook hands and took turns expressing their admiration for the swift, riveting game they'd just witnessed. "What a pleasure, what an outstanding game," Rice enthused. "Drysdale sure pitched great." He had called all-star games in 1959 and 1962, would eventually go on to call another in 1970, and would work three other World Series — but umpiring this particular championship contest would remain the highlight of Rice's nineteen-year career. Looking back much later, he would judge the fourth game of the 1966 Series to be the best game he ever saw.[42]

"You did a great job," Humphrey told him, adding, with a wink, "I hardly complained at all during the game."

The vice president exchanged a few more hellos, waved and nodded, and then, accompanied in the passageway beneath the stands by his Secret Service agents, crossed to the

Baltimore dressing room and poked his head inside. It was as expected — jubilance and delirium, a scene of absolute anarchy, men in all states of undress scampering and screaming. Someone had a radio turned up loud, blasting soul music. Blefary was furtively lathering NBC's Joe Garagiola with shaving cream. Drabo was planting snakes and igniting hotfoots, while Boog was launching big buckets of ice water at unsuspecting teammates. Shivering pleas to the first baseman of "Enough, Tubby!" earned indignant responses: "It's Mr. Tubby from now on," Boog asserted between bursting booms of triumphant laughter. "I'm a World Champion!"[43] Jim Murray of the *Los Angeles Times*, nearly drowned and thoroughly drenched by one of Boog's bucketfuls, was being dressed down for having called Baltimore "a fly-blown old strumpet of a city" and having written, "The only thing major league about the Orioles is their rightfielder."[44] Paul Blair was dancing around the lockers, giggling and saying, "Beautiful, beautiful, beautiful." A glowing Hank Bauer was advising newsmen to go easy on the Dodgers.

Surveying the bedlam, Humphrey spied the lithe Latin figure of Luis Aparicio. "I told you to hit me a home run," the vice president called out, as indeed he had before the game.

"I know, I know." The little shortstop winced. "I disappointed you, sorry!"[45]

Humphrey pushed his way in and cut a swath through the revelers to get to Frank Robinson. "We went out to win this for the city," Frank was telling Chuck Thompson. "We really wanted to win for Baltimore." The vice president tapped his shoulder, then extended a hand in congratulations.

"Good job," he said.

"Thank you," Robby replied.[46]

It was simply too crowded and chaotic for the vice president to speak with every Oriole. After a minute of halfhearted maneuvering, he quit the room and led his entourage over to the Dodger clubhouse.[47] It would be, he assumed, the quickest of visits. He ended up staying a half hour. The mood there was not nearly as gloomy as one might have imagined. It had been a far bigger blow to the boys when they'd lost the 1962 play-off to the Giants. There had been a good many tears that raw October night — drunken rage, fistfights, and frustration. By contrast, the Dodgers now appeared rather blasé. Walter Alston sat in his office near the locker room slowly pulling off his shoes. "I'm not going to jump off a bridge," the gray-haired manager was muttering to a huddle of reporters, "if that's what you think."[48]

The vice president shook Alston's hand and inquired enthusiastically about the Dodgers' imminent Asian trip. Humphrey had recently written the manager a letter that emphasized how very much the visit could accomplish in the furthering of East-West relations. Humphrey was smart and loquacious, speaking so fast now to the Dodger manager that, as Barry Goldwater once observed, listening to him was like trying to read *Playboy* while your wife turned the pages.

Turning from Alston, the vice president greeted Dick Stuart as he emerged from the shower. Stuart was naked but for a towel slung about his hips. They shook hands regardless, and Stuart requested an autograph. Humphrey located a pen, tracked down some paper, and happily obliged.

Humphrey spotted Willie Davis and flashed on his miraculous catch of the fourth inning. "By gosh, the last time I saw you, I thought you were going over the fence," the vice president said with great feeling. The previous October, Humphrey had been rooting against these Dodgers, to no effect. "What," Humphrey asked Willie, with a whine in his voice, "did you have against the Twins last year?"

Lou Johnson recalled that the vice president had also thrown out the first ball in Game One of that Series, another game they'd lost. "When you threw out the first ball today," Johnson confided to Humphrey, "I knew we were going to have to fight like hell."

Humphrey found Sandy Koufax surrounded by sportswriters. "I've seen you pitch many times," the vice president told him. "I saw you fan fifteen Yankees in the World Series."

A small smile crossed Sandy's lips. "I did pretty good against the Twins last season, too," the southpaw teased.

Humphrey laughed. As he turned away, he heard the reporters begin to joke with Koufax.

"You guys may be in real trouble," one reporter pointed out. "Four games down and only three to play."

"Yeah." Schooling his features, Koufax kept a straight face. "We might as well give it to them."

"What are your plans now?" another asked.

"I'm flying back to Los Angeles. I hope it's a real slow plane."

"You're lucky. You won't have to fight off a mob at the airport."

"Yeah," Koufax responded, "but I'm afraid of the rocks."[49]

Humphrey found Drysdale slumped in front of his dressing cubicle. His sweat-covered head hung almost to his knees. The last half inch of a burning cigarette threatened his fingers, and he was working on his second soothing beer.

"Hello, I'm the vice president!" Humphrey exclaimed, and stretched out a hand. "You know, you pitched a great game today."

Drysdale nodded. He had thrown just seventy-eight pitches that afternoon, had delivered his strongest performance of the year, and yet had lost. Dazedly, he got to his feet and thanked Humphrey.

"You have nothing to regret," insisted the vice president, looking steeply up at the tall right-hander. "You're a great champion in your own right and you don't have to win any more to prove it."

Drysdale shuffled his cleats. He opened his mouth to speak, then closed it again.

The vice president empathized with the discouraged pitcher. He vividly recalled how low he'd felt after Drysdale had defeated his team in the fourth game of the 1965 World Series. "You broke my heart when you beat the Twins last year," Humphrey told him softly.

For the first time all day, Big D smiled.[50]

Mayor McKeldin was out of town, attending a conference, but as soon as Blair's catch finalized the four-game sweep, he wired his congratulations to Bauer and "to every member of the world's best team."[51] That night in the town of Baltimore, they gonged the bell at City Hall sixty-six times in celebration. Drunks shook their fists at the sky and howled, "We did it!" while strangers kissed and cars honked incessantly. Colorful specks of confetti swirled about War Memorial Plaza. Shredded newspaper floated from hotel windows. Pedestrians drank openly. Traffic ground to a halt.

"It was great," Barry Levinson recalled. "Not only did we win, but we totally humiliated an LA team. Sometimes it's good not just to win but to humiliate. You know, the fact that you beat them in four games, and they couldn't score any runs against you — that went down very well. That was the beginning of Oriole pride. We had arrived."[52]

Sadly, what began as Baltimore's biggest party since V-J Day turned riotous when a shrieking, swarming mass of twelve thousand Baltimoreans descended upon the downtown streets, running wild in the flashing neon of the strip clubs, ripping signs off street poles, chanting "Birds! Birds! Birds!"[53] This was less the "lazy-lidded" Baltimore of contemporary Anne Tyler novels and more the "Mobtown" made famous in nineteenth-century broadsheets. Impromptu parades sputtered to life — fifty frenzied fans marching behind a police car, long motorcades back and forth to the stadium — until the impatient participants were drawn to greater mayhem.[54] Dodger pennants were gleefully set ablaze. Amid the deafening bang and blast of cherry bombs and firecrackers, fights broke out. Produce trucks were raided and cabbages flung.[55] Packs of youths smashed store windows around the Civic Center, opened fire hydrants, hurled beer cans at police, and turned over cars. Eventually, inevitably, the blare of sirens filled the early-morning hours, as riot police and canine units arrived, accompanied by a steady stream of emergency vehicles. By then, a new dawn was on its way, and a soft, fortuitous rain had begun to fall. The mob melted away, the many thousands straggling home. They left behind them streets littered with smashed cars, broken windows, and beat-up placards that read LOVE THEM BIRDS.

The historic 1966 Dodger lineup would never see another postseason, while the Oriole team would go on to vie for the championship again in 1969, 1970, and 1971.

These two dynasties — one arriving as the other left — would never again battle for the crown. Their Series had ended so swiftly and astonishingly that Bob Prince hardly had time to prepare for the sudden sign-off. As the Gunner rasped statistical totals and game summaries into his headset, his jackhammer voice almost softened with surprise. No one had expected this championship series to fall out as it had, least of all the veteran Prince. "Lots of tremendous thrills and great plays," he concluded at last, "and certainly they'll be talking a long, long time about this World Series."

The Gunner was often right, but on this the Hall of Fame broadcaster was dead wrong. Ask a casual baseball fan about classic postseason matchups of the 1960s, and you'll probably hear about the Pirates versus the Yankees in 1960 or the Cardinals versus the Red Sox in 1967. Suggest the Dodgers and the Orioles, and perhaps you'll hear about the Dodgers versus the Yankees in 1963 or the Mets versus the Orioles in 1969. Remind this fan that the Dodgers and the Orioles once competed *against* each other, and there will ensue a lengthy pause, after which you'll likely be asked, "Uh, what year was that again?"

The strange and abrupt upheavals of 1966 may have contributed to this amnesia, for few years have ended so differently from how they began. At the start, diplomats and statesmen still were heroes, the Vietnam War and the civil rights movement were popular causes, and either the Dodgers or the Yankees (or both) were expected to appear in the postseason. In a way, it was still the 1950s, despite what the calendar read when the baseball season opened. "Decades are not so clearly defined," Barry Levinson observed. "'Sixty-six was a huge transitional period, the beginning of this kind of cultural revolution. All of a sudden, the war became a hot topic. Music began to shift. Drugs started to become more prevalent. Protests began to break out. All these things began to explode."[56]

By year's end, the noisy 1960s had arrived, and the Great Society had unraveled. The old folks cowered; the youth were massing. "Flower Power" and Nixon's "silent majority" were on the horizon. No baseball game — no matter how dramatic, no matter how many "tremendous thrills and great plays," no matter what it said about the rise and fall of classic baseball dynasties — could gain much of a foothold in the common consciousness just then. In a world grown suddenly large, the World Series was diminished to an inconsequential speck.

If, as the adage goes, "those who can remember the sixties weren't really there," then it was 1966 when memories dimmed and went out. The astounding events that characterized baseball's championship series that season, the reason they welcome forgetting, seem inextricably bound up with the race riots, NASA debacles, and Vietnam War deceptions that so aggrieved and altered the country at the time. It was an in-between year, overshadowed in popular recollection by what came before and after. It was a season of transition, in the nation as in the national pastime, a time of comings and goings. That year no American arrived more loudly than Frank Robinson, and none would depart more quietly than Sandy Koufax.

EPILOGUE

Arrivals and Departures

A glance at the results — the record number of consecutive shutout innings, the sweep by the team picked to lose — underscores the impression of the day that the 1966 World Series constituted one of baseball history's biggest upsets. It had been presumed, at the least, that this would be a replay of the 1965 World Series. It wasn't. Six hurlers over four games pitched some of the best baseball of their careers. Sandy Koufax was not among them.

Still, many Orioles believed that the experts weren't so far off. "I think we still have the lowest team batting average for a winning team, and they've got the lowest team batting average for a losing team," Brooks Robinson noted years later.[1]

"It was just a fluke," Wally Bunker agreed. "Everybody says we weren't that good and they weren't that bad, and well, that's about right, you know what I'm saying?"[2]

The Dodgers attributed their poor performance to the wear and tear of the tight National League chase. Unlike the Orioles, they'd had no chance to adjust to the idea of a post-season contest — to catch their breath, raise their sights, and ready themselves for a fight. "By the time we flew all the way back from Philadelphia," Ron Fairly recalled, in an assessment confirmed by most of his former teammates, "we were mentally done. We were whipped. I think there were eight or nine teams that could have beaten us. I'm not taking anything away from the Baltimore Orioles, because they had one heckuva club. But it was such a strain on us just to get to the World Series."[3]

After winning the pennant on the last day of the season, Phil Regan remembered, "there was just a sense of *phew!*" They had hardly rested for two weeks and needed "time to regroup."[4] But they couldn't afford the luxury. Instead, Wes Parker remembered, "all of a sudden, two days later we run out on the field — and there's Baltimore."[5]

In their autobiographies, both John Roseboro and Maury Wills wrote that they fully expected the team to return to form at any moment. Nate Oliver, however, remembered that after losing the first two games in such embarrassing fashion — unable to hit Drabowsky or Palmer, unable to field the ball behind Koufax — the team was "hit with a case of shock."[6]

"Before we knew it," Fairly added, "hell, they'd beat us four straight. It was quick. And the games didn't even last very long."[7]

It wasn't only that the Dodgers lost, of course, but that they established records for fewest runs, fewest hits, lowest batting average, and most errors in an inning. The Dodgers may have been tired, but could they conceivably have been more tired than any other club in the history of the World Series?

"These guys won their ninety-five games," one of the Dodger brass told a reporter before Game Three. "They won the pennant. They could care less about this thing."

"Two swings won two games," noted Oriole reliever Eddie Fisher, summarizing the Baltimore half of the series. Bunker figured that it had to be luck, more than anything else, that allowed his team to defeat LA's vaunted staff of champions. "If that series went ten more games," Wally would contend, "Koufax and Drysdale might have won the last six. And Osteen too."[8]

Wes Parker disagreed, later saying, "Even if that World

Series had gone ten games, I don't think we would have scored a run.[9]

"A lotta guys were very upset, because O'Malley had made plans for us to go to Japan right after the World Series," continued Parker. "If the World Series had gone seven games, we would have left the next day. And when we lost the first game of the World Series, nobody said this, but it was almost like we felt, 'Okay, well, since we lost the first game, we might as well lose four straight, because then we'll get three or four days off before we have to go to Japan.' Everybody was really mad about that Japan trip. Really mad."[10]

Parker, of course, did not suggest that the Dodgers threw the Series, nor did anyone associated with the team. And he was careful to distinguish that the team's lack of motivation in the Series sprang from a desire for some rest and respect rather than revenge and recompense. "If we'd won the first game, it would have changed everything for us," he explained. "We would have been much more fired up about sweeping them and getting our four days off before going to Japan."[11] But it was not to be.

Four days off would not have been enough for Claude Osteen, who did not particularly want to go to Japan at all. In October 1966, his wife was pregnant with their third child and near the end of her last trimester. Osteen desperately wanted to be present for the birth. In addition, including Game Three, he'd already pitched in forty games that year. He needed time off. His arm was exhausted, his fastball laughable.

Don Sutton, however, was in even worse shape. Neither the still-injured Sutton nor Koufax or Drysdale would be accompanying the team to Japan.

"I need you to go over there," Buzzie Bavasi informed Osteen. "The first game's gonna be on *Wide World of Sports*. I need you to pitch that one. If you want to come home after that, you can. It's up to you."

Reluctantly, Osteen assented. After a brief stopover in Honolulu, during which the NL champs played two games against a team of Hawaiian all-stars, they flew on to Tokyo. There, on October 22, Osteen started the opener of the exhibition tour. He pitched well, he hit a home run, and his team won. But *Wide World of Sports* did not elect to broadcast that particular victory. Instead, ABC aired the next day's game, when a diminutive southpaw from the Yomiuri Giants shut out Los Angeles 5–0.

"So that," Osteen would later observe drily, "wasn't very pleasing." A consummate team player, he nonetheless decided to remain with the Dodgers for a little while longer. He pitched two more games and lost them both. It wasn't just his tired arm that was to blame. The pitching mounds in Japan were flat, the strike zone high, and every batter unfamiliar.[12]

In midtour, after traveling north to Sapporo, Sendai, and Toyama, the Dodgers came around to rest again in Tokyo. With his wife back in the States due any day, Osteen decided that this represented an opportune moment to depart. Unfortunately, Maury Wills felt the same way. The shortstop's bad knee had been getting worse. When the Dodgers refused him permission to return home for a medical consultation, Wills jumped the tour and vanished.

Osteen was preparing to pack when he was hastily summoned to Walter O'Malley's suite in Tokyo's New Otani Hotel. Wills had just been located. While flying home, he'd stopped off in Hawaii and apparently stayed. Osteen was shown photographs that had been wired to Japanese newspapers. Instead of receiving X-rays and heat treatments, Maury had been caught singing on a bandstand beside Don Ho, playing banjo with a Dixieland band. The Dodgers' hosts had also received pictures of the supposedly injured Don Drysdale. He was golfing.

O'Malley had been visiting the official residence of the premier of Japan, who had interrogated him thoroughly about

Wills's disappearance and the absence of Drysdale and Koufax. The Dodger owner had felt humiliated. "Look," he told Osteen, "I need you to stay." The owner's bright eyes popped flashbulb-like behind large, flat, wire-rimmed spectacles. He was a tall, wide man, his black hair silvering at the temples. "I'll get you home immediately if there's an emergency with your wife. You can call home every day; I'll pay the telephone bills. But I'd like for you to stay."

Osteen didn't see O'Malley too often. The owner rarely made personal pleas. He stayed. Ten days later, with Osteen and his teammates in Shizuoka, his third son was born.

By now it was apparent that all the Dodgers were weary and homesick. "I didn't dig sitting cross-legged on the floor and chewing raw fish," Roseboro would grumble afterward.[13] They were playing far sloppier than any Americans had ever played in Japan. No previous major-league visitors had dropped more than four games; the Dodgers had lost eight. Of their last nine games, they had won but two.

Then, just as this rotten tour thankfully neared its end, things really deteriorated. A knock came on Osteen's hotel door. A Japanese journalist stood there. After exchanging polite greetings, the journalist inquired, in halting English, "Have you heard? Mister Koufax, he retire."[14]

In Los Angeles the previous afternoon, November 18, seventy-five reporters had been summoned to a suite in the Beverly Wilshire Hotel, where Sandy Koufax momentously revealed that he'd just asked the Dodgers to place him on the voluntary disabled list. "I've got a lot of years to live after baseball," Koufax announced into a battery of microphones, "and I'd like to live them with the complete use of my body."[15]

He paused, glancing down at his hands, folded serenely on the table before him, his fingers interlaced. It was his oversize hands and lengthy digits that had given him his second pitch, his magnificent breaking ball, which as much as anything had established him as a success. "Sandy has the longest fingers I'm sure in the league, if not in all of baseball," Vin Scully had observed during the second game of the 1966 World Series. "That's one reason why he gets such fantastic rotation on the pitch. He has the fingers of a concert pianist."

Employing a slightly different patois, John Roseboro confirmed Vinnie's assessment. "To throw a curve hard overhand, you have to let it roll off of your index finger," the Dodger catcher would explain to Koufax biographer Jane Leavy. "As they say in the ghetto, shit, he had great big fucking hands. He could wrap that ball. He wrapped it."[16]

Koufax's left hand could hold six baseballs, but it could not throw one without further aggravating the arthritis in his elbow. So he was quitting.

The reporters in the suite were as thoroughly flummoxed as were the nation's sports fans. "Nobody believed it," Roseboro remembered, "except the ballplayers who knew he always meant what he said."[17] The farewell scene was not without humor. When the newsmen pressed for specifics about his financial well-being, Koufax smiled. "Well," he responded, as if deep in thought, "I have enough for lunch and dinner . . . today."[18]

They wondered about his plans for the future. He had none. "Right now," he said with a chuckle, "I guess you'd have to say that I'm unemployed."

One reporter teasingly inquired whether the Dodgers might be interested in keeping the southpaw (a career .097 batter) around as a pinch hitter. At this Koufax roared with laughter.[19]

More jarring Dodger changes were to occur when baseball officials convened in Pittsburgh at month's end. Tommy Davis had seen only limited use during the exhibition tour, garnering just thirteen at bats. Still, he'd hit .462 in Japan, better than any other Dodger — but not, apparently, good enough. On the morning of November 30, while golfing with Willie

Davis, Tommy was met at the ninth hole by a television camera and crew. They wanted his reaction to the trade.

"What trade?" he asked.

"You've been traded to the Mets."[20]

Walter O'Malley, in the meantime, found that he could not forgive Maury Wills for the embarrassment he'd caused the team in Japan. He instructed GM Buzzie Bavasi to get rid of their superstar shortstop.

A day after the trade of Tommy Davis was announced, Maury's home phone rang. "The rumor," said the reporter on the other end, "is that you've been traded to the Pirates."

Wills was inconsolable. "I don't want to be traded," he insisted, close to tears. "I've spent all my life playing for the Dodgers. The Dodgers are my life. Tell the people of Los Angeles that I'm praying I won't be traded."[21]

His prayer went unanswered. A moment later, the rumor was confirmed.

In less than two weeks, the Dodgers had lost their best pitcher, their best runner, and their best hitter.

Even as Bavasi aggressively continued with more off-season deals and demotions, he steadfastly denied that the Dodgers were entering a rebuilding phase. Such an admission might adversely affect attendance in such a fidgety and forgetful place as Southern California. If they performed poorly just once, Bavasi mused to a reporter, "do you think this club would survive in Los Angeles, a town which demands, and is entitled to, a winner?"[22] Dodger fans were notorious for arriving late and leaving early. Would they show up at all if their team wasn't competitive? The answer would come soon, for in dealing Wills, Bavasi had both dispatched the spark plug of their offense and dissolved the glue of their infield. In losing Koufax and Davis, the two Brooklyn boys who had blossomed so beautifully out west, more links to the past had been severed, more franchise history erased. By the beginning of 1967, of the forty men listed on the Dodgers' 1966 spring training roster, only twenty-seven remained. That year the team would finish in eighth place, attendance would drop by almost a million, and the rebuilding would begin in earnest.

Wills would go on to play two years as a third baseman in Pittsburgh, then a few months in Montreal, before returning to Los Angeles in 1969, in a midseason trade. There he'd finish out his playing days as a Dodger.

As for Tommy Davis, he would never fully recover from his ankle injury. Traded frequently, from one league to the other, from contenders to expansion teams and back again, he would limp his way around the majors for another decade. The American League's implementation of the designated hitter would help extend his career several seasons. Increasingly, he would become a one-tool player. His motto, he joked, was "Have bat, will travel." John Roseboro recalled, "He was a straight, clean fellow, who loved just playing more than anything else."[23] Although Davis would never win another batting championship, he would retire, at age thirty-seven, with the highest pinch-hitting average of any player in baseball history.

On November 1, 1966, Brooks Robinson headed for South Vietnam. Accompanying him on this tour were Stan Musial — one of the very few major leaguers who had played in more games and possessed more at bats than Brooks eventually would — as well as Harmon Killebrew, Hank Aaron, Joe Torre, and broadcaster Mel Allen. The six of them visited troops throughout the war zone, at frontline outposts and airstrips, in field hospitals and encamped villages.[24] They traveled in C-130 transports whose wings were riddled with bullet holes, or in helicopters that descended from three thousand feet in a corkscrew spiral in order to avoid sniper fire.[25] They heard constant gunfire and watched the countryside being bombed. Gazing down at the unfamiliar terrain of plains and deltas, of saturated rice paddies, elephant grass, and sticky, airless jungles, they were informed that the people in pointed lamp shade hats who were running for cover were the enemy. The rest, the ones who didn't flee, were friendly. That was the only way to discern who was on the side of the Americans. "A strange war," Joe Torre recalled, "where there were no lines drawn." The ballplayers had presumed the Vietnam War to be akin to the Korean conflict of the early 1950s. It was infinitely less straightforward than that. Fighting there, Brooks realized, was "like trying to grab at quick-silver."

Over three weeks, the six men ran what were termed "baseball clinics" at Da Nang, Pleiku, Banmethuot, Nha Trang, and Phan Thiet, as well as in encampments near the Cambodian border. For the most part, these involved chatting, shaking hands, signing autographs, and showing a film of 1966 World Series highlights. The troops had avidly followed the postseason contest on Armed Forces Radio. Still, they couldn't fathom how the Dodgers had lost four straight. Pressed about this at every battle station, Brooks would always beam and say, "They underestimated us. And we outplayed them."

"You Orioles cost me money," complained one GI who had bet on the favorite.

"That's why I had to come over," Brooks replied. "To get you on the right horse next year."

The baseball representatives were repeatedly assured that they were in little danger, only to discover otherwise. The site on the infamous "Marble Mountain" where they lunched one day with Marine commanding general Lewis W. Walt was leveled by mortars the next day. Torre came across a soldier staring dazedly at his helmet. A bullet had entered in the front and exited from the side while miraculously just grazing his head.[26] This was an amorphous conflict; no one's safety could be guaranteed. One night Torre and Musial visited a unit bunkered in a cemetery. At nine o'clock, when the troops began firing off rounds to scare the Vietcong, they almost shot Musial by accident.[27] Stan later concluded that touring Vietnam had been a foolish adventure.[28] Similarly, Robinson recalled, "I wasn't scared at the time, but the more I think about it now, I should have been."

Brooks was impressed by the courage of the servicemen but distressed by the carnage he saw. "I met a lot of brave American kids who were badly shot-up," he remembered. "It shook me to see them — arms and legs missing, faces shattered, blind." In one ward, he found a young soldier who'd lost both legs after stumbling into a booby trap. Musial approached. "How you doin', son?" he inquired softly, extending a hand. "I'm Stan Musial of the St. Louis Cardinals." Brooks watched as the soldier, in his hospital bed, jerked to attention. "Oh, Mr. Musial!" he exclaimed, profusely apologetic. "I'm sorry I didn't recognize you!"

Brooks swallowed hard as he remembered the incident. "I'll tell you that just tore me up. My lasting impression of Vietnam is that kid lying there without any legs, apologizing because he didn't recognize Stan Musial."[29]

Ultimately, Brooks was led to rethink the war. Having viewed the conflict as a representative of the national pastime, he developed a response that was representative of his countrymen. "I came back pretty gung-ho about our participation then," he conceded in his 1971 autobiography, "but like many others, I believe we've stayed long enough and paid a dear price — we should be gone already. But that's just a balding third baseman's opinion."[30]

Brooks Robinson would eventually go on to become a balding (and highly popular) Oriole broadcaster. His would not be the only fortunes changed by 1966, nor would he be the only veteran of that World Series who would find a livelihood in the game after his playing days were over. Others likewise would become announcers — Drysdale and Ron Fairly, most successfully, as well as Wes Parker. Many would end up as professional bench coaches, pitching coaches, or scouts. A select few — Jim Lefebvre, Jeff Torborg, Davey Johnson, Phil Regan, and Maury Wills — would take on the job of big-league manager, with varying success.

Undoubtedly, the biggest beneficiary of the 1966 World Series would be its MVP, Frank Robinson. Having capped his phenomenal season of vindication by succeeding so notably in the postseason, in plain view of America, Frank unhesitatingly jumped at the chance to reintroduce himself to the country. "I hope I'll be invited to a lot of cities this winter," insisted a champagne-drenched Robby, speaking with great earnestness in the clubhouse after the fourth game. "I want to meet people. A man matures that way."[31]

Robby, like Koufax, had always been as private off the field as he was competitive on. What had changed? In the wake of the championship sweep, Frank — brimming with confidence and flushed with joy, having a second time been named a league's Most Valuable Player — glimpsed opportunity. It wasn't just the chance for greater fame and fortune, although on this point he was not coy. The Orioles owed him. He'd earned $68,000 that year and desired $100,000 in 1967. A $32,000 raise might have sounded outrageous at the beginning of 1966, but no more. "There's no doubt but that Koufax and Drysdale, with their double holdout last spring, helped all ball players," Frank explained. "Now it's possible, after a good season, to go in and ask for a $20,000 to $50,000 raise. A few years ago, such a request would get you thrown out of the office by the general manager."[32]

It wasn't only about the money. Around the time that Koufax announced his retirement, Robinson was elsewhere in Los Angeles speaking with a reporter. Robby and Sandy were both the same age, both "an old thirty," but one was bowing out while the other was calling attention to his entrance. "If I play seven or eight more years," Frank mused, "then I think I'd have sufficient baseball knowledge to step directly into managing."[33]

It seemed so simple: he had strong opinions; he understood the game. But for all his credentials, he may as well have announced that he wanted to become an Apollo astronaut or president of the United States. No African American had ever expressed publicly such an ambition, much less actually been handed the reins of a major-league team. In 1966, however, Emmett Ashford had become the first black umpire in the major leagues, and Frank's former basketball teammate from high school, Bill Russell, had been named to coach the Boston Celtics, becoming the first black American to run a major sports team.

Emboldened by all he was accomplishing, Frank assured reporters that there would soon be a black manager, and he named four active players — Jim Gilliam, Maury Wills, Willie Mays, and Ernie Banks — who he felt already had enough experience and skill to do the job.

As a teen, Frank had suffered the taunts of racism. In his twenties, he'd felt tainted by that night when he'd brandished a gun in anger. Now, in his thirties, he spoke like a man emerging from a bitter isolation, determined to reengage with the world at large. Whatever the cause — whether it was his exposure to sincere humanitarians such as Mayor McKeldin and Brooks Robinson, his warm acceptance by the players and fans of Baltimore, his wife talking him through the summer's tumultuous events, or his near-death experience in the deep end of an undertaker's pool — Frank no longer spoke of racism as intractable. The civil rights movement suddenly didn't seem so futile. He was optimistic about change. He could do anything, and anything could happen. Gradually, he settled into a role as a leader in the clubhouse and, from there, of the black community.

Early in 1966, disillusioned ex-Dodger Jack Robinson had stated flatly that baseball's owners lacked nerve, and for that reason he didn't think there would ever be a black manager in the major leagues.[34] Frank had made a career out of proving people wrong — first the dad who doubted his son's talent, then the racist minor-league customers, then the boobirds in Cincinnati, then Bill DeWitt. Now Frank set out to prove that his hero, Jack Robinson, also was wrong.

Robby focused on fulfilling his managerial ambitions the same way he ran the bases: determined, single-mindedly, unafraid, spikes up. He spent nine winters working as manager of the Santurce Crabbers in the Puerto Rican league, giving up spending his off-season with his beloved family. Between March and October, Robby studied his own managers in the major leagues, questioning and prompting them, watching and learning. During the other months, he tried to translate what he'd learned onto the diamonds of Santurce, San Juan, Caguas, and Mayagüez, twisting into shape a theory of tactics and strategies that felt wholly his own. He had the good fortune, over the next decade, to study under some of the most respected managers in baseball.

After Earl Weaver replaced Hank Bauer at the Baltimore helm halfway through the 1968 season, Frank observed how successfully Weaver sacrificed everything for the big inning, how willingly he overlooked bad fielding by someone who wielded a crucial bat. Weaver was a bold, emotional micromanager. He fidgeted and bellowed, kept statistics, and used the entire roster more inventively than Bauer.

In the winter of 1971–72, Weaver allowed the Orioles to trade Robby to the Dodgers. In Los Angeles, where Frank played but one season, he found Walter Alston's reserve baffling. He ran the game cautiously. In his quiet way, he was also versatile and shrewdly adaptable. He'd been victorious with radically different teams using radically different talents in radically different home parks. But after the theatrics of Earl Weaver, Alston seemed to be made of stone.

Gradually, Frank came to understand that Alston was not dead, but he would give him scant more praise than that. A few times a season, the strong silent manager would erupt in

rage and dress down the team, after which his players predictably would straighten themselves out — for a while.

From the Dodgers, Robby headed inland to play most of
the next two seasons in Anaheim. Though nearly forty and
looking ahead to his next job, he nonetheless kept putting up
historic numbers. As a Dodger, he'd homered enough to sur-
pass Mel Ott, Eddie Mathews, and Ted Williams on the all-
time home run list. As an Angel, he passed first Jimmie Foxx
and then Mickey Mantle to claim fourth in the record books.
His address changed again at the end of 1974, when he was
traded to Cleveland. Before the next season began, he was
named player/manager, thus becoming the game's first black
manager. In the season opener, in his first at bat, he hit a
home run. His team won. He added eight more home runs
that season, and three the next, to end up with a total of 586,
behind only Hank Aaron, Babe Ruth, and Willie Mays. He se-
curely held that position for almost three decades.

By the time Barry Bonds surpassed him, in 2002, Frank
had managed three teams — the Orioles, Giants, and Indians,
each for three years. While he was managing in San Francisco, in 1982, he was voted into the Hall of Fame (as a
player) on the first ballot. In his induction speech, Frank
thanked first his wife and family and then Jack Robinson.
"Without Jackie," he said, turning to Jack's wife, Rachel
Robinson, "I don't know if the door to baseball would have
opened again for a long, long time. I know I couldn't have put
up with what Jackie put up with."

Robby's team performed well that season, and United
Press International (UPI) named him Manager of the Year. He
was praised for his aggressive managerial style. He routinely
accomplished a lot with very little, was a fantastic motivator,
and had an intense, commanding presence in both the locker
room and the front office. He'd even learned how to engage
the press.

As a manager, however, Frank Robinson was no Hall of

Famer. After eleven years of managing a lot of mediocre ballplayers, he'd lost more games than he'd won. Baltimore fired
him on May 21, 1991, and for nine years he remained on the
game's fringes, a hearty, hale figure, much respected and admired, until Major League Baseball found the perfect post for
him. They consolidated the handling of on-the-field discipli-
nary matters into the hands of one "discipline czar" and offered Frank the position. He accepted. Everyone agreed that
it suited him.

In the summer of 2002, Barry Bonds hit his 587th home
run, passing Robby on the all-time list. At age sixty-seven,
Frank was back out on the field that season, managing the
Expos on behalf of Major League Baseball, which had assumed control of the dying Montreal franchise. Needing instant credibility, they'd asked Frank to leave his desk job to
manage the team. Only Frank Robinson could climb back
down into the dugout and make it look like a promotion.

Notes

PART ONE: Robby's Revenge

1. Robinson, *My Life Is Baseball*, p. 163.

2. Ibid., p. 164.

3. Beard, *Birds on the Wing*; Robert Harris Walker, *Cincinnati and the Big Red Machine*; Robinson, *My Life Is Baseball*.

4. *Sportscentury: Frank Robinson*, ESPN Classic.

5. Robinson, *My Life Is Baseball*, pp. 31–35.

6. Robinson and Stainback, *Extra Innings*, p. 24.

7. Robinson, *My Life Is Baseball*, p. 33.

8. Robinson and Stainback, *Extra Innings*, p. 25.

9. Robinson, *My Life Is Baseball*, p. 57.

10. Robinson and Stainback, *Extra Innings*, pp. 26–29.

11. Wills and Celizin, *On the Run*, pp. 163–64.

12. All Robinson quotes in paragraph from *My Life Is Baseball*.

13. Robinson and Stainback, *Extra Innings*, p. 33.

14. Roseboro, *Glory Days with the Dodgers*, p. 186.

15. Robinson and Stainback, *Extra Innings*, p. 33.

16. Bill Ford, "Names Called before Fight, Robbie Says," *Cincinnati Enquirer*, August 16, 1960; Lou Chapman, "Eddie Decks Robinson in Brief Brawl," *Milwaukee Sentinel*, August 16, 1960.

17. Robinson, *My Life Is Baseball*, p. 113.

18. Robinson and Stainback, *Extra Innings*, pp. 50–51.

19. Robinson, *My Life Is Baseball*, p. 119.

20. Robinson and Stainback, *Extra Innings*, p. 52.
21. Robinson, *My Life Is Baseball*, p. 122.
22. Wally Bunker, telephone conversation with author, November 2003.
23. Gildea, *When the Colts Belonged to Baltimore*, p. 169
24. Barry Levinson, telephone conversation with author, August 11, 2004.
25. John Fialka, e-mail correspondence with author, November 12, 2003.
26. Levinson conversation.
27. Sobel, *Civil Rights 1960–66*, p. 242.
28. Jackie Robinson, *I Never Had It Made*, p. 47. See also Tygiel, "Il a gagne ses epaulets," in *The Jackie Robinson Reader;* Simon, "Minor Leaguer," in *Jackie Robinson and the Integration of Baseball;* Rampersad, "A Royal Entrance (1946)," in *Jackie Robinson: A Biography.*
29. Doug Brown, "Bauer's Pet? That's How Birds Ribbed Paul Blair," *Sporting News*, November 5, 1966.
30. Robinson and Stainback, *Extra Innings*, p. 60.
31. Beard, *Birds on the Wing.*
32. Eisenberg, *From 33rd Street to Camden Yards*, p. 162.
33. Bob Maisel, conversation with author, June 2, 2004.
34. Ibid.
35. Ted Patterson, *The Baltimore Orioles*, p. 87.
36. Jim Palmer, telephone conversation with author, July 31, 2004.
37. Doug Brown, " 'Old Maid' Hurlers Say, 'We Do' — Hank Blushes Fetchingly," *Sporting News*, May 14, 1966.
38. Brooks Robinson, telephone conversation with author, December 2003.
39. Doug Brown, "It Was Word of Lau That Put Drabowsky in Orioles' Flannels," *Sporting News*, October 22, 1966.
40. Alan Goldstein, "Drabowsky Becomes Latest Polish Hero," *Baltimore Sun*, October 6, 1966.
41. Bob Addie, "Palmer vs. Koufax in Second Game Today," *Washington Post*, October 6, 1966.
42. Beard, *Birds on the Wing.*
43. Ibid.

44. Lou Hatter, "Orioles Beat Indians Twice to Gain Tie for Lead," *Baltimore Sun*, May 9, 1966.

45. Eisenberg, *From 33rd Street to Camden Yards*, p. 163.

46. Cairns, *Pen Men*, pp. 196–97.

47. Jim Elliot, "Boy Having Ball with Ball F. Robinson Hit Out of Park," *Baltimore Sun*, May 9, 1966.

48. Ibid.

49. *Sportscentury: Frank Robinson*, ESPN Classic.

50. Eisenberg, *From 33rd Street to Camden Yards*, p. 163.

51. Lou Hatter, "Robinson Banquet Hits," *Baltimore Sun*, May 10, 1966.

52. Ibid.

53. Robinson, *My Life Is Baseball*, p. 183.

54. Eisenberg, *From 33rd Street to Camden Yards*, p. 164.

55. Ibid., p. 165.

56. Doug Brown, "Handy Andy Pressure-Proof Bird Prize," *Sporting News*, October 8, 1966.

57. John, *TJ: My 26 Years in Baseball*, p. 100.

58. Jim Elliot, "Mele, Mates Laud Brooks," *Baltimore Sun*, July 13, 1966.

59. Beard, *Birds on the Wing*.

60. Eisenberg, *From 33rd Street to Camden Yards*, p. 163.

61. Ibid.

62. Robinson and Stainback, *Extra Innings*, p. 63.

63. Sobel, *Civil Rights 1960–66*, pp. 443–44.

64. John S. Carroll, "Racist Pushes White Supremacy," *Baltimore Sun*, July 26, 1966.

65. "Racist Rally Ignites Angry Outbursts," *Baltimore Sun*, July 28, 1966.

66. George J. Hiltner, "Negro Describes Assault by Mob," *Baltimore Sun*, November 17, 1966.

67. Robinson and Stainback, *Extra Innings*, p. 64.

68. Jack McDonald, "Frisco Civic Leaders Salute Baseball TV as Riot Queller," *Sporting News*, October 29, 1966.

69. Earl Lawson, " 'Only Fair I Use Needle on DeWitt' — Robinson," *Sporting News*, November 12, 1966.

70. "Fans Hang DeWitt Effigy in Downtown Cincinnati," *Sporting News*, July 2, 1966.

71. Lou Hatter, "Bauer Reflects on Season," *Baltimore Sun*, October 2, 1966.

72. Eisenberg, *From 33rd Street to Camden Yards*, p. 167.

73. Robinson and Stainback, *Extra Innings*, p. 61.

74. Doug Brown, "F. Robinson's Jibes, Pranks Enliven Trips," *Sporting News*, August 27, 1966.

75. Doug Brown, "F. Robby's Fast-Flying Needle Helps Keep Orioles in Stitches," *Sporting News*, July 9, 1966.

76. Ibid.

77. Eisenberg, *From 33rd Street to Camden Yards*, p. 167.

78. Brown, "F. Robinson's Jibes."

79. Sobel, *Civil Rights 1960–66*, pp. 435–37.

80. Cairns, *Pen Men*, pp. 189–91.

81. Ibid., p. 189.

82. Doug Brown, "It's Fun Time If Moe Picks Up the Phone," *Sporting News*, June 11, 1966.

83. Ibid.

84. Bunker conversation.

85. Cairns, *Pen Men*, p. 195.

86. Ibid., p. 192.

87. Michael Ruck, telephone conversation with author, July 30, 2004.

88. Eisenberg, *From 33rd Street to Camden Yards*, p. 156.

89. Ibid., p. 168.

90. Robinson and Stainback, *Extra Innings*, p. 66.

91. Robinson, *My Life Is Baseball*.

92. Roseboro, *Glory Days with the Dodgers*, p. 17.

93. *Sportscentury: Frank Robinson*, ESPN Classic.

94. "Frank Robinson Almost Drowned at Swim Party," *Los Angeles Times*, October 12, 1966.

95. *Sportscentury: Frank Robinson*, ESPN Classic.

96. Phil Jackman, "Orioles' Andy, the Busiest Backstop," *Sporting News*, March 25, 1967.

97. "Frank Robinson Almost Drowned."

98. Hatter, "Bauer Reflects on Season."

99. Beard, *Birds on the Wing.*

100. Eisenberg, *From 33rd Street to Camden Yards*, p. 172.

101. Characterizations of McKeldin's thoughts and feelings regarding CORE, integration, Frank Robinson, Spiro Agnew, and other issues he confronted in 1966 (as well as testimonies to his integrity) come from a variety of sources. Particularly enlightening in this regard were Daniel Drosdoff, formerly of the *Baltimore Sun*, and the interviews with David Glenn, Marshall W. Jones Jr., Judge Watts, Judge Harry A. Cole, and Mr. Marudas, conducted as part of the McKeldin-Jackson Project of the Maryland Historical Society.

102. Daniel Drosdoff, e-mail correspondence with author, November 11–12, 2003.

103. Daniel Drosdoff, "C.O.R.E. Vote Shifts View on Violence," *Baltimore Sun*, July 7, 1966.

104. Daniel Drosdoff, "City-C.O.R.E. Cooperation Now Believed a Possibility," *Baltimore Sun*, October 5, 1966.

105. Richard H. Levine, "800 Attend 'White Man's Rally,'" *Baltimore Sun*, July 28, 1966; "Racist Rally Ignites Angry Outbursts."

106. "Ex. Gov. T. R. McKeldin Dies; Dominated G.O.P. in Maryland," *New York Times*, August 11, 1974.

107. Beard, *Birds on the Wing.*

108. "McKeldin, Robinson Team Up," *Baltimore Sun*, September 27, 1966.

109. Frederic C. Wood Jr., Letter, *Baltimore Sun*, October 1, 1966.

110. "McKeldin, Robinson Team Up."

111. Eisenberg, *From 33rd Street to Camden Yards*, p. 172.

PART TWO: Sandy's Swan Song

1. Sid Ziff, "Sandy Would Rather Pitch Than Fight," *Los Angeles Times*, March 28, 1966.

2. Jim Murray, "Sandy Eager to Play, Waits for Buzzie's Call, But . . . ," *Los Angeles Times*, March 17, 1966; "Don't Let 'Em Fool You; Koufax Wanted to Pitch," *Los Angeles Times*, March 31, 1966.

3. Bavasi, *Off the Record*, pp. 103–5.

4. *The Limey*, written by Lem Dobbs, directed by Steven Soderbergh (Artisan Entertainment, 1999).

5. "Reagan 'Incredibly Ignorant' on State Laws, Brown Says," *Los Angeles Times*, October 9, 1966.

6. Sid Ziff, "Sandy, Don All Alone," *Los Angeles Times*, March 1, 1966.

7. Charles Maher, "K&D Will Wow 'Em in Show Biz," *Los Angeles Times*, March 29, 1966.

8. Ibid.

9. Sid Ziff, "Dodgers Amused," *Los Angeles Times*, March 18, 1966.

10. Ibid.

11. Charles Maher, "Drysdale Ponders Seven-Year TV Offer," *Los Angeles Times*, March 15, 1966.

12. Ziff, "Sandy, Don All Alone."

13. "K&D Rejects Dodgers' Final $210,000 Offer," *Los Angeles Times*, March 30, 1966.

14. Ibid.

15. Frank Finch, "Ailing Tom Davis Due for Pinch-Hitting Duty," *Los Angeles Times*, March 5, 1966; "Improving Tommy Davis in Cleanup Position against Braves," *Los Angeles Times*, March 11, 1966.

16. Russell, *The Tommy Davis Story*, p. 70. This is how Davis remembers the events, but in fact he was signed several months before the Dodgers announced their move.

17. Drysdale, *Once a Bum, Always a Dodger*, p. 4.

18. Jim Murray, "Lou Johnson Is Man in Motion," *Sporting News*, October 8, 1966.

19. Jerome Holtzman, "Life Sweet for Lou Johnson without Drugs, Booze," *Chicago Tribune*, May 27, 1993.

20. Bob Hertzel, "Dodger Pair Fights Drugs," *Cincinnati Enquirer*, July 21, 1971.

21. Bob Hunter, "Johnson at Third Base? Dodgers Think Maybe That's Good Idea," *Sporting News*, January 8, 1966.

22. Ryan, *Kings of the Hill*.

23. "2 Veterans, Rookie Astronaut Will Fly First Apollo Craft," *Los Angeles Times*, March 22, 1966; Richard West, "Manned Apollo Flight to Be First 'Open End' Space Trip," *Los Angeles Times*, August 3, 1966.

24. "2 Gemini IX Astronauts Killed in Crash of Supersonic Jet," *Los Angeles Times*, March 1, 1966.

25. Marvin Miles, "Gemini Makes Emergency Splashdown after Docking," *Los Angeles Times*, March 17, 1966; Rudy Abramson, "Officials Can't Explain Why Gemini Went Out of Control," *Los Angeles Times*, March 17, 1966; Arthur J. Dommen, "Astronauts Land in Okinawa; Were Seasick Awaiting Rescue," *Los Angeles Times*, March 18, 1966.

26. "K&D Rejects Dodgers' Final $210,000 Offer."

27. Claude Osteen, conversation with author, June 6, 2004.

28. Frank Finch, "Osteen, Podres Exchange Tips," *Los Angeles Times*, March 16, 1966.

29. Paul Zimmerman, "What Quiet on the Set?" *Los Angeles Times*, March 30, 1966.

30. Jim Murray, "Forget about 'Em," *Los Angeles Times*, March 6, 1966.

31. Ziff, "Sandy Would Rather Pitch Than Fight."

32. Sid Ziff, "How the Fans Feel," *Los Angeles Times*, March 3, 1966; Charles Maher, "L'Affaire Drysdale-Koufax: Villains or Heroes?" *Los Angeles Times*, March 27, 1966.

33. Ziff, "Sandy Would Rather Pitch Than Fight."

34. Frank Finch, "Club Jubilant, Alston Expects Aces to Pitch during Season's First Week," *Los Angeles Times*, March 31, 1966.

35. "The Dandy Dominican," *Time*, June 10, 1966.

36. Bob Hunter, "Wills Re-Crowns Dodgers Kings — It's Just Case of Togetherness," *Sporting News*, June 25, 1966.

37. Phil Regan, telephone conversation with author, May 26, 2004.

38. Jeff Torborg, telephone conversation with author, June 30, 2004.

39. Mandel, *SF Giants: An Oral History*, p. 133.

40. Roseboro, *Glory Days with the Dodgers*, p. 215.

41. Palacios, Robin, and STATS, *Ballpark Sourcebook*, p. 92: "Dodger Stadium helps pitchers by allowing the worst batting average, the fewest homers, the fewest runs and basically no triples. The power alleys are flyball cemeteries."

42. "Big D Can Still Chuckle," *Sporting News*, June 25, 1966.

43. Dick Young, "Bavasi Has a Warning for Salary Balkers," *Sporting News*, June 25, 1966.

44. Torborg conversation.

45. Ibid.

46. Bob Hunter, "L.A.'s New Big D Sutton Death to Foes," *Sporting News*, May 14, 1966.

47. Roseboro, *Glory Days with the Dodgers*, p. 197.

48. Drysdale, *Once a Bum, Always a Dodger*, pp. 226–29.

49. Torborg conversation.

50. Drysdale, *Once a Bum, Always a Dodger*.

51. Torborg conversation.

52. Hal Lebovitz, "Skeptics Can't Believe It, but Brown Won't Return," *Sporting News*, July 30, 1966.

53. Charles Maher, "Modell Claims Jim Brown, Team Victims of Cheap Publicity Stunt," *Los Angeles Times*, July 27, 1966.

54. Ziff, "Sandy Would Rather Pitch Than Fight."

55. Bob Hunter, "Lineup Card Biz Booms as L.A. Injuries Rocket," *Sporting News*, May 28, 1966.

56. Jim Elliot, "Mele, Mates Laud Brooks," *Baltimore Sun*, July 13, 1966.

57. "St. Louis Sparklers," *Sporting News*, July 23, 1966.

58. Gaylord Perry, *Me and the Spitter* (New York: Signet, 1974), pp. 148–49.

59. Ibid.

60. "St. Louis Sparklers."

61. Patterson, *The Baltimore Orioles*, p. 88.

62. Miller, *A Whole Different Ball Game*, p. 79.

63. Ibid.

64. Ibid.

65. Ibid.

66. " 'Perfect' McLain Was Hungry for Triumph," *Baltimore Sun*, July 13, 1966.

67. Bob Burnes, "When Maury's Miffed, the A.L. Must Pay," *Sporting News*, July 23, 1966.

68. Wills, *How to Steal a Pennant*, p. 50.

69. Ibid., p. 19.

70. Frank Finch, "Bavasi Waits for Wills," *Los Angeles Times*, March 10, 1966.

71. Al Wolf, "Wills Spurns Offer, Remains in L.A.," *Los Angeles Times*, March 12, 1966; Frank Finch, "Wills Going to Camp, Will Talk with

Bavasi," *Los Angeles Times*, March 14, 1966; "Wills Ends Holdout, Signs with Dodgers," *Los Angeles Times*, March 16, 1966.

72. Miller, *A Whole Different Ball Game*.

73. Ibid.

74. "Wills Injures Right Knee in Trying to Run Out Bunt," *Sporting News*, July 30, 1966.

75. Charles Maher, "Wills' Stealing Days Over for '66," *Los Angeles Times*, August 15, 1966.

76. "Wills Points to Two Changes," *Baltimore Sun*, October 9, 1966.

77. Frank Finch, "Sandy's Left Arm Hurt, Given Shot," *Los Angeles Times*, July 25, 1966.

78. Roseboro, *Glory Days with the Dodgers*, p. 188.

79. "O'Malley Pinpoints Injuries as Hurting Dodgers' Moves," *Sporting News*, August 6, 1966.

80. Hunter, "Lineup Card Biz Booms."

81. Bob Hunter, "Regan 'Mr. Regal' of L.A. Blue Berets," *Sporting News*, September 3, 1966.

82. Jerome Holtzman, "Chisox Youth, Spirit Impress Vet Reliever Regan," *Sporting News*, July 8, 1972.

83. Jim Murray, "Phil Regan — the Man Who Came to Dinner," *Los Angeles Times*, September 24, 1966.

84. Gary Herron, "Phil Regan: Former Relief Ace Came By His Unusual Nickname Honestly," *Sports Collectors Digest*, June 27, 1997.

85. Frank Finch, "Sandy Foiled Again, Homers Come Too Late in 5–1 Win," *Los Angeles Times*, August 2, 1966; "Mota Knocks LA Out of Lead," *Los Angeles Times*, August 3, 1966.

86. Bob Hunter, "L.A. Kingpin Sockers Cost Total of 9 Gs," *Sporting News*, March 28, 1962.

87. *Los Angeles Times*, June 9, 1963.

88. Wes Parker, telephone conversation with author, October 2003.

89. Ibid.

90. Jim Murray, "Willie Davis' Motto: Run . . . DON'T Walk," *Los Angeles Times*, August 15, 1966.

91. Nate Oliver, telephone conversation with author, October 7, 2003.

92. Charles Maher, "Willie D. Credits New Bat, Stance," *Los Angeles Times*, August 6, 1966.

93. Parker conversation.

94. Ross Newhan, "Willie Davis: Both a Frustration and a Joy," *Los Angeles Times*, June 17, 1973.

95. Parker conversation.

96. Dick Young, "Willie's Bat Got Well in Hospital," *New York Daily News*, September 5, 1969.

97. Nora Zamichow and Ross Newhan, "Arrest of Ex-Dodger Davis Spotlights a Troubled Life," *Los Angeles Times*, March 16, 1996.

98. John Kennedy, telephone conversation with author, October 9, 2003.

99. Roseboro, *Glory Days with the Dodgers*, p. 193.

100. Ron Fairly, telephone conversation with author, October 2003.

101. Phil Collier, "Willie D. Has New Incentive — Buzzie," *Sporting News*, March 27, 1976.

102. Wills and Celizin, *On the Run*, p. 148; Wills, *How to Steal a Pennant*, pp. 131, 217.

103. Bob Hunter, "Will Willie D Ever Live Up to Hopes?" *Sporting News*, August 31, 1968.

104. Sid Ziff, "King of Confusion," *Los Angeles Times*, August 29, 1966.

105. Philip Norman, *Shout! The Beatles in Their Generation* (New York: Fireside, 2003), pp. 267–68.

106. Jerry Cohen, "Once-Glamorous Strip Now 'Kiddieland' — Big Beat Drives Adults from Erstwhile Haunts," *Los Angeles Times*, March 10, 1966; Dave Larsen and Dick Main, "Huge Officer Force Breaks Up Crowd in Strip Showdown," *Los Angeles Times*, November 20, 1966.

107. Norman, *Shout!*

108. Press conference in *The Beatles Anthology*, Apple Corporation, 1995.

109. "Regan Authors Ballad about Relief Corps," *Baltimore Sun*, October 9, 1966.

110. Holtzman, *The Commissioners*, pp. 123–25.

111. Ibid.

112. Ibid.

113. "Yorty May Not Make Governorship Choice," *Los Angeles Times*, September 22, 1966.

114. Frank Finch, "Dodgers Lose It in Clutch, 4–3," *Los Angeles Times*, September 1, 1966.

115. Milton Gross, "L.A. 'Revolt' Is Reported," *Baltimore Sun*, October 10, 1966.

116. Wills, *How to Steal a Pennant*, pp. 165–66.

117. Phil Regan, telephone conversation with author, May 26, 2004.

118. Kevin Steiner, telephone conversation with author, February 2004.

119. Regan conversation.

120. Dick Kaegel, "A Report That Led to a Dodger Disaster," *Sporting News*, October 29, 1966.

121. " 'We Didn't Low-Rate Koufax, Took Realistic Look at Him' — Scout Russo," *Sporting News*, October 19, 1966.

122. Sid Ziff, "Dodgers in Trouble," *Los Angeles Times*, September 9, 1966.

123. Didion, *The White Album*, pp. 14–15.

124. Leavy, *Sandy Koufax*.

125. Ibid., p. 232.

126. "Wills Admits Beef with Tommy Davis during Giant Game," *Los Angeles Times*, September 9, 1966.

127. Regan conversation.

128. Sid Ziff, "Why Not Punch?" *Los Angeles Times*, September 11, 1966.

129. Frank Finch, "Blank, Blank — Dodgers Lead Loop," *Los Angeles Times*, September 12, 1966.

130. Roseboro, *Glory Days with the Dodgers*, p. 250.

131. Dick Kaegel, "Even Writers Toss Bouquets at Scully, Dodger Ace on Air," *Sporting News*, July 16, 1966.

132. Fairly conversation.

133. Don Page, "Scully Sing-Along Tops Hit Parade," *Los Angeles Times*, October 2, 1965.

134. Fairly conversation.

135. King Kaufman, e-mail conversation with author, May 20, 2004, clarifying Kaufman's *Salon* article "Brilliant Careers: Vin Scully" October 12, 1999, http://www.salon.com/people/bc/1999/10/12/scully/.

136. Fairly conversation.

137. Ibid.

138. Ibid.

139. Ibid.

140. Kaufman correspondence.

141. Don Page, "Transistors from Ear to Eternity," *Los Angeles Times*, August 27, 1966.

142. Don Page, "Who's That What Slud into Third?" *Los Angeles Times*, September 17, 1966.

143. Charles Maher, "Want to Build a Rating? Get Scully," *Los Angeles Times*, June 2, 1966.

144. Sid Ziff, "Sweet Lou on a Tear," *Los Angeles Times*, September 22, 1966.

145. "Baltimore Mayor Gets Invitation to Series," *Los Angeles Times*, September 28, 1966.

146. McKeldin did agree to bet Yorty "a barrel of Chesapeake oysters against some comparably juicy California product" that Baltimore would take the championship ("People," *Time*, November 25, 1966).

147. Charles Maher, "Giants Win 2, Knock Bucs Out of Race," *Los Angeles Times*, October 2, 1966.

148. Bob Addie, "Koufax Is Human," *Washington Post*, October 4, 1966.

149. "Mauch Fires Up Phillies for Final Series," *Los Angeles Times*, September 30, 1966.

150. "Alston: 'Got Away with It Every Time,'" *Los Angeles Times*, September 30, 1966.

151. Leavy, *Sandy Koufax*, p. 234.

152. Addie, "Koufax Is Human."

153. Ibid.; "Victory Bath: Champagne and Shaving Cream," *Los Angeles Times*, October 3, 1966; Frank Finch, "Sandy Ends the Agony — Dodgers Do It," *Los Angeles Times*, October 3, 1966.

154. Leavy, *Sandy Koufax*, pp. 235–36.

155. Charles Maher, "Giants Play Waiting Game at the Airport," *Los Angeles Times*, October 3, 1966.

156. Leavy, *Sandy Koufax*, p. 236.

157. Torborg conversation.

158. Osteen conversation.

159. Regan conversation.

PART THREE: Then Came Moe

1. Bob Addie, "Koufax Is Human," *Washington Post*, October 4, 1966.
2. Bob Maisel, conversation with author, June 2, 2004.
3. Ibid.
4. Ibid.
5. Jim Palmer, telephone conversation with author, July 31, 2004.
6. Eisenberg, *From 33rd Street to Camden Yards*, p. 175.
7. Bob Maisel, "The Morning After," *Baltimore Sun*, October 4, 1966.
8. Bob Burnes, "First Game Flashes," *Sporting News*, October 22, 1966.
9. Bob Addie, "Eckert Ignored," *Washington Post*, October 6, 1966.
10. Alan Goldstein, "Frank Robinson Admits Orioles Were Peeved about Remarks of 'Inferior' League," *Baltimore Sun*, October 6, 1966.
11. Robinson, *My Life Is Baseball*, p. 206.
12. Burnes, "First Game Flashes."
13. Addie, "Eckert Ignored."
14. Lowell Cohn, "A Love of the Game," *San Francisco Chronicle*, March 27, 1981.
15. Allen and Whitaker, *Crash*, p. 135.
16. Ross Newhan, "Dodgers Feel the Pain of Death Again," *Los Angeles Times*, July 4, 1993.
17. Brooks Robinson, telephone conversation with author, December 2003.
18. Goldstein, "Frank Robinson Admits."
19. Robinson, *My Life Is Baseball*, p. 208.
20. Ibid., p. 209.
21. Eisenberg, *From 33rd Street to Camden Yards*, p. 176.
22. Bob Maisel, "The Morning After," *Baltimore Sun*, October 6, 1966.
23. Bob Burnes, "West Coast Clouts," *Sporting News*, October 22, 1966.
24. Jeff Torborg, telephone conversation with author, June 30, 2004.
25. Jim Murray, "Series Opener: Exciting as Seeing Grass Grow," *Los Angeles Times*, October 6, 1966.
26. Earl Lawson, "DeWitt Stands Ready to Swap, Despite Robinson-Deal Fiasco," *Sporting News*, October 22, 1966.

27. Larry Claflin, "Busted to Private — Ex. Capt. Yaz Faces Threat of Transfer," *Sporting News*, October 22, 1966.

28. Maisel conversation.

29. Doug Brown, "It Was Word of Lau That Put Drabowsky in Orioles' Flannels," *Sporting News*, October 22, 1966.

30. Doug Brown, "Moe's Wit as Sharp as His Series Pitching," *Sporting News*, November 26, 1966.

31. Brown, "It Was Word of Lau."

32. Wally Bunker, telephone conversation with author, November 2003.

33. Wes Parker, telephone conversation with author, October 2003.

34. "Goose Eggs from the Orioles," *Time*, p. 79, October 14, 1966.

35. Paul Zimmerman, "Alston's Faith in Big D Unshaken Despite Bad Start," *Los Angeles Times*, October 6, 1966.

36. Ibid.

37. Ted Patterson, *The Baltimore Orioles*, pp. 85–86. In her biography of Sandy Koufax, Jane Leavy provides a different response from Bauer, but contemporary accounts indicate he simply departed.

38. Doubtless Mele was thinking of their legs as well as their bats, seeing how the Dodger running game could be slowed if Oriole pitchers tossed mainly fastballs. (This would, in theory, give Etchebarren extra time to pick off — or throw out — a runner.)

39. John Hall, "Stunned Drabowsky Modest in Series Victory," *Los Angeles Times*, October 6, 1966.

40. Bob Addie, "Palmer vs. Koufax in Second Game Today," *Washington Post*, October 6, 1966.

41. Beard, *Birds on the Wing*.

42. Sid Ziff, "Birds Get Quick Lift," *Los Angeles Times*, October 6, 1966.

43. Charles Maher, "Day to Forget at Dodger Stadium," *Los Angeles Times*, October 6, 1966.

44. "Sandy Meets an 'Old' Fan — Palmer," *Los Angeles Times*, October 6, 1966.

45. Ibid.

PART FOUR: That's Not Sandy Koufax

1. Sid Ziff, "Bullpen Does It," *Los Angeles Times*, September 15, 1966.

2. Alan Goldstein, "Koufax Wises Up," *Baltimore Sun*, October 5, 1966.

3. Sid Ziff, "Series Fever," *Los Angeles Times*, October 4, 1966.

4. Bob Burnes, "West Coast Clouts," *Sporting News*, October 22, 1966.

5. Gordon Beard, "Birds Confident No Return Trip," *Baltimore Sun*, October 7, 1966.

6. Ibid.

7. John Hall, "Birds Not Crowing Yet, But . . ." *Los Angeles Times*, October 7, 1966.

8. Jim Palmer, telephone conversation with author, July 31, 2004.

9. "Tavern Light Opera Troupe Sings to Birds' Final Score," *Baltimore Sun*, October 7, 1966.

10. Ibid.

11. John Hall, "Stunned Drabowsky Modest in Series Victory," *Los Angeles Times*, October 6, 1966.

12. "Dugout Dope," *Los Angeles Times*, October 5, 1966.

13. Burnes, "West Coast Clouts."

14. "Tavern Light Opera Troupe."

15. Jim Murray, "Willie D. Played Center Just Like It Owned Him," *Los Angeles Times*, October 7, 1966.

16. Ibid.

17. Bob Burnes, "Davis' Three Boots Help Palmer Put Birds Two Up," *Sporting News*, October 22, 1966.

18. Dick Kaegel, "A Report That Led to a Dodger Disaster," *Sporting News*, October 29, 1966.

19. Charles Maher, "Willie: 'If I Can See Them, I Can Catch Them,'" *Los Angeles Times*, October 7, 1966.

20. Tommy Davis, telephone conversation with author, December 2003.

21. Wes Parker, telephone conversation with author, October 2003.

22. Maher, "Willie."

23. Ibid.

24. Sid Ziff, "Sad Day for Willie," *Los Angeles Times*, October 7, 1966.

25. Ron Fairly, telephone conversation with author, October 2003.

26. Leavy, *Sandy Koufax*, p. 237.

27. "Tavern Light Opera Troupe."

28. Gordon Beard, "Birds Confident No Return Trip," *Baltimore Sun*, October 7, 1966.

29. Hall, "Birds Not Crowing Yet."

30. Ibid.

31. John Hall, "It's Only a Game?" *Los Angeles Times*, October 8, 1966.

32. Betty Grissom, telephone conversation with author, March 2003.

PART FIVE: Bunker's Just Not That Good

1. "Baltimore's Mayor Bids Bar End Bias," *New York Times*, October 5, 1966.

2. Gildea, *When the Colts Belonged to Baltimore*, p. 112.

3. "Oriole Fans Stay Up Late to Greet Team," *Los Angeles Times*, October 8, 1966.

4. Richard H. Levine, "City Officials, Hotels — Even the Block — Campaign for World Series Spoils," *Baltimore Sun*, September 22, 1966.

5. Eisenberg, *From 33rd Street to Camden Yards*, p. 178.

6. Claude Osteen, telephone conversation with author, June 6, 2004.

7. Paul Zimmerman, "Alston Frets over Bats, Not Boots," *Los Angeles Times*, October 7, 1966.

8. Ibid.

9. Wally Bunker, telephone conversation with author, November 2003.

10. Frank Finch, "Bunker, Blair Blitz Lifeless Dodgers, 1–0, to Foil Osteen," *Los Angeles Times*, October 9, 1966.

11. "Banners Rib the Dodgers," *Sporting News*, October 22, 1966.

12. Richard H. Levine, "First for the Fans Is Third for the Orioles," *Baltimore Sun*, October 9, 1966.

13. Lou Hatter, "Curt Makes Fielding Gem," *Baltimore Sun*, October 9, 1966.

14. Osteen conversation.

15. Ibid.

16. Ibid.

17. Roseboro, *Glory Days with the Dodgers*, p. 175.

18. Osteen conversation.

19. Ibid.

20. Bunker conversation.

21. Lou Hatter, "Elbow 'Hurt Like Devil,' before Bunker Took Hill," *Baltimore Sun*, October 9, 1966.

22. Eisenberg, *From 33rd Street to Camden Yards*, p. 178.

23. Osteen conversation.

24. Jim Murray, "Bats Are Just Props for Blankety-Blank Dodgers," *Los Angeles Times*, October 9, 1966.

25. Levine, "First for the Fans."

26. Ibid.

27. Alan Goldstein, "Alston to Start Drysdale Today," *Baltimore Sun*, October 9, 1966.

28. Hatter, "Elbow 'Hurt Like Devil.'" As for Pelekoudas, he later observed, "Bunker was throwing the ball over the plate so much of the time that I wanted to get a bat and go up and hit against him" ("Umpire Pelekoudas Salutes Wally for Excellent Control," *Sporting News*, November 12, 1966).

29. Bob Burnes, "Bunker, Blair Boost Birds Nearer to Topmost Branch," *Sporting News*, October 22, 1966.

30. George Minot Jr., "Osteen Claims Home-Run Pitch Was Outside Where He Wanted It," *Washington Post*, October 9, 1966.

31. Goldstein, "Alston to Start Drysdale Today."

32. Bob Maisel, "The Morning After," *Baltimore Sun*, October 9, 1966.

33. Lou Hatter, "Paul Blair Admits He Was Guessing When He Cut at Homer Pitch Off Osteen," *Baltimore Sun*, October 9, 1966.

34. "Sinker Foils Kennedy," *Sporting News*, October 22, 1966.

35. Minot, "Osteen Claims."

36. "Bunker's Six-Hitter, Blair's Homer Give Orioles Third Series Game, 1–0," *Baltimore Sun*, October 9, 1966.

37. Bunker conversation.

38. Eisenberg, *From 33rd Street to Camden Yards*, p. 180.

39. John Hall, "Blair Gets Even for Rejection by Dodgers in '61," *Los Angeles Times*, October 9, 1966.

40. Ibid.

41. Shirley Povich, "Orioles Can Wrap Up Series Today," *Washington Post*, October 9, 1966.

42. Eisenberg, *From 33rd Street to Camden Yards*, p. 178.

43. Ibid., p. 179.

44. Bunker conversation.

45. Eisenberg, *From 33rd Street to Camden Yards*, p. 176.

PART SIX: We Regret to Announce . . .

1. Maryann Hudson, "News Shakes Team Again," *Los Angeles Times*, July 4, 1993.
2. Larry Stewart, "Don Drysdale, Hall of Fame Dodger Pitcher, Dies at 56," *Los Angeles Times*, July 4, 1993.
3. Ross Newhan, "Dodgers Feel the Pain of Death Again," *Los Angeles Times*, July 4, 1993.
4. Ibid.
5. Charles Maher, "L.A. Takes It Calmly," *Los Angeles Times*, October 10, 1966.
6. "Forestry Service Lauds Dodgers: Conserve Wood," *Los Angeles Times*, October 5, 1966.
7. Alan Goldstein, "L.A. Hears 'Taps' before Finish," *Baltimore Sun*, October 10, 1966.
8. "Bird-Watching," *Sporting News*, October 22, 1966.
9. Bill Plaschke, "To Drysdale, Dodgers Meant Winning," *Los Angeles Times*, July 4, 1993.
10. Anthony Lewis, "U.S. Baseball Is Sticky Wicket to Britons Watching the Telly," *New York Times*, November 4, 1966.
11. Bob Burnes, "Bunker, Blair Boost Birds Nearer to Topmost Branch," *Sporting News*, October 22, 1966.
12. Beard, *Birds on the Wing*.
13. Doug Brown, "Orioles, as Observers, Get New Kicks Out of Series Flickers," *Sporting News*, December 31, 1966.
14. Brooks Robinson, telephone conversation with author, December 2003.
15. Bob Maisel, conversation with author, June 2, 2004.
16. W. Lawrence Null, "Humphrey Lauds Losers," *Baltimore Sun*, October 10, 1966.
17. "Predicted Robby's Clout," *Sporting News*, October 22, 1966.
18. "F. Robinson Proves Point," *Baltimore Sun*, October 10, 1966.
19. Roseboro, *Glory Days with the Dodgers*.
20. "Wrapping It Up," *Sporting News*, October 22, 1966.
21. Richard H. Levine, "Birdville Jubilant as Fans Find Way to Say 'We Done It,'" *Baltimore Sun*, October 10, 1966.

22. "Robby Sees Series Homers as His 'Greatest Thrills,'" *Sporting News*, October 22, 1966.

23. Lewis, "U.S. Baseball Is Sticky Wicket."

24. Seymour Smith, "Birds Claim Few Jitters in Ninth," *Baltimore Sun*, October 10, 1966.

25. John Hall, "Baltimore Lives It Up," *Los Angeles Times*, October 10, 1966.

26. Lewis, "U.S. Baseball Is Sticky Wicket."

27. Ibid.

28. Eisenberg, *From 33rd Street to Camden Yards*, p. 179.

29. Maher, "L.A. Takes It Calmly."

30. Lewis, "U.S. Baseball Is Sticky Wicket."

31. Lou Hatter, "Brecheen's No. 1 Thrill," *Baltimore Sun*, October 10, 1966.

32. "Stu Scares Etchebarren," *Sporting News*, October 22, 1966.

33. Maher, "L.A. Takes It Calmly."

34. Lou Hatter, "Family Roots McNally On," *Baltimore Sun*, October 10, 1966.

35. Norman Miller, "Birds Laud Scout Report That Said: Challenge 'Em, Bats Can't Hurt You,'" *New York Daily News*, October 22, 1966.

36. "Dodgers Hit New Low," *Washington Post*, October 10, 1966.

37. Ibid.

38. Goldstein, "L.A. Hears 'Taps.'"

39. Smith, "Birds Claim Few Jitters."

40. "Lou Went for Distance," *Sporting News*, October 22, 1966.

41. Smith, "Birds Claim Few Jitters."

42. Skipper, *Umpires*.

43. Hatter, "Brecheen's No. 1 Thrill."

44. "Wrapping It Up."

45. Hatter, "Family Roots McNally On."

46. "F. Robinson Proves Point."

47. George Minot Jr., "Humphrey Clears Air," *Washington Post*, October 10, 1966.

48. W. Lawrence Null, "Walt Alston Not Planning to Jump off Any Bridges," *Baltimore Sun*, October 10, 1966.

49. Goldstein, "L.A. Hears 'Taps.'"

50. Null, "Humphrey Lauds Losers."

51. However, Los Angeles Mayor Yorty did send McKeldin a case of California wine to pay off the bet he lost ("People," *Time*, November 25, 1966).

52. Barry Levinson, telephone conversation with author, August 11, 2004.

53. Stephen A. Bennett, "Biggest Gala Since V-J Day," *Baltimore Sun*, October 10, 1966.

54. "Police Call Riot Squad to Quell Oriole Rooters," *Los Angeles Times*, October 9, 1966.

55. Beard, *Birds on the Wing*.

56. Levinson conversation.

EPILOGUE: Arrivals and Departures

1. Brooks Robinson, telephone conversation with author, December 2003.

2. Wally Bunker, telephone conversation with author, November 2003.

3. Ron Fairly, telephone conversation with author, October 2003.

4. Phil Regan, telephone conversation with author, May 26, 2004.

5. Wes Parker, telephone conversation with author, October 2003.

6. Nate Oliver, telephone conversation with author, October 7, 2003.

7. Fairly conversation.

8. Bunker conversation.

9. Parker conversation.

10. Ibid.

11. Ibid.

12. Lee Kavetski, "Dodgers Suffer an Eclipse in Land of the Rising Sun," *Sporting News*, November 26, 1966.

13. Roseboro, *Glory Days with the Dodgers*, p. 154.

14. Claude Osteen, telephone conversation with author, June 6, 2004.

15. Charles Maher, "Koufax Quits Because of Ailing Arm," *Los Angeles Times*, November 19, 1966.

16. John Roseboro, interviewed by Jane Leavy, May 1999.

17. Roseboro, *Glory Days with the Dodgers*, p. 218.

18. "Too Many Shots, Too Many Pills," *Time*, p. 64, November 25, 1966.

19. "Sandy Koufax Retires from Game at Career Peak Due to Arthritis," *Baltimore Sun*, November 19, 1966.

20. Russell, *The Tommy Davis Story*, pp. 131–33.

21. Wills, *How to Steal a Pennant*, pp. 172–73.

22. Bob Hunter, "One Bombshell after Another — Dodgers Shake," *Sporting News*, December 3, 1966.

23. Roseboro, *Glory Days with the Dodgers*, p. 170.

24. "A Trip That's Really Worth While," *Sporting News*, November 19, 1966.

25. Lou Hatter, "Brooks Robinson Returns from 2-Week Vietnam Tour," *Baltimore Sun*, November 24, 1966.

26. Torre, *Chasing the Dream*, pp. 98–100.

27. Ibid., p. 99.

28. Lansche, *Stan the Man Musial*, pp. 299–300.

29. Robinson conversation.

30. Robinson, *Putting It All Together*, p. 51.

31. Sandy Grady, "A Warmth Like Willie's, F. Robinson's Next Goal," *Philadelphia Evening Bulletin*, October 29, 1966.

32. Bob Hunter, "MVP Robby Shooting for Skipper Post," *Sporting News*, November 19, 1966.

33. Ibid.

34. Edgar Munzel, "A Negro Skipper in Big Time? 'Bound to Happen,' Says Banks," *Sporting News*, May 21, 1966.

Selected Bibliography

Allen, Dick, and Tim Whitaker. *Crash: The Life and Times of Dick Allen.* New York: Ticknor & Fields, 1989.

Alston, Walter. *A Year at a Time.* Waco, Tex.: Word Books, 1976.

Bagli, Vince, and Norman L. Macht. *Sundays at 2:00 with the Baltimore Colts.* Centreville, Md.: Tidewater Publishers, 1995.

Bavasi, Buzzie. *Off the Record.* Chicago: Contemporary Books, 1987.

Beard, Gordon. *Birds on the Wing: The Story of the Baltimore Orioles.* Garden City, N.Y.: Doubleday, 1967.

Beirne, Francis F. *The Amiable Baltimoreans.* New York: E. P. Dutton, 1951.

Brown, Jim, with Steve Delsohn. *Out of Bounds.* New York: Kensington Publishing, 1989.

Cairns, Bob. *Pen Men: Baseball's Greatest Bullpen Stories Told by the Men Who Brought the Game Relief.* New York: St. Martin's Press, 1992.

Carmichael, Stokely, with Ekwueme Michael Thelwell. *Ready for Revolution: The Life and Struggles of Stokely Carmichael (Kawme Ture).* New York: Scribner, 2003.

Carter, Dan T. *The Politics of Rage: George Wallace, the Origins of the New Conservatism, and the Transformation of American Politics.* New York: Simon & Schuster, 1995.

Davis, Tommy, with Paul Gutierrez. *Tommy Davis' Tales from the Dodgers Dugout.* Champaign, Ill.: Sports Publishing, 2005.

Delsohn, Steve. *True Blue: The Dramatic History of the Los Angeles Dodgers, Told by the Men Who Lived It.* New York: William Morrow, 2001.

Didion, Joan. *Slouching towards Bethlehem.* New York: Farrar, Straus & Giroux, 1968.

———. *The White Album.* New York: Simon & Schuster, 1979.

Drysdale, Don, with Bob Verdi. *Once a Bum, Always a Dodger: My Life in Baseball from Brooklyn to Los Angeles.* New York: St. Martin's Press, 1990.

Eisenberg, John. *From 33rd Street to Camden Yards: An Oral History of the Baltimore Orioles.* New York: Contemporary Books, 2001.

Ferguson, Franklin Fields. *Negro American: A History.* Ypsilanti, Mich.: Ferguson, 1969.

Foner, Philip S. *The Voice of Black America: Major Speeches by Negroes in the United States, 1797–1971.* New York: Simon & Schuster, 1972.

Forman, James. *The Making of Black Revolutionaries.* New York: Macmillan, 1972.

Giglio, James N. *Musial: From Stash to Stan the Man.* Columbia: University of Missouri Press, 2001.

Gildea, William. *When the Colts Belonged to Baltimore: A Father and a Son, a Team and a Time.* Baltimore: Johns Hopkins University Press, 1994.

Goldblatt, Andrew. *The Giants and the Dodgers: Four Cities, Two Teams, One Rivalry.* Jefferson, N.C.: McFarland, 2003.

Grissom, Betty, and Henry Still. *Starfall.* Springfield, Ohio: Crowell Publishing, 1974.

Grissom, Virgil. *Gemini.* New York: Macmillan, 1968.

Gruver, Edward. *Koufax.* Dallas: Taylor Publishing, 2000.

Hayward, Mary Ellen, and Charles Belfoure. *The Baltimore Rowhouse.* New York: Princeton Architectural Press, 2001.

Holtzman, Jerome. *The Commissioners: Baseball's Midlife Crisis.* New York: Total Sports, 1998.

John, Tommy, with Dan Valenti. *TJ: My 26 Years in Baseball.* New York: Bantam Books, 1991.

Joseph, Paul. *Baltimore Orioles.* Minneapolis: Abdo & Daughters, 1997.

Koppett, Leonard. *The Man in the Dugout.* New York: Crown, 1993.

Lansche, Jerry. *Stan the Man Musial: Born to Be a Ballplayer.* Dallas: Taylor Publishing, 1994.

Leahy, Leo. *Lumber Men: Nontraditional Statistical Measurements of the Batting Careers of Over 900 Major League Regulars from 1876 to 1992*. Jefferson, N.C.: McFarland, 1994.

Leavy, Jane. *Sandy Koufax: A Lefty's Legacy*. New York: HarperCollins, 2002.

Levinson, Barry. *Sixty-six*. New York: Doubleday-Broadway, 2003.

Lifson, Hal. *1966!* Chicago: Bonus Books, 2002.

Mandel, Mike. *SF Giants: An Oral History*. Santa Cruz, Calif.: Self-published, 1979.

McNeil, William F. *The Dodgers Encyclopedia*. Champaign, Ill.: Sports Publishing, 2001.

Meier, August, and Elliott Rudwick. *CORE: A Study in the Civil Rights Movement, 1942–1968*. Urbana: University of Illinois Press, 1975.

Miller, James Edward. *The Baseball Business: Pursuing Pennants and Profits in Baltimore*. Chapel Hill: University of North Carolina Press, 1990.

Miller, Marvin. *A Whole Different Ball Game: The Sport and Business of Baseball*. New York: Carol Publishing, 1991.

Murray, Jim. *The Last of the Best*. Los Angeles: Los Angeles Times, 1998.

Palacios, Oscar, Eric Robin, and STATS, Inc. *Ballpark Sourcebook: Diamond Diagrams*. Skokie, Ill.: STATS, 1998.

Palmer, Jim, and Jim Dale. *Palmer and Weaver: Together We Were Eleven Foot Nine*. Kansas City, Mo.: Andrews & McMeel, 1996.

Patterson, Ted. *The Baltimore Orioles: Four Decades of Magic from 33rd Street to Camden Yards*. Dallas: Taylor Publishing, 2000.

———. *Football in Baltimore: History and Memorabilia*. Baltimore: Johns Hopkins University Press, 2000.

Peary, Danny. *We Played the Game: Memories of Baseball's Greatest Era*. New York: Black Dog & Leventhal Publishers, 1994.

Plaut, David. *Chasing October: The Dodgers-Giants Pennant Race of 1962*. South Bend, Ind.: Diamond Communications, 1994.

Rambeck, Richard. *The History of the Baltimore Orioles*. Mankato, Minn.: Creative Education, 1999.

Rampersad, Arnold. *Jackie Robinson: A Biography*. New York: Knopf, 1997.

Riley, Dan, ed. *The Dodgers Reader.* Boston: Houghton Mifflin, 1992.

Roberts, Russell. *Stolen: A History of Base-Stealing.* Jefferson, N.C.: McFarland, 1999.

Robinson, Brooks. *Putting It All Together.* New York: Hawthorn Books, 1971.

Robinson, Frank, with Dave Anderson. *Frank: The First Year.* New York: Holt, Rinehart & Winston, 1976.

Robinson, Frank, with Al Silverman. *My Life Is Baseball.* Garden City, N.Y.: Doubleday, 1968.

Robinson, Frank, and Berry Stainback. *Extra Innings.* New York: McGraw-Hill, 1988.

Robinson, Jackie. *I Never Had It Made.* Hopewell, N.J.: Ecco Press, 1995.

Robinson, Rachel. *Jackie Robinson: An Intimate Portrait.* New York: Abrams, 1996.

Roseboro, John, with Bill Libby. *Glory Days with the Dodgers and Other Days with Others.* New York: Atheneum, 1978.

Russell, Patrick. *The Tommy Davis Story.* Garden City, N.Y.: Doubleday, 1969.

Russo, Jim, with Bob Hammel. *Super Scout: Thirty-five Years of Major League Scouting.* Chicago: Bonus Books, 1992.

Ryan, Nolan, with Mickey Herskowitz. *Kings of the Hill.* New York: HarperCollins, 1992.

Schneider, Russell J. *Frank Robinson: The Making of a Manager.* New York: Coward, McCann & Geoghegan, 1976.

Simon, Scott. *Jackie Robinson and the Integration of Baseball.* Hoboken, N.J.: John Wiley & Sons, 2002.

Skipper, John C. *Umpires: Classic Baseball Stories from the Men Who Made the Calls.* Jefferson, N.C.: McFarland, 1997.

Sobel, Lester A. *Civil Rights 1960–66.* New York: Facts on File, 1967.

Sporting News. *Official 1967 Baseball Guide.* St. Louis: Sporting News, 1967.

Thompson, Chuck, with Gordon Beard. *Ain't the Beer Cold.* South Bend, Ind.: Diamond Communications, 1996.

Thorn, John. *The Relief Pitcher.* New York: E. P. Dutton, 1979.

Torre, Joe, with Tom Verducci. *Chasing the Dream: My Lifelong Journey to the World Series*. New York: Bantam Books, 1997.

Tygiel, Jules, ed. *The Jackie Robinson Reader: Perspectives on an American Hero*. New York: E. P. Dutton, 1997.

Walker, Robert Harris. *Cincinnati and the Big Red Machine*. Bloomington: Indiana University Press, 1988.

Westcott, Rich. *Splendor on the Diamond*. Gainesville: University Press of Florida, 2000.

Wills, Maury, and Mike Celizic. *On the Run: The Never Dull and Often Shocking Life of Maury Wills*. New York: Carroll & Graf Publishers, 1991.

Wills, Maury, with Don Freeman. *How to Steal a Pennant*. New York: G. P. Putnam's Sons, 1976.

Index

Also by Tom Adelman

The Long Ball

The Summer of '75 — Spaceman, Catfish, Charlie Hustle,
and the Greatest World Series Ever Played

"One of the best baseball books I've ever read. . . . Adelman's portrayal of both American and National League championship series, and the ultimate Reds–Red Sox final matchup, are riveting."

— Katherine Pushkar, *Newsday*

"A gripping closeup of the 1975 World Series, considered by many to be the greatest ever played."

— *Reader's Digest*

"Tom Adelman's evocative retelling brings it all back."

— Boris Kachka, *New York*

"The games, characters, and moments of that unexpected baseball joyride in 1975 are chronicled in intense detail in Tom Adelman's *The Long Ball*."

— Christopher Walker, *Patriot Ledger* (Boston)

"This may be the best baseball book ever written."

— Randolph Giudice, *Oahu Island News*

BACK BAY BOOKS
Available wherever paperbacks are sold

TOM ADELMAN chronicled the legendary 1975 World Series in his bestselling *The Long Ball*. He has also written several novels and works of music criticism. He lives with his family in New Jersey.